Reaching Your Teenager

Also by Elizabeth C. Winship

Ask Beth: You Can't Ask Your Mother

Masculinity and Femininity

Reaching Your Teenager

Elizabeth C. Winship

Houghton Mifflin Company · Boston 1983

The charts on pages 4 and 5 are copyright © 1980 by Ross Laboratories and are adapted from: P. V. V. Hamill et al., "Physical Growth: National Center for Health Statistics Percentiles," *American Journal of Clinical Nutrition* 32: 607–629, 1979. (Data from the National Center for Health Statistics [NCHS], Hyattsville, Maryland.) Reprinted by permission.

The photograph on page 6 is from J. M. Tanner, *Growth at Adolescence,* 2nd ed. London: Blackwell Scientific Publications, 1962, and is reprinted by permission of J. M. Tanner.

The chart on page 20 was drawn by Lucy Bartholomay.

Library of Congress Cataloging in Publication Data

Winship, Elizabeth C.
Reaching your teenager.

Bibliography: p.
Includes index.
1. Youth — United States. 2. Junior high school students — United States. 3. High school students — United States. 4. Parent and child — United States. 5. Parenting — United States. I. Title.
HQ796.W4992 1983 649'.125 83-143
ISBN 0-395-32219-7
ISBN 0-395-34033-0 (pbk.)

Printed in the United States of America

V 10 9 8 7 6 5 4 3 2 1

To Ann Barnes,
who knows all about how women work

Acknowledgments

I am most grateful to all the people who advise me about teenagers, and are the real wisdom of Ask Beth. I am especially thankful to the following, who helped me directly with this book:

Doctors Ann Barnes, gynecologist at Harvard Medical School and Massachusetts General Hospital; John C. Coolidge, senior psychiatrist at Judge Baker Guidance Clinic; Thomas B. Fitzpatrick, dermatologist at Harvard Medical School and Massachusetts General Hospital; Lester Grinspoon, psychiatrist at Harvard Medical School and Massachusetts Mental Health Center; Richard C. Pillard, psychiatrist at Boston University Medical Center; John P. Remensnyder, plastic surgeon at Shriner Burns Clinic and Massachusetts General Hospital; Norman Spack, specialist in adolescent medicine at Children's Hospital Medical Center and Chestnut Hill Medical Center.

Thanks also to attorneys Edward T. Bigham and Tom Schiavoni; Judge Kevin Doyle of the Waltham District Court; and officer George Norton of the Wayland Police. Also to Buddy Henderson, drug counselor at Bridge Over Troubled Waters; to Polly Wilson, Coordinator of Alcohol Services, Emerson Hospital in Concord; and to Bernie Jenkins, for allowing me to infiltrate her group for parents, How to Survive Teenage.

I am grateful to Richard B. McAdoo, Editor Emeritus of Houghton Mifflin, who started me off writing books, and I would like to say very special thanks to my overworked editor, Stella Easland, but she will cross out the "very."

Finally, my everlasting gratitude to my husband, Tom Winship, for reading everything and keeping me on the track, and to my sons and daughters, Larry Winship, Peggy Winship, Josie Ramstad, and Ben Winship, who not only helped greatly with this manuscript but whose very being made my work possible.

Contents

Introduction

Everyone in my group smokes pot and drinks a lot. I don't do these things yet. Should I try, to be one of the gang?" "My boyfriend asked me to sleep with him. He says everyone else is doing it, but I'm scared. I am only thirteen." "My friends are ripping-off stores, and they call me chicken because I won't." "I went home with my boyfriend after school, and no one else was there. Now I've missed my period for almost two months. How can I tell my Mom? She'll kill me!"

These are excerpts from letters I get every day. They're addressed to Ask Beth, an advice column for teenagers that I write for the *Boston Globe* and is syndicated nationally. The young people who write to me are naturally the ones who are most troubled, but their problems differ only in degree from the problems adolescents are facing all over the world.

Teenagers have a tough time in our country. It doesn't seem that our society loves them very much. Take a three-year-old into a store and everyone coos and smiles. Take a thirteen-year-old and people look suspicious and start guarding the merchandise. We are missing the boat.

We have cut our teenagers out of the mainstream of our lives. We park them in academic institutions on the fringes of our communities, we give them little useful work, and we throw them almost entirely into their own age group for company, advice, and role models. Alienation is inevitable. Much of this is due to things beyond our control, including technocracy, population growth, and socioeconomic changes. But parents can still do a lot. In reading the hundreds of thousands of letters written to my column, I hear kids crying out for good, honest communication, for clear and rational limits, for true responsibility, and for respect as individuals. These are things parents can provide.

Communication. Adolescents are pulling away from parents, and often don't confide in them much anymore. Parents, in turn, tend to criticize and nag more than listen and really talk with their teenagers. Adults often do not talk honestly with children, anyway. Serious subjects such as money and sex are seldom discussed with candor. Adolescents need a sympathetic ear from their parents, and they need facts on which to base their decisions. In good, two-way discussions, thrashing out issues with wise and loving parents, children learn how to make intelligent choices.

Limit setting. If parents set too few boundaries, kids flounder. If their rules are too rigid, however, adolescents cannot learn how to run their own lives. Freedom needs to be payed out, bit by bit, and failure is often lesson enough in itself. When punishment is necessary, it should be swift, appropriate, and clearly understood. Extreme or unfair punishment does not produce self-discipline — it fosters rebellion.

Responsibility. True responsibility means being liable for the outcome of what you do. This is not permissiveness, which allows kids to do or try anything without demanding that they be accountable for the results. The more true responsibility teenagers have, the more reliable they become. Opportunity must match maturity and experience, but in general we underestimate teenagers' abilities.

Respect. Love and respect are different and don't always go hand in hand. Teenagers come up with such crazy ideas sometimes that they hear more criticism than admiration. While they often sound cocky, adolescents are seldom really self-confident. If you build them up rather than cut them down, they learn to respect themselves. It is kids with healthy self-respect who are least easily persuaded to risk harm to their minds or bodies from drinking too much, driving too fast, or being careless about sex.

My formula isn't radical. It isn't magic. But it has worked for me and for many parents who have asked me for help.

In this book, I hope to help parents guide their teenagers

through the complexities of junior high and high school life. The changes puberty brings to children's emotions and behavior create problems for both them and their parents. Parents are often relieved to know which of these problems are developmental, and will be outgrown. Early chapters, therefore, identify and describe which behaviors are typically adolescent and temporary.

Adolescents *must* strive for independence; this is part of sound psychological growth, but it brings predictable struggles between them and their parents. Fewer of the old methods of control work anymore, yet there is more pressure on children to grow up faster than ever. Kids face more temptations, yet society has fewer guidelines to help them make wise choices. The second half of this book discusses the issues that modern teenagers run into and suggests ways that parents may be able to head off trouble by applying liberal doses of communication, responsibility, limits, and respect.

Adolescence is a *wonderful* age, full of energy, curiosity, and high spirits. When we get in tune with our teenagers, listen and laugh and share their fresh, clear-eyed view of the world, we have good times and learn something about our old assumptions, too. When we reach our kids, it pays off all around. It helps create good companions for us and gives them a better leg up on life.

Reaching Your Teenager

1. Puberty

The changes that take place during puberty are stupendous. In a brief time, a child's skeleton, internal organs, muscles, and glandular system all grow extremely fast. These changes profoundly affect the whole personality.

Many of the problems kids write to my column about have to do with these changes: "I'm getting too tall!" "I'm not growing at all!" "I'm too big, too curvy." "I'm too small, not curvy enough." "Am I normal?"

Puberty is not well understood by most adults. They can't remember how and when and in what order the changes all occurred, or how it felt. So parents tend to pooh-pooh their children's anxieties, saying, "You'll outgrow it." And usually, but not always, the children will. Children undergoing puberty often feel that their bodies are changing wildly and that it's all out of their control. They need sympathy and reassurance to feel secure during such an unnerving transformation.

The Preadolescent Growth Spurt

Puberty is triggered by a sudden rush of hormones, those mysterious chemicals produced by certain glands, which control changes in all parts of the body. One of the most obvious changes is a sudden burst of growth.

Girls begin growing fast somewhere around age nine or ten. The first faint swelling of the breasts may also be seen at this time. The beginning of breast enlargement is usually, but not always, followed by the widening of hips, appearance of pubic and underarm hair, light down upon the upper lip, a slight lowering of the voice, and lastly, menstruation.

Some girls develop early and fast, some much more slowly. This unevenness creates some of the hardest trials of puberty, because girls who leap ahead or lag far behind their friends feel abnormal. The speedy growers need constant assurance that their peers will catch up. The ones who lag behind usually feel there is something desperately wrong with them, and that they will *never* grow up. They need assurance that showing any signs of puberty, such as the tiniest swelling of the breasts or genitalia, means that the growth process will go on and be completed.

Parents should emphasize, however, that the changes of puberty have different outcomes for different people. If adolescents look around at adults they know, they will see how different "normal" people can be: some tall, some thin, some muscular, some busty, some flat, some downright squatty. Kids often assume they will each attain some mythical "perfect" figure, and if they don't, it's somehow their fault. They take it very hard if they find they are destined to be rather different, so parents need to help them have more realistic expectations, and realize that your figure doesn't make or break you as an adult.

Little boys and girls grow at about the same rate, but most girls begin their prepubic, or adolescent, growth spurt at about ten or eleven years of age, two years earlier than most boys. A girl may grow three and a half or four inches or more in a single year. The fastest growing period is over by age twelve for many girls, and by thirteen, their growth rate is usually slowing down. At twelve or thirteen the average girl is taller than the average boy.

The growth pattern for boys is similar, but doesn't usually accelerate until age twelve and a half. At the time of their fastest growth, boys too may add four inches a year, or even six, eight, or more.

During this spurt, both sexes grow about eleven or twelve inches, which is roughly 20 percent of their adult height.

Charts can be used to get some idea of the usual rate of growth and range of normalcy, but they should not be used to try to find one's "perfect" height or weight. In reality, practically no one is "average." Parents need to explain to teenagers, probably several times, how "averages" are figured out. For example, if you took eight girls, four of whom were five feet two inches and the other four five feet six inches, their average height would be five feet four inches. But *none* of the girls would be that exact height.

A look at a sixth- or seventh-grade class will show immediately how wide the range can be. Some girls are as tall and shapely as mature women. Others still have the small, straight bodies of little children. Most fall somewhere in between. All of them are "normal."

Growth certainly doesn't always follow the normal line. "Help!" a girl writes, "I'm too tall, and I'm still growing. I'm only twelve and I'm the tallest person in the whole seventh grade. I look tall and feel tall, too. Is there anything I can do to stop growing? — Giraffe." The answer is no. Except in really extreme cases, nothing can be done. Height is largely determined by heredity, so a child from a tall family is likely to be above average. Severe illness or starvation can interfere, but contrary to folklore, neither smoking, drinking, nor masturbation will stunt growth.

Alas, those who are destined to grow tallest usually grow soonest. This is especially difficult for the tall girls and the short boys. The girl who signed herself "Giraffe" undoubtedly has tall parents and grandparents. She will be a tall woman, but not always so much taller than her peers. In fact, she is near the end of her adolescent growth spurt.

Early maturing girls, like Giraffe, are usually within an inch of their full height by age thirteen, while most boys are far from it. Boys don't get close to adult height until age fifteen, so the taller girls go through one or two interminable years of towering over the boys. This affects girls strongly. They aren't considered cute, and boys may be embarrassed to dance with them. Some girls try to compensate by becoming tomboys or going out for sports in which they can compete. Some develop terrible posture, slumping down in an attempt to appear shorter. Parents have to emphasize again and again that the size differential is temporary and will correct itself in a year or two. It seems like an endless time to a teenager, so remind girls that they won't be permanently out of scale. Point out successful and happy women who are taller than average — fashion models, for instance.

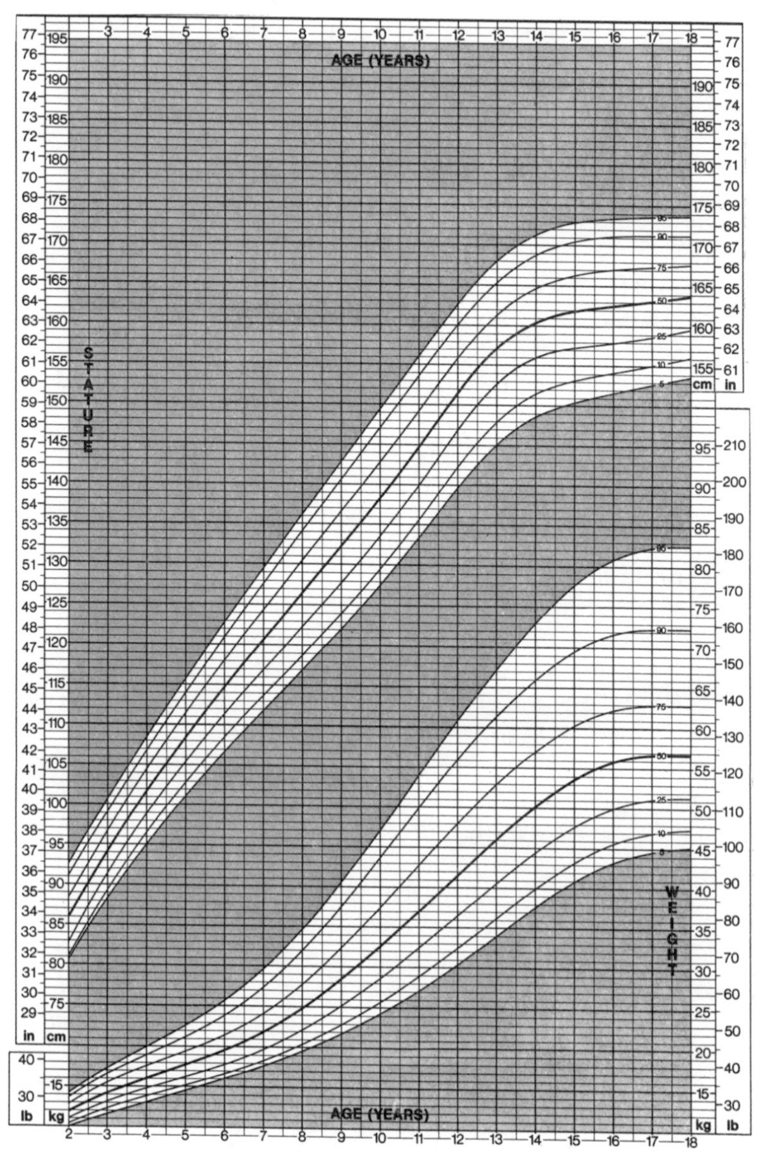

Physical growth of girls, aged two to eighteen

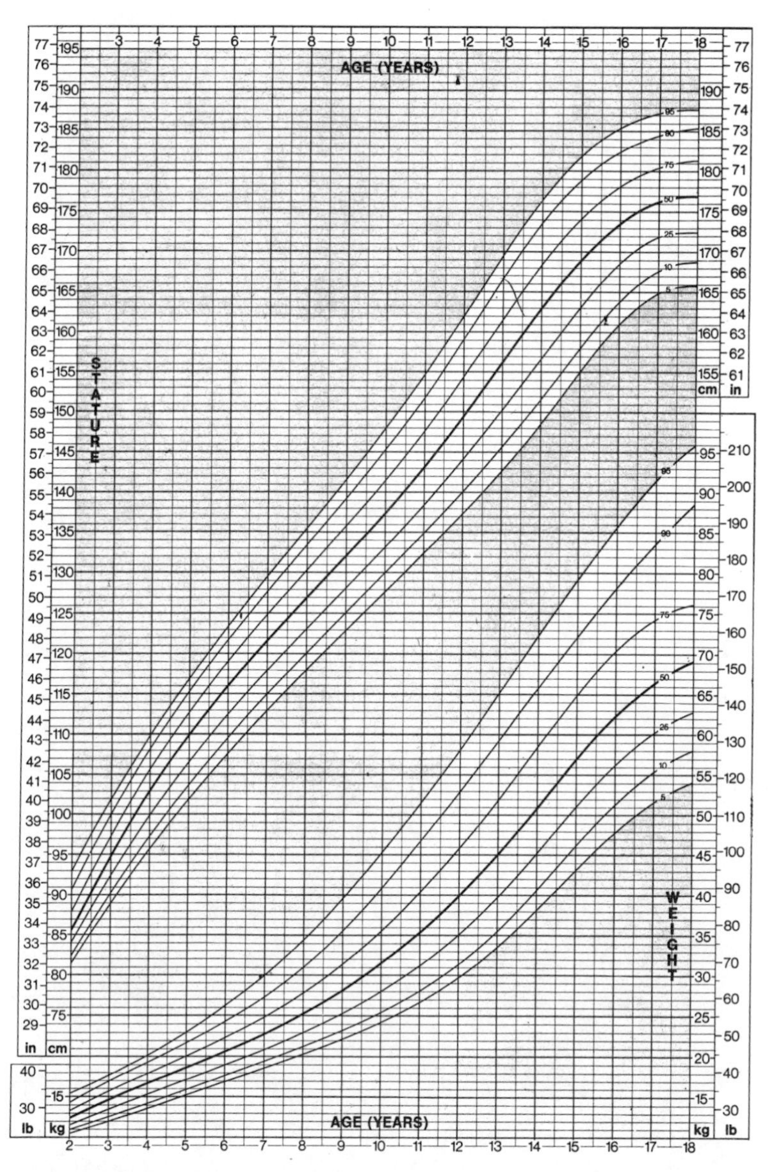

Physical growth of boys, aged two to eighteen

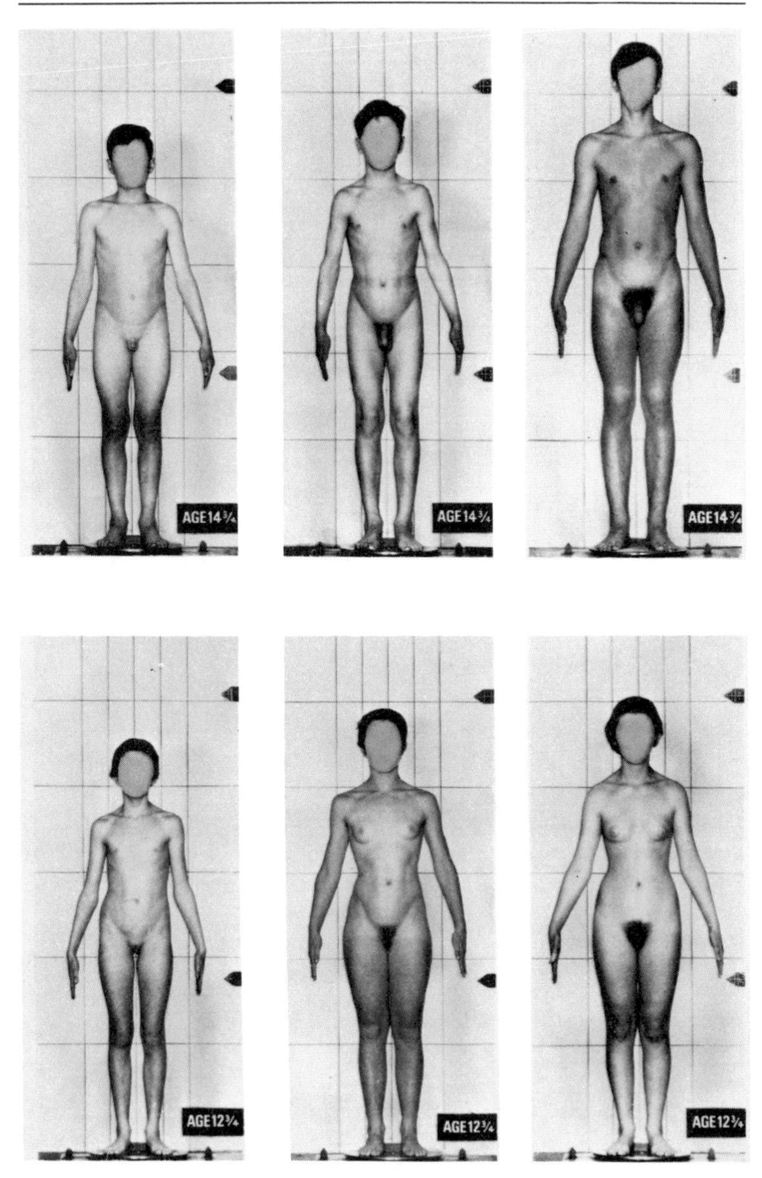

Three normal but very different body types in twelve-year-old girls and fourteen-year-old boys

People who are destined to be short often don't even start growing until others have got a big head start. Some boys don't catch up with the girls until age eighteen, nineteen, or twenty, and some remain very short always. The slower maturers also grow more slowly when they do start. This is especially hard on the short boys, who endure humiliating nicknames, like "Shrimp," "Small Fry," "Pee wee," etc., which can hurt their self-esteem. They may be ineligible for certain sports, despite real athletic ability, and unable to compete in varsity football or basketball or even soccer against their longer-legged and heavier classmates. Parents should steer them into individual sports, like tennis, track, and skiing, in which they stand a better chance.

Parents may need creative ingenuity to help short sons or tall daughters through this difficult period. Ridicule or ostracism by their peers is a crippling blow to a fragile ego. "I'm real short," a boy writes, "and everyone in my class thinks I'm nothing but a clown. It's true. I'm apt to come up with the fast remark, and can usually make kids laugh, but sometimes I wish they would treat me like a real person, not just a joke." This boy's reaction to his lack of height is quite common. Some short men have become famous comedians. Others compensate by becoming the school brain or a high achiever in other ways, like Napoleon and Mayor La Guardia. Parents can help their kids channel their energy into useful and rewarding activities, so they will have the satisfaction of being successful in some area. Parents also need to give these kids constant reassurance that they are appealing and lovable people and will be attractive to others romantically, too, when everyone has reached maturity and size has sorted itself out.

You have to walk a careful line with kids who are not average size. You need to be aware, but a little matter-of-fact, too. Constantly mentioning teenagers' size or repeatedly measuring their growth will exacerbate worries they already have. Yet you should not be afraid to have the doctor check your child's growth if it really is very early or very late. Probably this will result in the advice that the child is fine and will grow, or stop growing, in good time. It is helpful for the teenager to have this assurance.

In rare cases, medical intervention may be advised. Children who haven't started puberty at all by the appropriate age may have a hormonal imbalance that can be corrected. Those who seem to be growing much taller than heredity would predict can be given treatment to slow growth. These cases are extremely uncommon, however, and the ordinary tall girl or short boy should not be given false hopes that a doctor can "fix it."

Female Changes in Puberty

The Breast Develops

The first visible sign that a girl is on the road to sexual maturity is a faint swelling of the breasts. This "bud stage" is the first of three stages. The nipple projects, ever so slightly, and there is a firming up of tissue under the area surrounding it. The bud stage usually occurs between the ages of nine and a half and eleven, when rapid growth is beginning, but it may happen earlier or later. Menstruation will predictably begin about two to two and a half years later.

In the second stage, the dark area around the nipple, called the areola, begins to enlarge and spread. This causes a double-bumped effect that may obscure the nipple and cause the girl to worry that her breasts are the "wrong" shape, or that her nipples don't protrude properly. Many girls won't mention their fears, but parents who sense a concern can explain that this is a normal phase, and the breasts will soon fill out more as they reach the third and final stage.

Most girls' breasts are pretty well developed by about age fourteen, though they may continue filling out for several more years. Some girls find that one breast is larger than the other. While development is never exactly even in any part of the body, the differences are usually unnoticeable except to the individual herself. Daughters who worry that they are lopsided should know that this almost always works itself out with maturity. Occasionally a girl has an obvious disparity. Because breasts are so noticed by peers, this ought to be concealed if it bothers her. Consult the lingerie department of a reliable store about a bra with extra padding on one side. Extreme cases can be corrected by plastic surgery, once growth is completed.

By far the most common complaint I hear is this: "I'm fourteen years old and I'm flat. I have less on top than any other girl in my whole class. I was wondering, is there any exercise I can do, or stuff I can send for to make me bigger? — Flat as a Board." Alas, there is not. None of those treatments, lotions, creams, or other things really work. The size of the breast is largely determined by heredity, though as the breast is mostly composed of fat, chest size can be increased by adding weight all over. Popular exercises to develop the bosom are designed to strengthen the pectoral muscles, which lie under the breasts. Exercise may help prevent sagging, but it cannot increase the size of the breast itself. Surgery, called augmentation, designed to make breasts larger, is not usually recommended until girls have reached a more mature age, partly because surgeons don't want them to have false expectations of what this will do for them. The augmentation is not necessary for physical reasons, however, and not likely to be covered by health insurance. Flat as a Board may grow a little more over the next few years, but she's probably never going to have a very large bosom. Parents should try to help a girl with this trait to accept the situation and to understand that small breasts work every bit as well for nursing babies and for lovemaking, too.

Our society is so hipped on breast size that girls who have a small bra size are made to feel that they are failures. Young boys don't help. The breasts are the first noticeable sign of sexual development among their girlfriends, and immature sixth- or seventh-grade boys can make the crudest remarks, snap bra straps, and even pinch and squeeze. The girls soon realize that boys are superconscious of who's "stacked" and who is flat. Parents may not realize how much this matters, but some girls actually fear they will be skinny and unpopular and alone all the rest of their lives. As most kids are low on self-esteem at this age, their egos need a lot of bolstering. Try to help these girls see things in better perspective and to bring out other aspects of their figure and personality. And help boys see that this kind of teasing is really sexual harassment, and not at all acceptable.

What about "stuffing"? Girls sometimes tuck socks or Kleenex into their bras, but this is seldom successful, because other kids can see that the curves are not real and may poke fun. A lightly padded bra looks much better. In today's almost braless society, it may be hard for a girl to get away with such a bra, however. Their peers find out and word gets around. Why teenagers are so bent on destroying each other with ridicule is another problem, but it's a fact. There's just no hiding place under a skintight T-shirt. A mother might point out that a looser, button-front shirt would give a girl better cover, but there's such pressure on teens to avoid notice by dressing exactly like everyone else that her daughter may decide it's not worth it. Any mother who's ever agonized over whether to wear a long or a short skirt to some special dinner will understand how the girl feels.

The best and most lasting way to overcome the sensitivity of being small is to have a good attitude: "OK, so I'm flat. But that's not the only thing I am. I am pretty, have nice hair, good legs, an interesting face. I'm a good talker and quite witty." Parents can help a girl discover what she does have going for her, and help her learn to bring these good points out.

The young girl with an extra large bosom may also be in for a rough time. Girls who grow tall early often develop in the breast early, too, and may be wearing a 36B at age eleven or twelve. Boys often stare and make rude remarks, or give embarrassing nicknames such as "Stack house" or "B.B." (for big boobs). Most young girls who are prematurely big breasted are mortified, and their life is hell for a while. "I want to crawl in a hole and die!" one such girl complained. "Everyone thinks I'm this big sexpot and I'm not at all. I hate boys! What can I wear to hide my horrible breasts? My parents say I'm much too young for any operation."

A positive way of thinking about herself helps a large girl as well as a small-breasted one. A girl calling herself "Big Ones" said she was twelve, but had the figure of an eighteen-year-old. The boys on the bus all kidded her, so she just laughed along with them. So long as the boys weren't crude, her laughter kept them on her side. Later, when she is old enough to date, the boys will remember her as a friendly and genial girl. Of course, having a large bosom is an advantage in getting attention from boys, there's no sense denying it, but a flat girl who is also genial and friendly will get her share of attention, too.

A girl who wants her breasts to look smaller should look into bras called "minimizers." They can be fitted at most good lingerie counters. Clothes can help a lot too: Tight belts, blouses made of clingy, thin, and especially see-through materials, and button-front shirts that gape should be avoided. Vertical stripes, pale-colored tops, subtle designs, and fairly straight styles deemphasize large breasts, and give a more balanced-looking figure.

Some large breasts may require plastic surgery. Even with a good support bra and extra wide straps, the weight of large breasts may cause painful shoulders, backache, and other physical problems, as well as the real misery of constant attention and comment from peers or even insensitive adults. Breast reduction surgery may be performed on quite young teenagers who have true problems with heavy breasts, and this is usually covered by insurance.

The subject of bras is of great importance to young girls. The big question used to be when to get her first bra. A girl might want to involve her mother in this decision, but feel shy about asking her, so a sensitive mother should try to make it clear that she is available to go shopping for the first bra. Some girls would like to try a training bra before the need is very obvious. Their motive may be for comfort, for protection (tiny young breasts are often extremely tender), or simply for social status. All of these are valid reasons. Some parents tend to discount status, but how a young person gets on with her peers makes a big difference in the formation of self-esteem, so if a bra will help, why not make it easier? The sales personnel in a good lingerie department can be of great help in assuring proper fit, and a mother can be of help in assuring that the salesperson is kind and attentive, something a young teenaged girl may not be able to request for herself.

The first question about a bra nowadays may, however, be whether to wear one at all. As bralessness becomes increasingly popular, more and more girls write wondering if it is harmful to jettison all support of the breasts. Doctors are divided on this issue. Some say lack of support hastens sagging. Others say that without the bra, the muscles that support the breast must do the work of holding it up, so that bralessness actually postpones sagging. Photographs of certain tribes where women wear nothing on top show both extremes of breast condition, from firm to flabby, so it seems to be a moot point.

A more basic objection many mothers feel to their daughters' shedding their bras concerns the effect it may have on boys. The moving breast used to be considered a come-on, but this becomes less true as males grow accustomed to the unsupported female form.

A girl with young, firm breasts probably does not need support, and if encouraged to be reasonably modest about gaping shirts and see-through T-shirts, has no reason to wear a bra. Even girls with larger breasts are discarding bras, however, and time will have to show whether this is wise or not. The old wired-up job that made a woman look like the prow of the *Queen Mary* is definitely out. More natural looking stretch bras are preferred today. Those who wear no bra have the added problem of what to do when nipples show or get sore from friction on their shirts. One answer is Band-Aids. Another is to wear a camisole under the blouse.

Body Hair

Though most girls notice the start of breast development first, in some girls pubic hair starts to appear before, or simultaneously with, breast development. Small amounts of straight, light hair first show on the outer labia. In time, this thickens and spreads out into the mature triangle. Pubic hair that grows down onto the inner thighs causes a problem if it shows beneath a bathing suit. Girls inquire if it is all right to shave it off, and the only apparent drawback is that there can be an annoying itch when stubble grows back in this sensitive area.

There is a gradual increase of body hair in general during adolescence, much of it unwelcome to girls. Underarm hair is often shaved, as is excess or dark hair on the legs, which parents usually are not concerned about. When down appears on the upper lip, it may bring the first hair removal crisis. "What can I do about this horrible mustache? I tried bleach, but it doesn't work. Shaving makes it worse. My mother won't let me get electrolysis until I'm eighteen. — Raven-Haired Unbeauty." Facial hair on a dark brunette can be really noticeable, and Raven-Haired Unbeauty could use depilatories until she can get electrolysis, the more permanent treatment. Depilatories are safe for all but the most sensitive skin, and do a better job than a razor. Still, electrolysis — in which hair follicles are killed electrically — is the most permanent method of hair removal. Competently done, it is safe and not very painful. It costs more than other hair-removal methods, but if you spread the expense over the years it will prevent hair growth, the price is not excessive. The results of electrolysis are much more satisfactory than those of other methods, and there is no medical reason to ask a teenager to wait.

Even boys can be concerned about facial hair, if it appears much sooner than that of their friends. They are afraid others will think they are trying to show off, if they are the first in their group to start shaving. Yet other boys complain about not getting a mustache soon enough. Beards come along at different times, and a boy with pale, fine hair may want to shave when there's no real need for it. Parents can be sympathetic and let him go ahead.

Most boys don't have noticeable hair on their chests until later in their teens. The fate of most males is to grow more and more hair on their bodies, while less and less grows on their heads. Early balding is hereditary. The only consolation you can offer a balding boy is that the process is caused by high levels of the male sex hormone androgen, so he can brag, with some justification, that he's a real he-man.

Bragging will grow hair as fast as remedies from a bottle or tube. These are all a waste of money. The only artificial treatment that will help baldness is a hair transplant, which is an expensive and lengthy process.

Figure Changes

A girl's body not only adds height and weight during teenage, but her proportions change, too. A girl may worry, like this writer: "What's going on? I'm growing tall, and my waist is practically under my armpits. Nothing fits me right. Am I always going to be like this?" Every part of the body can't grow at exactly the same rate. It is common for legs to lengthen out of proportion to the trunk. Arms may seem long too, or feet, or noses, or ears. This is why a youth may be called gangly, but it's a temporary state of affairs, and the answer in this case is "Yes, you will outgrow it."

By the end of puberty teenagers have the figures they will be living with, pretty much, the rest of their lives. Most people find fault with some part of their anatomy. It pays to stress to growing kids that they must not expect perfection but accept what comes. If they become preoccupied with some aspect of their physique, you can suggest — lightly and in passing — that being hung-up on such a thing exaggerates its impact on others by drawing attention to the "flaw."

Furthermore, people who are preoccupied with themselves are uninteresting and boring.

Extremes of height or weight or figure type can make a difference, of course, but even these variations can be lived with. The vast majority of kids will not have to cope with serious problems.

Menstruation

Roughly two years after the first signs of puberty appear, a girl reaches menarche, the time of her first menstrual period. This big moment signals that she has reached womanhood in the physical sense — from now on she can become a mother — though she may not actually be fertile for several more months.

How a girl feels about this event depends a great deal upon how she has been prepared for it. Amazing as it may seem, there are still girls reaching menarche who have been told nothing at all about menstruation beforehand. These unprepared girls are shocked at the onset of uncontrolled bleeding, and believe that it is a sign that something is seriously wrong. They fear that they have a terrible disease, but may be too frightened to tell anybody.

Some mothers don't prepare their daughters in time because they don't realize at what a young age menarche now occurs. In 1900, the average age was around fourteen and a half years, but now it is less than twelve and a half. This means half of all girls start *before* this age, many at eleven, ten, or even younger. So the answer to the question "When should I tell my daughter about menstruation?" is "Now!" Practically speaking, it is never too early. If you explain the simplest facts to a little girl, even by first grade, it will be that much easier to fill in the details later on. By age eight or nine, girls are very curious about reproduction and how it works. This is the right time to start giving them useful information. You can start by giving little girls a simplified version of the story of reproduction. Explain to them that about once a month the ovary releases an egg that is ready to be fertilized if a woman wants to have a baby, and that, meanwhile, the uterus gets ready to nourish the fertilized egg by growing a lining rich in blood. If the egg is fertilized, it will plant itself in this lining and develop into a fetus; it the egg is not fertilized, the lining is unnecessary and will simply pass out of the body through the vagina.

You should also tell young girls that although this fluid looks like blood it is actually only partly blood, and although it may seem like a lot of fluid there are only three or four tablespoons of it in the four or five days of a normal period.

Menstruation still has a bad image and, while a girl needs to know how to cope with the discharge and cramps, it's a mistake to let her grow up feeling that menstruation means getting sick or being subject to a "curse." It's not unclean or shameful in any way. The human race depends on women's reproductive powers and it is vital to teach girls that menstrual bleeding is simply a healthy, natural part of this miraculous system.

The whole process is controlled by an intricate system of hormone production. It is a fascinating system, and a girl will feel much more positive about herself if she understands it. If a parent doesn't feel comfortable about explaining it fully, there are books and articles, or you can talk with a sympathetic nurse or doctor.

"All my friends have their periods and not me," a girl writes. "I was thirteen last month, and I've got hair under my arms and wear a 34B bra and everything, but all I get is some white sticky stuff on my underpants. Is this a sign it's coming soon? — The Last Infant in Grade 7." Probably yes, and she will soon be complaining to classmates about what a nuisance it all is (one subtle way to let them know that she, too, gets her period now). There is no sure way to tell when it will start, though a mother can predict it somewhat. The age of menarche is related to height, weight, and skeletal age as well as heredity. Girls who start their period early are usually taller, heavier, and more advanced in skeletal development than their peers.

The appearance of a little clear vaginal discharge may or may not foretell the start of menstruation. A mother can promise her daughter, however, that so long as she has had the other signs of development, such as breast growth and pubic hair, the rest will surely follow. If by age fifteen or sixteen there is still no sign of menstruation, then a medical check on hormonal activity is in order, though in all probability the doctor will find that everything is perfectly all right — just slow.

Irregularity is the name of the game in most early menstrual cycles. "I had my period twice last summer, and haven't had it since, and it's over four months! Don't say I'm pregnant. I don't even talk to boys yet! What's wrong with me?" Youth, that's all. Like any delicate mechanism, it takes a while for the complex reproductive system to get finely tuned and running properly. The first periods may not actually involve true ovulation at all. So, in the earliest years of menstruation, it is not unusual to stop, start, or even skip as much as a whole year of periods.

Various other things affect menstrual regularity, and it's important for girls to know that health, nutrition, weight, and especially, stress can all delay their periods. Fear of pregnancy is the most common cause of stressful delays. But girls who are not sexually active can be reassured that unpredictability, though inconvenient, is not harmful in other ways.

Once a girl begins to menstruate, her big fear is that she will stain her clothes, and everyone will notice. What is the best way to prevent this? Pads are really inconvenient for the active girl. They may chafe or slip, and it's a nuisance to change them during a busy school day. But some girls write, "My mother won't let me wear tampons. She won't say why, she just says 'it isn't right' for girls my age, which is thirteen. — Hates Pads." Many mothers fear that tampons will damage the hymen. The old myth that an unbroken hymen "proves" virginity doesn't make sense nowadays — if it ever did. Hymens come with large holes as well as tiny ones or can be thin or flexible enough to permit either a tampon or a penis to penetrate without tearing. Today's active girls may already have stretched or torn their hymens by riding bikes, taking gymnastics, or other such activities. So there is no reason for even the youngest girl not to at least try a tampon.

The most serious concern about tampon use is toxic shock syndrome. This rare disease was recently discovered to be associated with the wearing of tampons, especially the extra-absorbent ones. The problem is not understood completely, but the infection seems to come from a type of parasitic bacteria (staphylococcus) found normally in the vagina. When tampons are worn for long periods, the vaginal fluid is held in one place, giving the germ an opportunity to make its way into the blood stream. Toxic shock syndrome produces flu-like symptoms, with a sudden, very high fever, nausea, and a sunburn-like rash. As this illness is very uncommon, doctors recommend that it is all right to wear tampons if they are changed frequently and alternated with pads. It is wise, for instance, for all women to use pads at night.

Some mothers discourage tampon use because the idea of handling one's own genitals is taboo. Women have been brainwashed with the idea that they are somehow bad or dirty "down there." This, I believe, is an excellent reason *in favor* of tampons. We want our girls to grow up being proud of their bodies, and to feel that their sexuality is wholesome and good. This doesn't mean becoming sexually active at thirteen. It means feeling good about themselves as women, and as sexual women too. Mothers who are open-minded about tampons help foster this wholesome attitude.

Some girls find it difficult or even impossible to insert a tampon because the hymen has too small an opening or is too rigid. They need to know that a doctor can fix this, if it's important enough to them to wear tampons. The opening can be enlarged through a quick procedure done with a local anesthetic. This little operation will also make first intercourse a great deal more comfortable when that time comes.

Practical information about personal hygiene is especially important during menses. This is a time when menstrual fluid and perspiration can have a particularly strong odor. Frequent pad and tampon changes, and showering, as well as regular use of underarm deodorants, will ward off the odor stigma that is often the topic of conversation among teenagers.

"I hate my period! First I feel like crying all the time and then I get such bad cramps I want to die. I stay home and lie down and take aspirin, but nothing helps. What causes this, and what should I do about it?" Most young girls are not plagued by serious problems during menstruation, but about 80 percent feel one or two of the various symptoms that glandular changes may produce at this time, such as mild depression, edginess, tearfulness, tenderness and swelling in the breasts or other parts of the body, headache, nausea, and heaviness or pain in the lower abdomen. Such discomfort is not "just in her head." There are physical reasons for it. In most cases, lying down is not the answer. Adolescents may have more discomfort than mature women, but doctors say that normal exercise helps pain. It certainly does no harm — Olympic swimmers have won medals while menstruating. There are also exercises designed specifically to help cramping, such as those outlined in Hilary C. Maddux's book, *Menstruation.* Over-the-counter pills are perfectly all right for teenagers, although you may have to try several before finding one that works for you. Cramps have a three-fold cause: contraction of muscles in the uterus, release of prostaglandin, and the interaction of the nervous system. Different drugs affect different causes. Recently, anti-prostaglandin drugs have been widely used. Severe cramping—or any other bothersome symptom—should be discussed with a physician.

Heavy bleeding may occur in adolescence, although what seems like an unusual amount of blood for one girl may be perfectly normal for someone else. A girl who soaks more than six or eight pads or tampons in one day or who finds very large clots should be examined, even if it's just for assurance that everything is normal. That is what most menstruation is — normal — and the key to a girl's peace of mind is not to let her worry about it in silence.

Boys' Sexual Development

Some boys, like some girls, are embarrassed when they start to develop sexually and try to hide it, while others are extremely proud and show themselves off. Whether their reaction is positive or negative, it is bound to be profound. As with females, male development has a general order, but it does not always follow the so-called norm, nor does it happen at the same time or same rate of speed for each boy. Without the help of a menarche, fathers are less able than mothers to remember the timing of their own sexual development in order to reassure sons that everything is fine and developing "like father, like son."

The first sign of sexual maturing in boys is the beginning of the enlargement of the testicles. This usually happens at about age eleven or twelve, the mean age being eleven and a half. The growing testicles produce androgen, which stimulates growth. Unlike girls, who have reached almost their full height by menarche, boys are just beginning their very rapid growth at the time puberty starts. They spurt up for several more years, and reach peak velocity at around age fourteen.

Rapid growth is accompanied by growth of the penis, the beginning of sperm production, appearance of pubic hair, and change in the voice. Finally, the nocturnal emission, or wet dream, signals that the boy has become a man. These changes may not appear in this exact order, and as the following chart shows, there is much overlap.

Boys are intensely concerned about their newly enlarging genitals and may not be sure just what to expect. "What's wrong with me?" they sometimes write. "My left testicle hangs down more than my right one. I'm afraid it is something serious, but I don't dare tell my parents." It is not unusual for one testicle to be lower than the other, and it's important for parents to discuss this with sons who may be agonizing in silence. During puberty, most boys are shy about going naked in front of others in the family, and parents aren't able to observe development. They would do well to inquire tactfully if the boy is worried about his developing body. Mention the fact that some unevenness in development is natural, but any very obvious size difference should be brought to the doctor's attention, as it could be reason for concern.

The problem might be caused by an old injury, an undescended testicle, or perhaps a hydrocele, which is a benign water cyst that requires medical attention since it will not cure itself and could jeopardize the boy's fertility. An undescended testicle also requires medical attention because it will not produce sperm and is forty to fifty times more prone to developing cancer. Undescended testes can be brought down into the scrotum through a relatively simple operation.

The most pressing worry to an adolescent boy is whether his penis will grow to the "proper" size. "Is there anything I can take to make my penis grow?" boys often write me. "I'm fourteen, and the smallest of all the guys in my class. They kid me so much I can't take showers after sports anymore. Aren't there some hormones or something that would help? — Humiliated." Humiliated will be relieved to know he probably will continue growing, and that if his sexual organs have started to grow at all, it is virtually certain they will go on to reach a predetermined adult size. The time it takes to reach adult penile size varies between two and four years after puberty starts, so a boy who still feels that his penis is too small at age thirteen or fourteen can be assured that it may go on developing

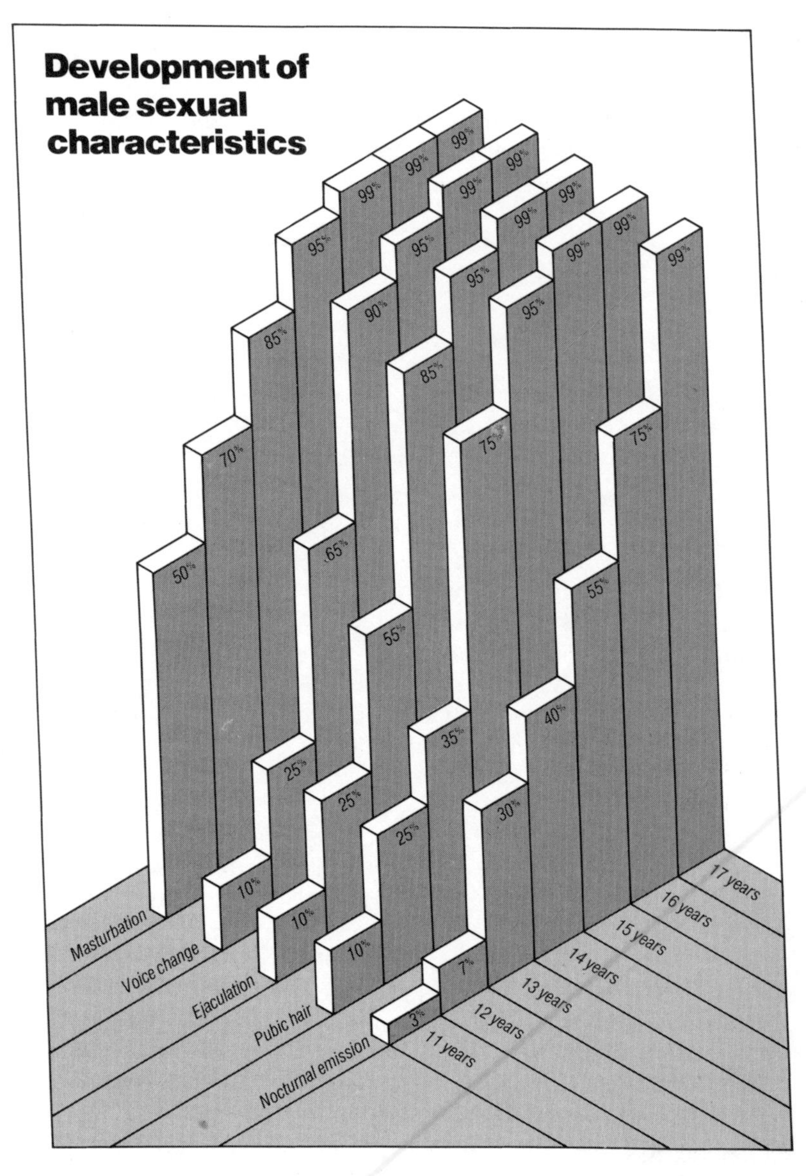

Development of male sexual characteristics

until he's fifteen, sixteen, or even older. Boys who are late developing may not reach full size until they are twenty or even twenty-two. Occasionally a boy's puberty is delayed, and in such a case hormone replacement therapy can make a dramatic difference. If there is any question at all about development, have the boy checked by a physician, as late development has ruinous effects on the psyche. Hormone therapy will not help once puberty has begun. There is nothing that can make the penis grow any bigger than nature has programmed it to be.

Boys do need to know the range of "average" penile size, which is from four to six inches, in the flaccid state. Those whose organs are larger or smaller are not abnormal. It's especially important to the boy who feels small to understand that the small penis almost always compensates by expanding more during erection. Parents should seek ways to explain to sons that penis size in no way affects a man's fertility or the pleasure he will get, and give, in sexual relations. Any penis is the right size. Skill and tenderness and caring are what matter, not the size or shape of the equipment involved. If it is difficult to say this directly, refer your son to one of the many books available that debunk the myth that a small penis is inadequate (see Suggested Reading).

"You may think I'm kidding, but my penis is too big. It's nine inches in a relaxed state. The guys all call me names like Super Stud and worse, and they say I'll never be able to marry a normal woman. Is this true?" We make such a fetish of bigness in the male that it's hard to imagine a boy worrying that he is too large, but it does happen. His friends usually envy him, so they try to cut him down to size by teasing or inventing stories about his future difficulties. Of course it's not true, and it should be pointed out to both boys and girls that the vagina is essentially empty space. It can clasp something as small as a tampon or stretch enough to allow a baby's head to pass through. So it can accommodate a penis of any possible size.

Occasionally, I get letters from worried boys who find that their penis is constantly crooked when erect. This is not just a quirk to be ignored. There are several possible causes, ranging from injury to certain diseases, and this needs to be checked by a urologist promptly.

For many years in this country, most baby boys have been

routinely circumcised shortly after birth. There is a trend away from such unnecessary operations in some circles nowadays, unless religion dictates otherwise. Uncircumcised boys need to be taught how to keep themselves clean. Smegma, an accumulation of oils and secretions, can collect under the foreskin and may cause an odor or even set the stage for disease, so boys need to develop the habit of pulling back this skin and washing themselves regularly with soap and water.

Another problem uncircumcised boys sometimes write to me about is that other kids think they "look funny." These boys should be helped to see that they are as normal as a boy can be. They can tell the people who make comments that they are pretty ignorant if they don't recognize the natural state when they see it.

A common problem among young teenage boys is probably this one. "I'm having trouble with erections. If I have to stand up in class, sometimes everyone can see, and I'm too embarrassed to talk. I can't always wear my shirt outside my pants. What can I do to keep from having this happen?" There is probably no adult male who hasn't been surprised by an erection at a most inappropriate time. The situation does come under control as a boy grows older. Men have written my column offering help stemming from their past experience, and they usually advise boys to avoid wearing tight pants, as these promote erections through constant friction and make the condition more noticeable. Jockey shorts or athletic supporters worn under comfortably loose pants will disguise the situation pretty well.

At about fourteen or so, when penile growth usually reaches its peak, most boys have their first ejaculation. This is a big moment, and their pals will probably hear about it, though their parents may not. At about this time, boys usually start to have wet dreams. Among adolescent boys, nocturnal emissions are taken as the sign that a boy has become a man, so they are very important. "When will I have my wet dream?" I am often asked. "I have grown a lot and I've got pubic hair and everything, but I haven't had this yet, so kids say I'm not really a man. — Anxiously Waiting." As the chart on page 20 shows, the majority of boys have not had a nocturnal emission until age fifteen or so. Anxiously Waiting is well within the normal range. A few boys never have a wet dream that they are aware of. Very little fluid is actually ejaculated, and consequently it's undetectable.

Sometimes it is all too evident, though. "My mother is after me for having wet dreams. She says I must be doing or thinking something dirty. I try not to have them, but it doesn't help. I even washed out my own sheet, but she can always tell. Don't say to ask my Dad, because my parents are divorced. What can I do? — Sam." All Sam can do is try to educate his mother. She really should know that wet dreams are totally involuntary. Sam can't stop them no matter how hard he tries. Nocturnal emissions are not "dirty," they may not even be the result of sexy dreams. She should be glad she has a normal, healthy son, and she should try to find a nice, warm, and sympathetic man who could stand in for Sam's father and talk with him about problems like this.

Hair

It's rather amazing that something so useless as hair should matter so very much. Parents who can remember how exposed they felt when they had to undress in the shower room at school will understand how preoccupied their adolescents may become with their body hair. "Help!" writes George. "I don't have any pubic hair that shows. The boys call me 'Baldy' and the girls want to know why, and it's so embarrassing. I'm fourteen, so shouldn't I have it by now?" The first hair that appears around the base of the penis is apt to be straight and not the stiff, curly hair it will become later. George will be getting satisfactorily hairy in a year or two, most probably, though if he is very blond, or a redhead, his pubic hair will never be as noticeable as that of his darker-haired friends.

Underarm hair comes along at about the same time as pubic hair, but chest hair, which is sometimes falsely assumed to be a sign of virility, and is therefore of more interest to males, does not appear until after adolescence. Facial hair does appear during adolescence, however, starting with down on the upper lip, then on the chin and along the line of the jaw. "I'm only thirteen, but I'm darker than the other guys, and my mustache is beginning to show. I'm afraid they will think I'm trying to act big if I shave, because none of them do. — Gorilla." We sometimes assume that a boy would be proud to be the first in his class to have to shave, and some boys do carry it off with pride, but others don't have enough confidence to be different, even in such a presumably positive way. Gorilla's parents should be sympathetic to his situation but at the same time let him see that they think it's good he is so mature. They can explain that any kidding he gets comes from envy. A father can advise about razors and shaving cream, yet do it in a matter-of-fact way so as not to inflate the importance of the whole issue.

Voice Change

The deepening of a boy's voice comes along with all these other changes. It's usually gradual, but can also be abrupt and dramatic, like this boy's. "How long does it take for a guy's voice to change? Every time I open my mouth, I can't tell what's going to come out, a normal sound or a squeak. I don't dare call my girlfriend, because she breaks up laughing. — Trumpet of the Swan."

As the larynx enlarges, a boy's voice eventually drops a whole octave. Usually at about age fourteen or fifteen, boys find their voice getting husky, or they may have embarrassing breaks. Teachers especially should go easy on asking boys to speak up in class at this time, and parents can try to mask their amusement somewhat, while tactfully suggesting that, as this is a temporary stage, the boy must endure it with good grace. After all, it's important to learn in adolescence how to cope with minor unpleasantness in order to deal with major problems in adult life. Ridicule does not help kids learn to cope.

Figure Changes

Boys worry just as much as girls do about their eventual physique. Will they be tall, strong, and muscular, or short, scrawny, and wimpy? Weight can be controlled and muscles developed to a certain degree, but, as in other areas of growing up, basic body type is a matter of heredity and something that has to be accepted.

During puberty, boys increase in thickness of bone as well as in height. Greater bone structure is noticeable particularly in the chest area. The body begins to show the broad shoulders and narrow hips of the typical adult male during the fourteenth and fifteenth years, and by about age sixteen, most boys have a pretty mature physique.

Some boys go through a prepubescent fat period, before puberty starts. Developing breast tissue can produce self-consciousness on the beach or may become embarrassingly apparent in the following situation: "Whenever we play basketball, the coach always puts me on the skin team [the side that takes off their shirts to distinguish them from the other team]. I hate this, because my chest is bigger than the other guys', and they all bug me about looking like a girl. Some of them act like I'm gay." Hormonal changes during puberty may overstimulate growth of breast tissue in boys, who find it excruciatingly embarrassing. School coaches should be sensitive to their predicament. Parents who know this is happening should tip off the coach. Then they should make an appointment for a hormone checkup. The problem will probably clear itself up in a year or so, but a busty boy does not need to tough it out alone — he needs help.

Even normal growth patterns often result in embarrassing moments. Newly enlarged legs and feet are hard to control. "Why don't you look where you're going?" complain exasperated parents as their son trips over the rug for the fourteenth time. But if parents suddenly had to wear a size 12 shoe, when last month they wore an 8 or a 9, they would understand how hard just maneuvering around the house can be. A complimentary word from Mom or Dad is not the perfect solution, but it's sure better than nothing.

Parental response to this whole gamut of sexual development goes a long way in shaping the way their children will respond to it themselves. During this stage parents have a great opportunity to foster pride and naturalness in their children's developing sexuality. By treating each change as normal, desirable, and wholesome, parents give their teenagers the necessary attitude for mature and loving sexual relationships in the future. Responding with fear, embarrassment, and secrecy, on the other hand, sets kids up for the sexual games that will thwart rather than enhance a fulfilling adult sex life.

2. Emerging Sexuality

Adolescents are preoccupied with sex. "I keep having these really sexy dreams," writes one girl. Another says, "Whenever a cute guy walks by, I get the strangest feelings." A boy asks, "Isn't there some pill I can take to make me stop thinking about sex all the time?" And a fourteen-year-old writes, "Having sex is all anybody around here ever talks about."

Parents and Teens Have Different Goals

Kids are driven by a compelling force to grow up as quickly as possible. Parents' instinct is to slow them down and keep them safe as long as possible. Thus dawns the generation gap. Teenagers often develop great reticence and even secrecy at this age, largely because their goals and those of their parents have become so different. The gap widens and makes communication very hard. It is a shame, because airing the confusing and scary feelings teenagers have about sex could prevent much of the pressure cooker effect that may result in explosive behavior.

Kids see their parents as overprotective, old-fashioned, restrictive, authoritative, evasive, insincere, and hypocritical about sexual matters. They complain bitterly that their parents have lost trust in them. "My father and I used to be so close, until I entered junior high school. Since then all we do is argue about things like my friends (especially boys), my social life, and 'What am I up to, anyway?' He doesn't seem to trust me at all anymore." Boys have similar complaints. "My parents don't seem to like me. They are always after me about my friends, and how I spend my free time. They seem to think all I want to do is drink booze and get it on with girls."

On the other side of the gap, parents find their teenagers too precocious, too curious, and too secretive about sex. "My daughter used to be such a happy and cheerful girl. Now she doesn't seem to like us anymore. She's always telling secrets on the phone. If I try to talk with her she clams up, or storms out of the room." Teenagers want more and more freedom, and when parents don't agree, they wail "You don't under*stand!*"

A major problem in parents' and teenagers' attitude toward sexuality is their disagreement over their short-term goals. Parents want their teenagers to be happy, responsible, and fulfilled sexual beings in adulthood, but this long-term goal often gets lost in worry about their immediate goal of keeping their children "safe." Teenagers share their parents' long-term goals, but their short-term goals are to satisfy their curiosity about sex, to affirm their maturity through exploration, and to seek pleasure right now.

Talking to Adolescents About Sexuality

Nobody doubts that teenagers need sex education, but when, where, what kind, and how it should be given is a matter of controversy. Since children now mature at an earlier age the need to arm them with information about the realities of sexual behavior is more urgent than before, and parents can help fill this need. Teenagers themselves wish their parents would teach them "the facts of life." "All my mother ever tells me about sex is the birds and the bees. I'm twelve years old, and I need to know about menstruation and stuff like that," writes one girl. A boy, signing himself "Know-Nothing," asked, "Why won't my parents tell me the facts? My Mom keeps saying 'Ask your Dad,' but he just says 'Ask her.' Where can I get the true information?"

Alas, most parents are like this Mom and Dad. A study of 1400 parents conducted in 1978 by the Project on Human Sexual Development disclosed that while all the parents believed they were the ones who ought to educate their own children about the subject, very few actually said much of anything at all. Less than 50 percent of mothers told their daughters about menstruation. Less than 15 percent ever mentioned intercourse or masturbation. Less than 6 percent mentioned contraception. And the fathers? They were virtually silent. The single most important thing that parents, both parents, can do about their children's sexuality is talk to them about it.

What parents do tell kids usually concerns only sin and anger. For generations, kids have been told by adults that sex is wrong and dangerous, trying to scare them out of having intercourse. It hasn't worked. The use of fear and guilt only confuses kids, because what they see happening all around is in direct conflict with this message. Trying to make kids feel guilty may lead to sexual hang-ups, irresponsible behavior, and/or exploitation, but it does not keep kids chaste, at least not today. The rise in rates of teenage intercourse, pregnancy, and sexually transmitted diseases all attest to this. Birth control use is deterred, but not intercourse. This puts the short-term goal ahead of the long-term goal, to the advantage of neither.

Why do parents have such a hard time talking to their children about sexuality? Partly because of ingrained reserve: Their parents never talked to them, either. Most adults find it difficult enough to talk to their partners with any ease or candor let alone their children. The words don't come easily, because adults never say them out loud, except in a locker-room situation. Even younger adults who have grown up in a time of increasing sexual freedom find it hard to get past the Victorian idea that sex is taboo.

Parents find sex education a difficult subject to teach to children, not so much from prudery, however, as from a real sense of uncertainty about what is right. One myth is that teaching kids about sex will make them want to go right out and try it. Parents hope that keeping their children ignorant will keep them innocent, but you can't control children by withholding information. Silence simply accentuates their conviction that sex is a mystery; it either frightens them or encourages them to experiment.

Most children are naturally interested at an early age. How can anyone not be fascinated by this most fundamental aspect of our very existence? How can any child avoid the constant titillation of sexual allusions in the media, the movies, and advertising? No, the giving of calm, factual, practical information by parents will satisfy not stimulate kids' excitement about sex.

Some adults say that kids today know everything about sex already, so they don't need any sex education. Kids may talk big, and even act big, but their information is not always accurate. When parents withhold the facts, kids turn to each other.

Teenagers assume they are the only ones in the dark, and all the other kids know everything. The others may act cool, but nine times out of ten, the answers they give are incorrect. When I receive a letter that starts out "My friend told me . . ." the ensuing fact is almost always wrong. Often the friend covers ignorance by acting superior: "Oh, you don't know that? What a little twit!" This leaves the questioner humiliated and still confused.

Kids learn about sex from many sources — songs, television, books, magazines, and of course, from each other. Consider the sexual lessons they get from television shows. Healthy, mutually caring, loving sexual relationships are seldom shown. When a couple is presumed to have such feelings for each other, their communication goes on behind closed doors. The sexual activity that does get portrayed is often distorted and almost always unwholesome, exploitative, and seductive. What kids need is the truth. And who is left to give it but the parents?

Parents wonder what to say and how to say it. "How much should a parent explain about human relations to a very curious nine-year-old? Larry 'digs' girls, and lots of his pals have girlfriends and even kiss them. He knows babies come out of a 'special place,' but he doesn't know how a man and woman go about 'making a baby.' When should he be told about sexual relations, and how does one go about it? — Mother Hubbard."

It is almost never too early to start. One should answer all a young child's questions simply and honestly. It is so much easier to talk about sexual matters with children before puberty, because they haven't become personally involved yet. Larry's kissing of girls is mostly play-acting, not real sexual behavior, and communication is easier at this younger age. This is the time to establish a give-and-take with children that will develop into a mutually comfortable exchange of information.

In general, you can begin giving your child some information concerning the basic facts of reproduction, pregnancy, and birth, including "making babies," by the time the child is seven. This is a big hurdle for most parents, but the longer they wait, the harder it is to talk about sex.

Parents usually get along all right with the plumbing part of reproduction, but bog down when it comes to coitus. Their embarrassment and confusion is obvious to the children and it sharpens their interest in the subject. If parents evade the questions, or say it is wrong to ask, a child realizes his parents think it is "naughty" and will not ask any more. Yet children need help to know and understand about internal differences and what will be happening inside them when puberty comes along.

Facts about masturbation, intercourse, homosexuality, and rape need to be explained as the child grows. A brief, calm, and simple explanation early on gives kids a basis for more understanding later.

Parents sometimes worry that giving younger children too much information may corrupt them. The truth never corrupts. Children absorb what they are ready to learn, and screen out the rest. It is good to keep answers short and simple. By answering the questions as they come up and avoiding unnecessary complications, the door is kept open for further questions.

It's important for parents to understand what the child is trying to find out. If your child has been told that "the father plants a seed," he or she may be curious about how that compares to gardening. Asking children for their ideas and opinions gives a parent a chance to sort out and correct misinformation.

Masturbation

One tough issue between parent and child may be masturbation. Children almost universally pick up some concern about it. "I masturbate sometimes. Will it really make me sterile when I'm grown up?" The myths about masturbation die hard. Current medical opinion is that it is the normal and healthy way for people to relieve sexual tension without intercourse. At least 99 percent of males and an increasingly large number of females masturbate at some time in their life. There is no physical or psychological harm in it. Frequency ranges from not at all to several times a day, and there is no such thing as "too much" from a physical point of view. The body has a built-in mechanism for protecting itself. If masturbation becomes a substitute for real-life relationships, however, parents need to discover what is inhibiting the child from normal contacts.

If a child is made to feel it is dirty or evil, he or she may become preoccupied with masturbation, and feel guilty about it. In general, however, excessive or flagrant masturbation in young children is not sexual. It may be due to lack of expressive physical affection from parents and extra hugging, attention, and love rather than scolding may ease the problem.

Masturbation ought to be private, naturally, and this may need some explaining to young children. Otherwise, it should not be an issue between parent and child. Accepting it as normal allows the child freedom from guilt.

Dirty Words

What should parents do when children first start using obscene language? Sometimes kids don't really know the meaning of words they hear, and repeat them in innocence, or try them out to test parental reaction. It is harder than it used to be to shock parents, since obscene language is commonplace in movies and books. Still, most of us don't like to hear four-letter words. Swearing is offensive, and a sloppy, boring way to express oneself.

Try not to overreact to such words. If you yell, "Never use that word in my presence again!" the child learns mainly how to get a big rise out of you. Instead, calmly explain what the meaning is: "*Fuck* is a slang word for having sex. Some people also say it when they are mad at each other. That's why it's not the pleasantest word to use for sex. We don't use such words in our house."

The deliberate use of swear words by teenagers can be very unpleasant. It is natural for teenagers to try to shock parents; it is one way they try to prove their growing independence. However, when use of foul language becomes excessive, the teenager may be trying to wrest more freedom from parents. If the need is reasonable, relaxing some rule may help. If it is unreasonable, parents will have to crack down and demand that swearing in their presence stops.

Pornography

Pornography worries many parents, who fear that "center-fold" magazines and "skin-flicks" will impel their children into sex faster than necessary. Psychiatrists feel this isn't likely. They would worry about a child who becomes obsessively involved with pornography, substituting such books and magazines for real-life relationships, but the occasional *Playboy* under the mattress is normal and harmless.

If you discover questionable literature hidden away, it can be a good opportunity to air opinions about such magazines, and the whole issue of sexuality. Gentle and tactful questioning may reveal missing facts your child wishes to know. Or you can suggest or simply provide a more informative and acceptable book on the whole subject.

Parents should protect children from hard-core pornography, such as explicit and violent sexual movies and television shows. They are harmful because they deal with sex only as physical gratification, reducing it to a valueless, mechanical exercise.

Pornography is exaggerated, distorted, often ugly and violent for the purpose of making money. The joys of normal sex are private, not exploited. Some misguided people, who can't participate in normal loving sex, get their kicks out of trying to shock others. Children who have had an adequate education about sex will be least affected, as they can spot the flaws.

Nudity

Nudity in the home troubles some parents. "My husband always walks back and forth from the bathroom naked when he showers. I worry that it is not good for our daughters, who are nine and eleven, to keep seeing an adult male in the nude." If he has always done this, the girls may not be shocked. But as kids usually become more modest at puberty, it would be kinder to the girls if he wrapped a towel around his middle.

On the other hand, it can make kids feel that their bodies are shameful if families make a fuss about nudity, gasp, and run for cover when accidentally discovered without clothes. Some psychiatrists say that parents should continue to behave as they normally do, but not flaunt their nakedness in front of children. Certainly nakedness in small children bothers no one. At puberty, natural modesty about their own growing bodies usually causes kids to cover themselves, and this ought to be respected by other family members.

How to Be a Parent Kids Can Ask

Younger kids want to know about the mechanics of sex and reproduction. As they get older, they want more specific, personal answers. They are curious about feelings, values, and relationships as well. The trouble is, this is the time when communication between parent and teenager is apt to weaken. The issue of sexuality has, in fact, a lot to do with the whole problem of the parent-teen communication gap, because it gets so involved in the struggle for control and independence. When a teenager seems secretive about sex, it may be due to his or her not wanting to appear childish or to a fear of upsetting the parent.

While parents should respect their adolescent's desire to be separate from them, there is still a need for parental understanding and trust. This can't be given blindly; it is necessary to learn something about the child's life and environment away from home. To help keep all lines of communication open, parents should keep in contact with other parents and teachers, do volunteer work in the school — something parents are called upon to do now more than ever, given the problems of our economy — and encourage visits from the child's friends.

"I'd like to tell my kids the facts of life, but they never ask" is a common complaint from parents. They have been turned off; now it is up to parents to turn them on. Sol Gordon, Professor of Child and Family Studies and foremost writer and lecturer on the topic of educating young people about sex, talks about becoming an "askable parent." Here are some suggestions:

1. ***Answer questions.*** What matters most is your attitude toward the child's asking. If you are responsive, it makes your child feel it is okay to come to you, no matter what. It doesn't matter if your answer is not perfect. You can improve on it later. "Remember what we talked about yesterday? I've been thinking about it, and I think a better answer would be . . ."

2. ***Be available.*** Plan to have time alone with your kids, so possibly embarrassing topics can be discussed in private. A child soon learns that it's not just you who considers sex a very special subject, but others do, too. You have to leave the door open so the child knows he or she is welcome.

3. ***Involve fathers.*** Sex has become a women's issue, and this is too bad. Children need the masculine point of view as well. The parent who spends most time with the child and/or is most at ease discussing sexuality will naturally do most of the responding, but it is very important for both parents to take some part in this. The old-fashioned notion that men can't talk sensitively about such matters can be easily refuted. Try!

4. ***Use real words.*** Euphemisms like "wienie," "down there," or "privates" are evasive and just add to confusion about sexuality. If you have never said penis or vulva or vagina out loud, practice doing it first, so you can speak naturally with your child. A proper vocabulary for the parts of the body and their actions is a good first step toward a healthy and informed attitude about sexuality.

Realistically, we don't have a very good vocabulary for sexual relations. Medical language, which is safest in "polite company," seems cold and impersonal. Street language needs to be understood, but many of the words are swear words that don't clearly explain what love is about.

5. ***Reduce embarrassment.*** Talk with your spouse. Decide what information you want to give your child, and then practice talking

about it together, using the right words. If you are a single parent, practice with a close friend. Even talking to the mirror will help, because watching yourself say highly charged words aloud — intercourse, clitoris, foreskin — takes a lot of steam out of them. A formal "giving the facts" session is uncomfortable for everyone, so give answers when the questions happen to come up. Young kids don't know what's a proper time and what isn't, but if they ask at an inappropriate moment, tell them you are glad they asked and you will explain at a better time. Follow up as soon as possible. Then they'll know their question wasn't wrong, just their timing.

Some parents can't be comfortable talking with their kids because they aren't comfortable about their own sexuality. Parents whose own parents gave them a heavy message that sex is evil and dirty can't easily shed these feelings. However, it is still possible to have a discussion. Say, "I can't help being embarrassed talking about this, but I will try." Your child will admire your candor and courage. You can also explain why you are embarrassed and that you hope your children won't have to feel this way.

Children are often embarrassed, too, so be sure to keep talk about sexuality completely impersonal. When they learn that you will neither reveal intimate details about your own life nor pry into theirs, your kids will become more at ease.

6. ***Utilize other sources of help.*** If you just can't bring yourself to talk about sex at all, turn to books. Some excellent ones written for children of different ages are listed in the Suggested Reading section at the end of the book. Another excellent source of help can be an adult with whom your child feels comfortable enough to ask questions. You can't order a teenager to go have a good dialogue about sex, but you can say, "If you ever have questions about such-and-such a subject, Dr. Jones or Uncle Fred (some relative, teacher, minister, etc.) would be a good person to ask." This plants the idea and registers your approval. Other resources are family counselors or community sex education programs in churches, schools, or youth organizations.

7. ***Get the child's ear.*** "I want to tell Lisa and Helen, who are eleven and nine, about sex, but they never ask. When our neighbor had a baby, I explained where babies come from, but they don't

seem to have any other questions at all!" Helen and Lisa must have questions — all kids do. Their mother, though willing, has somehow given them the feeling that it's not okay to ask. Parents will have to initiate the questions even if the children don't. Make use of events in stories, movies, TV, neighborhood births and marriages, etc., to lead into a discussion. Look for clues from your children. Listen for hidden questions. If they see animals mating, for instance, they may ask about it, which opens the door to questions about human sexual relations.

You can be a little oblique sometimes. If your child seems really embarrassed, be particularly careful not to become personal about the subject.

Listen as well as talk. When they find you pay attention to what they say, without judging, adolescents will speak. To find out what misconceptions children might have, encourage them to talk about their thoughts. For instance, ask, "What did you think about the way Dave was pushing Janie around in that television show?" "Why do you think it's not a good idea for kids to hitchhike alone?" "Is it all right for girls to ask boys out the first time?"

8. ***Use humor.*** You obviously don't want to tell kids dirty jokes: it would strain parent/child relationships and embarrass your children if you put sex into the category of "gutter" humor, even if they do it themselves. But you certainly can use a light tone whenever possible. Because sex is such an emotional subject, it makes us all want to giggle sometimes, and that's just fine. Kids will grow up feeling that their sexuality is natural and happy, not just serious, hard work!

9. ***Find the answers yourself.*** If you don't know the answer, say so. If you say, "What the heck does that mean?" your kids will be impressed that you have enough self-confidence to admit you don't know everything. You aren't diminished in their eyes; in fact, you rise in their esteem if you show your willingness to do research on their behalf. You may want to get a book in which to look up information, and let the child read it too. Sharing this way improves communication. If you have to ask a doctor or a health clinic, it's all the more impressive. The Planned Parenthood hotline is always glad to answer questions. This is a useful resource for children, too.

10. ***State your own values.*** This is the crux of parental concern

about sex education. One of the biggest fears parents have about family education classes in school is that their kids will be taught values that contrast with their own. Most teachers try hard to be nonjudgmental, to discuss values without dictating what is right and wrong. It is impossible for any individual not to convey some of his values inadvertently, but by the age of puberty, children know their parents' values very well.

Most parents want stricter morals for their kids than those which they in fact apply to themselves. The important thing to realize is that children pick up what your true beliefs are, through your comments, language, emotion, and feelings toward others. There ought to be a narrow gap, if any gap at all, between what you really believe is true and what you tell them is right. Don't be afraid to say what you really think. What is right for you, an adult, may not be right at all for a ten- or twelve-year-old, but he or she should know the difference. In other words, you needn't be afraid to sound too "liberal," but by the same token, don't be afraid of sounding too old-fashioned. Your children may not hold to your values, but they should respect yours as you would theirs. This teaches children to respect the concept of value systems, rather than to reject the whole system out of hand if they disagree with certain parts of it.

11. ***Talk about love and relationships.*** Talking to kids about sex only in terms of morality has not stopped them from becoming sexually active. Morality has become the buzz word for "genital sex," when what it should mean is acting so as not to hurt other people or oneself. Parents need to talk to children about a lot more than just the sexual part of relationships — talk also about trust and fidelity, caring, restraint, intimacy, and vulnerability. There will be more about this in Chapter 5, but it is important to stress that one should start this kind of talking before puberty so that children will always connect thoughts about sex with thoughts about loving relationships.

Young boys, especially, tend to think of sex only in the genital sense. We need to get them past the misconceptions that slick magazines and soap operas convey about love, to a realistic understanding of mature love, with its highs and lows, pleasures and pain, fun and hard work, and the knowledge that commitment is important to a relationship.

Sexual Identity

How people view themselves as males or females is an integral part of their identity. It colors the way they think about themselves, and the way they react to others.

People have to identify with their own sex first. What do men do? How do women act? Feel? Think? Trying to fit the role they are supposed to fill makes a big difference in boys' and girls' developing personality. Kids often start letters to me with "I am a girl . . ." or "I am a boy . . ." and then state their age, maybe their grade, and what the problem is. As adults, we too are constantly asked to identify ourselves as "M" or "F."

Whatever the innate difference between the two sexes, society sets the rules. Adults respond differently to boys and girls right from birth. A boy baby is spoken to in a firmer voice. A girl baby is more cuddled and cooed over. Parents have divergent attitudes, hopes, and expectations toward sons and daughters all through childhood. Schools educate boys and girls differently with stereotypical academic and social expectations for each.

Religious attitudes, health care, and social services are cultural influences that also affect sex roles. The law and the courts do not treat boys and girls in the same way for the same crime. Perhaps the most striking differences are found in the work place, where women's pay and promotions still lag far behind men's, and men's time off for child care lags far behind women's.

Double Standards

The old double standard is still very much in existence. Masculinity is defined by success in sex, in physical activity, and in the marketplace. Femininity is defined by success in love relationships and maternity. Girls are raised to be compliant, noncompetitive, passive, good-looking, and nurturing, in order to attract men and maintain their love. "Be a good girl" means don't fight, don't get dirty, don't be too aggressive or adventuresome. Girls are praised for being affectionate, sensitive, expressive, and docile. The fact that girls are more affected by their reproductive systems — that hormonal changes can make them moody and "unreliable" — is exaggerated. Though less now than a decade ago, they are still urged to be interested in domestic affairs, and to have careers in the service areas, such as nursing, teaching, and social work.

Boys are raised to be aggressive, active, assertive, curious, strong, courageous, and protective of the weak. "Be a good boy" means don't cry, don't complain, get up and hit 'em again. Boys are admired for achievement in sports, in jobs, in school. Boys are expected to be strong and silent, and not ask for help, or worry about feelings. They are supposed to be uninterested in ballet or painting, and instead to partake in "masculine" things like cars, power, speed, machinery, sex, war, and politics.

The women's liberation movement, spurred by the economic necessity of many women to work, is creating changes in society's attitudes toward males and females, and in sex roles. More men now help with child care and housework, and more women expect to have careers rather than just depending on their husbands to define their place in society. However, these changes are occurring very slowly: many of the old stereotypes about how boys and girls should behave still persist.

The effect of all these "supposed to be's" on a growing personality is enormous. Inborn traits and talents may be warped or inhibited. A girl's natural curiosity to test and explore is squelched. From an early age, she's taught to suppress her physical being, her desire to be independent, and especially any sexual curiosity. As a result, girls don't develop such effective inner controls or such an independent sense of self as do boys. Instead, they keep trying to "see themselves as others see them," in order to be loved. Their self-esteem needs constant reinforcement, through the approval of others rather than from their own achievements. Through life, women persistently value themselves according to the way they are rated by others. This is why women are said to take everything personally. They are taught to see issues in terms of how they will be affected by them, instead of trying to see things objectively. "How will they like me if I cut my hair?" (Not "How will I like myself.") "What will they think of me if I wear a long skirt?" (Not "How will I like it on myself.")

Boys enjoy more independence and self-assertion. They are encouraged to indulge their native curiosity and inborn energy, but may suffer from heavy pressure to compete, to get ahead, to succeed. This pressure, coupled with the assumption that boys never cry, complain, or talk about personal problems, means that they lose touch with their own feelings. "I'm a boy, fifteen, and for two years I've been wanting to quit football, but I don't dare tell anybody. They'd probably think I was a sissy or chicken. — Unshirted Hell." Boys are not encouraged to explore their own inner landscape, and find it more difficult to learn how other people feel. Their self-esteem depends more directly on achieving and winning than on intimate relationships.

This double standard affects children's behavior in many ways. Boys and girls are segregated so often in the school room and the gymnasium that they become rivals, if not enemies. "You walk like a girl!" is one of the worst insults one boy can hurl at another. "She's a tomboy" is usually a put down. A boyish girl is not "date bait." "They treat me like I'm just a pal," writes a talented eighth-grade ballplayer. "When will they see I'm really a girl?"

Girls are not supposed to be pals. Their place is to wait around, neat and clean, for boys to ask them out. The heavy differentiation between gender roles implies that it's better to be a boy. This pushes girls into earlier dating, which is the real testing ground for the adolescent girl. If many boys ask her out, she's made it. She's a desirable woman. Her esteem goes up. While it is true that girls mature sexually earlier than boys, this early dating isn't really motivated by sexual desire but by the need to prove desirability.

Stereotyping accentuates the differences between boys and girls, making genuine friendships hard for them. The traditional male-female point of view has encouraged the boys to think of the girls as sex objects and the girls to value themselves accordingly. "Why don't boys ever think of anything but making out?" they complain. "All my boyfriend ever does is paw me." All the while, these girls are doing their level best to attract the very attention they deplore. Alas, during their preteen years, these boys and girls have gotten out of touch with each other as equals. So now when they would like to communicate, they can't talk to each other with any ease at all. "What do girls like to talk about, anyway?" is the question I get most often from young teenage boys.

Such sex-role stereotyping takes a heavy toll when teenagers do start serious dating. Who is going to be responsible for their safety and health? Girls don't feel comfortable enough with the boys to bring the subject up. Boys aren't raised to feel any accountability for sexual exploits. If she gets pregnant, that's *her* problem. This is one big reason for the tragic rate of teenage pregnancy.

Parents will do well to down play sex-role differences in raising teenagers, and to help sons and daughters think of the opposite sex as being very much like their own rather than very different.

Homosexual Fears

The strong and persistent message to children that "boys will be boys" and "girls must be girls" places a big burden on teenagers, for people aren't really divided by gender into two distinct and totally different species, one *all* masculine and the other *all* feminine. Gender differences are strung out along a scale. There is some degree of bisexuality in all of us. We start out as embryos, exactly the same. We have parents of both sexes as role models, at least some of the time. We share common traits with the opposite sex, all the time. This makes the identity crisis hard for many kids. They wonder, what does being a man or woman really mean?

It is typical in early adolescence for teenagers to review past childhood phases of their life, and reject what is no longer appropriate for the adult-to-be. Parents will recognize some really infantile behavior at times. While this doesn't usually last long, it often involves a crush on someone of the same sex, which can be scary to kids. Crushes are normal, and usually transient, but a boy who finds himself admiring another boy extravagantly, even to the point of passion, can find this upsetting. "Kids laugh at me because I've got this thing about the coach. He's a really great guy, and they know it, but they say I must be gay because I talk about him so much. I don't think I am. Am I?"

Homosexuality is a key issue in the process of sexual identity. A father's greatest fear for his son is that he might become gay. This naturally communicates itself to the boy, and youthful crushes can be very unnerving.

The subject may come up through name-calling. Young kids hurl names like "gay," "fag," "queer" without knowing what they really mean. A boy who has a slight build, is studious rather than athletic, and perhaps effeminate in manner is frequently labelled a "homo." Mannish girls may be called lesbian, or "butch," though it is less common.

Homosexual fears may also be aroused by the common comparing of "masculinity" that often goes on in the locker room. Trying to prove "mine's bigger than yours" sometimes results in group experimentation, arousing fear and guilt. Girls are now having this kind of worry more often as the struggle for sexual equality has put lesbianism on the front page, too.

Parents need to assure teenagers that concerns about homosexuality are perfectly normal. They can do this by talking calmly and factually about what homosexuality really is, rather than presenting the issue only as an unnatural evil. Explain that there are people who prefer sexual relations with others of the same sex. Although the exact number isn't known, it is estimated that from 4 to 10 percent of the population is gay. This is a tough issue for parents to discuss, because society has such intense fear about it. In fact, some fathers are even afraid to hug or kiss their sons lest they turn them into homosexuals. This is just the point that needs to be made clear. A boy or girl can't be "turned into" a homosexual. Homosexuality is determined very early in childhood, though experts are not sure exactly how this happens. But even an actual homosexual experience will not change people's sexual identity if they are not gay to begin with.

By the same token, kids who are destined to be truly gay can seldom, if ever, be talked out of it. Sexual direction usually makes itself known at about the time of puberty. If a person is gay, the issue can't be dismissed by saying "it's only a phase." Homosexuality is not a matter of choice. Parents who discover that their child is gay will often take him or her to a psychiatrist for treatment. If the child has emotional problems accepting his or her sexual direction, this can be helpful, but it will probably not make the child heterosexual.

Parents of gays need a lot of help, too. There are several good books to enhance their understanding, as well as organizations for parents of gays that provide support and relief. Parents should learn to understand what being gay really does mean, so they will not "lose" their child through fear and disappointment. Parents can be helped to see that this is the same child they always had; only the matter of sexual preference, which is, after all, an entirely private matter, is different from what they had hoped or expected.

Fighting the Double Standard

Sex-role stereotyping has intensified our fears about homosexuality. By fearing to allow any so-called feminine traits in males, lest they tip into the homosexual category, we do boys a tremendous disservice. We deny them the softer, more tender aspects of their natures and exaggerate their competitiveness and aggression. In this sense, sex-role stereotyping tends to make enemies of men and women. Psychiatrists have found stereotyping to be one of the most devisive influences in relationships between the sexes, continuing to divide men and women right through adulthood. So in providing good sex education for our children, we should try to protect them from the damaging effects of the old double standard.

Kids will be much better off if we allow them to develop their genuine, personal interests, traits, and talents instead of trying to force them into preconceived molds of little men and little women.

Parents need to encourage their daughters to be curious, to explore, to take some chances, to compete, and allow them to assert themselves physically and intellectually instead of stifling them by saying "girls don't do that."

Boys can be helped to see that it's okay for men to be tender and sensitive. Allow your sons to express their emotions openly — even to cry. Girls don't cry as much when they grow up, because they find out it doesn't solve problems. Boys will learn that, too. If they are allowed to release their sadness, anger, or joy — in action as toddlers and by talking about these feelings as they mature — they will learn better how to handle their own emotions and to understand others' more deeply. Let your sons know that it is good to ask for help. Many men believe that admitting a problem is a sign of weakness, but no one is infallible. Knowing when you need help is a sign of maturity, for boys as well as girls.

Help daughters explore and develop talents, hobbies, and interests that might become careers. Today's girls are tomorrow's working women, not only because of liberation but because of economics. Girls as well as boys need opportunities to learn skills, in school, in part-time jobs after school, or during vacations. Volunteer jobs can be very productive. Parents should assume that their daughters will be doing something worthwhile and satisfying when they grow up, including being a wife and or mother. Don't set specific goals. Girls, like boys, have the potential and the will to work for whatever they want and feel is important.

Chores should be nonsexist. It's important to teach both sons and daughters how to cook, sew on buttons, change tires, and do yard work. Household and parenting skills will one day be useful to boys, too, when working mates will need and expect help from each other. Many of today's adolescents will be single heads of households. Girls as well as boys will need to repair their own appliances, keep their own cars running, balance their own checkbooks.

What does all this have to do with sex education? How boys and girls respect each other has everything to do with how they treat each other. For example, a girl who has healthy self-esteem can say no to unwanted sexual advances. She won't let herself be exploited. Similarly boys who are taught to appreciate the opposite sex as friends and equals won't be so likely to treat girls as sex objects.

Nonsexist upbringing doesn't make girls into amazons or boys into weaklings. A girl can enjoy machinery and sports and racing cars and still be feminine. A boy can enjoy poetry, ballet, and small furry animals and still be masculine. Society is moving toward a more egalitarian relationship between men and women, instead of sex-typed role-playing. Equality of the sexes is more demanding, but infinitely more rewarding, too.

Coping with children's sex education is one of the toughest jobs parents face. It helps to remember that we are all created as sexual beings. Even the Bible says that sexuality is to be honored, respected, and affirmed. Parents who can create an environment in the home in which children can like all aspects of themselves, including sexuality, pave a smoother road to maturity for their children.

There are many places parents can go for help. (See Suggested Reading for titles of books and pamphlets.) Look also for programs about sex education in your school, library, church, family planning clinic, or mental health agency. The Red Cross and March of Dimes have sponsored programs, as have cooperative extension services, 4-H Clubs, the Y, and other organizations. Your local Planned Parenthood League can help. Or you can write to Sex Information and Education Council of the United States (SIECUS), 1855 Broadway, New York, NY 10023.

3. Face and Figure

To be young, beautiful, and thin has assumed tremendous importance in our life today. If you look at ads or listen to commercials, you might conclude that it matters far more to be attractive than to be intelligent, resourceful, and skilled. The impact of this on teenagers is tremendous. Looking their best is an important goal, but at this time of life, their development doesn't always add up to smooth and chic. They are more likely to come up with oily hair, acne, fat hips, skinny muscles, or blackheads. Such problems are difficult at any age, but to the quivering teenage ego, they seem the ultimate disaster.

How seriously should parents take an adolescent's concerns about face or figure? Pretty seriously. If you try to shrug off these concerns, you are dealing another blow to an ego already suffering from pimples and baby fat. Complaints should be heeded. Don't say "You'll outgrow it," unless you know that the condition is definitely developmental. Do find out if there is a treatment that will help. The answer for the parent is to be sympathetic to the youngster's problems and realistic about resolving them.

Figure Problems

The changes in shape that puberty brings are discussed in Chapter 1. The following is a discussion of some figure problems adolescents face.

Proper Weight

A family's concern with good nutrition will pay off in the long run, even if kids have fat or thin periods along the way. In adolescence, parents have to rely heavily on their kids established eating habits and knowledge of nutrition, because teenagers do most of their eating away from home. Since kids do a lot of munching when they're with their friends, eating becomes a big social event in teen-age life. Many of them, especially rapidly growing boys, are bot-tomless pits. They eat a full dinner, including seconds, and then stand in front of the refrigerator, half an hour after the dishes are done, and complain that there's nothing to eat. Breakfast may be skipped, lunch eaten at school, after-school treats shared with friends at the local pizza or hamburger joint.

Parents should see to it that meals provided at home are well balanced. Healthy "whole food," such as fruit, raw vegetables, yogurt, and whole wheat bread, should be kept on hand for snacking. Par-ents need to discuss intelligent eating habits with their teenager, stressing that good nutrition makes a person look better and per-form better, in the classroom as well as on the playing field.

Girls are generally more conscious of their weight and the boys of their physique during teenage. A girl's average percentage of body fat increases to 20 to 24 percent of her total weight during puberty. A boy's decreases to 16 to 10 percent. Looking attractive is supposed to help a girl be appealing, get a man, get a job, even do better in school. So girls may think they are too fat, even when they aren't. One way to find out what weight is proper for your child is to consult an age-height-weight chart.

Such charts should be used as guidelines only. For one thing, the numbers vary somewhat from doctor to doctor. For another, they don't take into account a person's skeletal structure. You can't deter-mine the ideal weight for a fifteen-year-old, sixty-three-inch high girl unless you know whether she has heavy or fine bones. One way to tell is to try to close the fingers of one hand around the other wrist. If they don't overlap you have large bones. Another way to test for fatness is by the "skinfold test": Using the points of a caliper, or your thumb and forefinger, pinch a fold of skin on the underside of your upper arm. The thickness of the fold indicates the amount of fat under the skin. At fourteen, the average male skinfold thickness is 17 mm., the female, 23 mm. At sixteen, these measurements average 15 mm. for males, 25 mm. for females. A person with near-average skinfold thickness has about the right measure of total body fat.

Overweight

If your teenager is too fat or is clearly gaining too much, the first step is to see the doctor. Although teenage is probably the healthiest time of life, there are a few physical conditions, such as a malfunctioning thyroid or diabetes, that can cause weight problems. If, as is likely, there is no medical cause for the weight gain, the doctor can prescribe a good diet and give persuasive reasons why proper weight is important to health, vitality, and good looks. Helping a heavy teenager with weight control is a tricky proposition. Adolescents resent parents who try to tell them what to eat. Effective control requires the utmost tact, and ridicule is certainly no solution.

When parents tease or shame a chubby child into dieting, it almost always backfires. "My family keeps making remarks about my weight. I know I'm a little too fat, but when they say mean things, I feel so bad, I end up eating a big bowl of ice cream, or the whole box of cookies. How can I tell my mother she is only making me worse? — Miss Piggy." People often use food as a source of comfort when they are unhappy; nagging at kids only depresses them further, causing them to eat more. It's more effective not to attempt to control a child's diet but to find out what's depressing him or her in the first place.

Stress contributes to weight gain. Concerns about social life, sex, exams, drugs, physical development, and the future in general can cause a teenager a great deal of nervousness. Many students come home from a day at school and reach into the refrigerator for a reward. Those who get dull teaching, classwork that is stultifying or meaningless, and no relief by way of extracurricular activity or sports may be truly "bored out of their minds," week after week. Food may become the only high spot in their day. Trying to take away this pleasure by limiting sweets and ice cream might be a mistake. A much better answer is to help overeaters develop some areas of genuine interest and success.

"I'm a sophomore in high school and I'm not popular at all, especially with boys. I have some girlfriends, but I weigh close to 155, so no boy will look at me. Sometimes I am able to lose some weight, but then I seem to put it all back on again. — Elephant Woman." Feeling they have no friends is a common reason girls, and boys too, turn to food for compensation. Once more, the parents will be more effective attacking the reasons for the unpopularity, rather than the overeating itself.

Some teenagers eat too much because they don't feel ready for a more adult kind of social life. Being fat assures them of not being asked out socially. This response is usually subconscious. Girls or boys like Elephant Woman may believe their unpopularity is due to fatness, when in truth, they are fat because they don't dare risk the popularity game yet. With a little maturity and more confidence, these teenagers usually develop active social lives, and the fat melts away by itself.

Fear of success can also cause a young person to stay fat. If there is undue pressure to achieve, get on the honor roll, make the team, "get" the most desirable boy or girl, get into the Ivy League college, a teenager may become obese as an unconscious excuse for failing. Parents' vicarious efforts to satisfy their own longings or unmet needs through their children can cause these intense pressures. Children may, in turn, misinterpret their parents' hopes and set up impossible goals for themselves. Wise parents will reassess these goals and make sure they are realistic for their child. This may relieve the pressure and permit the child to stop overeating.

Dieting

When teenagers decide that they need to diet, and ask for help, it's a different story. Parents can help by planning tasty, attractive, and nonfattening meals. If the rest of the family feels gypped, let them eat their chocolate cake in private. Snacks, at least at home, can be limited to raw vegetables, fruit, fruit juices, and low-calorie beverages.

If a doctor's diet is being followed, there's no problem about nutrition. But a child who tries a crash diet is not getting the nutriments that are necessary for someone who is still growing. The right amounts of vitamins, minerals, and protein are important for good looks and vigor, as well as for good health. Vitamin substitutes, lean meat, fish, and vegetables can supply most of these needs with very few calories. The way to convince kids that this kind of wholesome diet is best is to talk in terms of friendship and success, glowing skin, shiny hair, a firm figure, and vitality on the playing field, as well as at school.

Exercise plays a key role in weight loss, but it's hard to make some teenagers believe it. Nutritional experts, such as Dr. Jean Mayer, have found that fat children may be eating no more than thin ones, but they use their bodies far less. They move slowly. Even during exercise periods, such as swimming, the lean kids are zipping around, while the fat ones may just hang on the side of the pool. A little extra walking, biking, swimming, or cross-country skiing can burn up a lot of extra calories.

Many girls have written to me about exercise: "I don't exercise because it will make me even hungrier. And anyway, I don't want to develop big muscles like an athlete. I want to stay slim." Such a girl needs to be told that far from making her bulge with muscles, normal exercise will make her slim and less hungry too. Of course, the best exercise of all is a vigorous thrust of the body away from the table, before too much has been eaten.

"I'm a few pounds overweight, but I can never stick to my diet. What about these pills you can buy? Are they dangerous?" The answer is yes, most diet pills contain some kind of amphetamine, or "speed." These powerful stimulants can "soup up" the body so that a person becomes full of energy and burns off extra weight, but the amphetamines are also habit forming and have toxic side effects. Regular use is dangerous, especially to teenagers, through loss of sleep and improper nutrition. There are no real short cuts — sauna baths, steam, body belts, etc. — to thinness. One simply must reduce calories and increase exercise.

A plan that works for some teenagers starts with keeping a record of everything they normally eat for a week, counting carefully how many calories they take in. If their weight stays the same, then this is a maintenance diet for them. To lose one pound a week, they need to cut back several hundred calories per day, depending on the exercise they get. Increasing exercise speeds the loss. But teenaged girls cannot go below 1000 or 1200 calories daily and boys cannot go below about 1500 without risking physical problems. With this system, the teenager controls his or her own diet and can pick favorite foods (taking into account nutritional needs). Not all teens have the patience to keep such records or portion their food so strenuously.

Kids who want to lose but are having trouble may find that a diet club is the answer.

Weight Watchers and Diet Workshop (commercial organizations) and Overeaters Anonymous (a nonprofit, self-help group) all have had good results with some adolescents. They work only if the program is something the teenager wants to do; a parent cannot push a child into it with expectations of success. The same is true of the so-called fat camps. Well-motivated campers may lose a lot; campers who are persuaded to go against their will may be shamed into losing some flab, but often it's gained right back. They may even gain more in defiance against being forced. Teenage is a time when developing one's own will is essential and threats to self-control are explosive.

"I'm not really too fat. My upper body is just about right, but I have fat hips and a big rear. What can I do about them, without losing weight on my chest? — Hippo." The hips, buttocks, and upper thighs are what doctors call the "depot area," where excess fat is stored first. A girl getting too large here (if she hasn't just inherited wide hips) is starting to get too fat. A little extra exercise will probably do the trick, though a small cut in daily calories will speed the process.

Stretch marks are associated with rapid weight gain or loss. Mothers know them only too well from pregnancy. Teenage girls may complain of little red lines on their hips, thighs, and breasts. They can be reassured that these will turn silvery and barely noticeable after a while. A beauty queen might resort to dermabrasion to remove them, but this is too expensive and unpleasant for most people to consider.

We have all heard that "inside every fat person there is a thin one, screaming to be let out." When the thin person does emerge she or he usually believes that all previous problems have been solved, and now she or he will be attractive, popular, and successful in every way. Alas, it isn't that simple. Weight is a matter of health, not personality. Reaching average weight doesn't automatically change teenagers' lives or friendships, so they need help in reshaping their self-image as well as their figures. To help with self-image a teenager might get into a new club or extracurricular activity, get a job after school to meet new friends, change a hair-do or clothing style, or try a new sport, instrument, or hobby. Parents can help with suggestions, being careful not to make *too* much over a teenager's weight loss. Dieting can get out of hand.

Underweight

Some people are just naturally thin. "I have no figure at all," wrote Sheila. "I keep eating everything in sight, but nothing helps. I'm fourteen. My arms and legs are like sticks, and as for a chest — forget it!" Boys, too, may be unhappy over their physiques. "I'm skinny and unmuscular. I keep getting taller, but I never fill out or get a better build. How can I shape up? — Bean Pole."

Thinness is not usually due to illness in adolescence. A sudden loss of appetite or weight ought to be checked by a physician, but kids who keep gaining normally, even though they stay at the bottom of the weight chart, are almost always healthy. There are other causes for being skinny.

Sudden growth in height stretches the body out so that it may appear unusually lanky for a while. Curves and muscles come with maturity. Most thinness is due to heredity. Kids who have lean body types with fine bones and long rather than round muscles are not going to change very much. Such "ectomorphs" seldom get fat. If your son, like Bean Pole, wants to develop a more muscular look, suggest he speak to his athletic coach about exercises, or get him a book on body building. He will never make himself into an Arnold Schwarzenegger, but he can improve his physique quite a bit. It is healthy to have an ectomorphic body type, and parents can console teens that everyone else is out there jogging their tails off, trying to look like them!

Anorexia and Bulimia

Anorexia nervosa and bulimia are two severe eating disorders that are becoming more common among teenagers and young adult women. Boys can get these disorders as well, but 90 percent of the cases are female.

This letter describes a fairly typical anorexic. "Last year I was happy in school, but this year my life is a torment. Kids teased me about being chubby, so I dieted down to a normal weight. Everyone said I looked so great, I thought it would be good to get just a little thinner, for insurance. Now I can't stop! I think about food all the time, but something seems to keep me from eating. My friends hate me, and my parents do, too." Anorexia sufferers literally starve themselves, and despite all the weight they lose, they look in their mirrors and still see a fat person. When 20 percent of their body weight is lost, girls stop menstruating. They look terrible, with toothpick arms and legs, huge eyes, dry skin, and thinning hair, but they may insist they feel fine and continue running and exercising. They are burning up their own muscle, however, and in a dangerous way. Some literally starve themselves to death.

Bulimia takes the form of alternate binging and purging. Bulimics can't stop themselves from orgies of eating and then ridding themselves of the loathed food, by self-induced vomiting, laxatives, or both. Bulimia can be an even more lethal disease than anorexia, as the body chemistry becomes severely unbalanced. In both cases, kids are depressed, feel guilty, and often have suicidal thoughts.

The causes of anorexia and bulimia are not yet clearly understood. Many of the girls who have the diseases were exceptionally docile as children. Perhaps they tried to please their parents at the expense of their own needs. Other factors seem to be a conflict over separation from family, a flight from sexual maturity and/or autonomy development. The disease may be a breakdown, a crisis, a call for help. In any case, it becomes a severe problem and it is important to get professional help. The sooner treatment begins, the better the chance of recovery.

Treatments vary with the individual. Some combination of medical and psychiatric therapy is usually recommended. Because the issue is so often one of control — the teenager versus the parent — adolescents may respond well to the self-help groups that are being formed in some communities. Your doctor or hospital may know of such groups, or you can write for information to the Anorexia Nervosa Aid Society, Box 213, Lincoln Center, MA 01773.

Posture

Faulty posture is fairly common in adolescence, and can lead to backaches and other problems. It is seldom due to a physical cause; like adults, modern teenagers seldom walk when they can ride, they slouch when they sit, carry loads badly, or slump deliberately to hide excess height or bustiness, and eventually, their muscles just don't hold them up straight anymore.

Nagging will not help. Parents can point out the consequences of bad posture, but the advice of a doctor will be more effective. Sometimes a doctor will even prescribe a brace, simply to remind young patients to keep their shoulders back and stand up straighter.

Scoliosis is one posture problem that does have a physical origin, and it most often makes its appearance in adolescence, particularly among girls. It is a side-to-side curvature of the spine. As the girl grows taller, the curve becomes more noticeable, sometimes making an obvious difference in the height of her shoulders. The spine may rotate as well as curving, so one breast may seem more pronounced, or the pelvis thrust more to one side than the other. Pediatricians usually check for straightness of the spine in routine physical exams, but sometimes the girl herself is the first to notice something wrong, perhaps because her clothes don't fit properly. Parents should consult an orthopedist right away, as treatment started early has the greatest chance of success. Exercises, braces, or surgery may be used to treat scoliosis.

Complexions

Whoever said "But my face — I don't mind it/For I am behind it;/It's the people in front get the jar" was a liar. Our faces are out there fronting for us all the time, and we mind about them very much. First impressions are very important to adolescents. But what do they get to work with? Zits! Blackheads! Pimples! Complexion troubles are the scourge of teenage, and until recently, acne was little understood. Now more help is available.

Acne

Almost all kids have some complexion trouble after puberty. This may last several years, but is usually, though not always, cleared up by early adulthood. "Help," wails Jim, "I've got blackheads on both sides of my nose and my forehead. I wash and wash. I never eat chocolate, but now I'm getting pimples, too. Why is this happening to me?" The hormonal activity in puberty brings changes in the skin, along with everything else. Little glands in the skin, called sebaceous glands, start producing more oil, so teenagers start having oily skin. This oil, or sebum, is supposed to flow to the surface of the skin, through little ducts, or follicles. In many persons, some pores, the openings of these ducts, become plugged, however. The oil can't get out and forms a whitehead, or comedo. If the duct stretches and air reaches the trapped oil, it gets darker. The comedo turns black and becomes a blackhead. It is not dirt but the trapped oil and dead cells that create blackheads.

Sometimes the follicle wall doesn't stretch. Oil and dead cells continue to be produced inside so they burst through the follicle wall under the skin. The skin becomes inflamed and bacteria multiply furiously, causing a pimple. Pus may form and cause the pimple to come to a head. This is acne. As it is the result of overactive sebaceous glands and clogged oil ducts, the treatment is first to get rid of what is doing the clogging, second to reduce the activity of oil glands, and third to kill the bacteria.

Regular home treatment can improve both blackheads and pimples. The skin should be washed, not scrubbed, with a mild soap twice a day, more in hot weather if the skin gets oily. After the soap is rinsed off, an acne product should be applied that penetrates the pores and kills the bacteria in the plugged-up ducts. Benzoyl peroxide is by far the most effective ingredient. Gels, which are thinner, are better than creams or lotions, but you may have to get a doctor's prescription for these. Directions must be followed carefully in order to build up tolerance gradually, as benzoyl peroxide irritates some skin at first. Products containing salicylic acid can help mild acne but do not prevent new blemishes from forming.

Exposing acne to light and air is also helpful. A little sun or *careful* use of a sun lamp is often healing. Keeping air away from affected skin by hiding it behind clothes or bangs only makes matters worse.

Squeezing pimples may force the inflammation further into the skin. Blackheads can be removed by centering an eye dropper or comedo extractor on them and forcing the plugged oil up into the tube. (For a more detailed description, see the books on skin care listed in the Suggested Reading section.) Touching the face with the hands, picking, and leaning the face on the hands are causes of acne flare-ups. Mothers *are* right about this. Trying to get kids out of this habit is as important for improvement as any treatment.

Home treatment works only if the person with acne has the will power to follow the routine daily. Parents can provide information and antiacne supplies if the teenager agrees, but bugging kids to use them will probably have a negative effect. It may take some weeks to see any improvement, and since adolescents are notoriously impatient, parents may need to provide a realistic estimate about how long it will take for the complexion to improve, so the kids don't give up in discouragement.

In the past, parents blamed acne on things like rich food, poor hygiene, even thinking "dirty thoughts" and masturbation. None of these affect the complexion. Two factors that do are stress and menstruation. "Dear Beth, Derek asked me to the prom. I was in seventh heaven. Got a dreamy new dress and then disaster! My face broke out like the Civil War. What am I going to do?? — Smallpox." Most of us can remember similar occasions. What Smallpox needs is parental sympathy plus wise advice about cover-up make-up. Dermatologists advise water-based make-ups because oil-based ones aggravate acne. Boys, too, may want and need some way to cover up pimples, and parents who endorse rather than ridicule their efforts to look better will make their lives that much pleasanter.

If consistent home treatment doesn't help the complexion significantly, take your child to a good dermatologist for topical antibiotic treatment. Lotions or gels that contain clindamycin or erythromycin and are applied directly to the skin are more effective than antibiotics taken by mouth.

A new treatment has just been approved by the Food and Drug Administration. It is a derivative of vitamin A, called 13-C1S retinoic acid (trade name Accutane). Taken as a pill, this drug is highly successful in severe cystic acne but is not used for mild acne. It does promise more help in the future.

While it is true that acne is usually outgrown, don't wait in the case of bad acne, because it can produce scars that *won't* be outgrown. Furthermore, bad pimples and scars can seriously interfere with social life. Adolescence is a critical time in the formation of self-image and you want to do everything you can to keep a teenager from developing an image that is scarred or pimply and therefore ugly.

Other Complexion Problems

Just plain oily skin, even without pimples, can be treated with the same drying gels used for acne. Another helpful product is the little towelettes for quick face wipes. They contain alcohol, which is drying, and can easily be carried to school.

Dry skin and chapping is less of a problem during teenage. If dry houses and cold winters do create this condition, using any kind of oil on the skin after washing will prevent chapping. Oil doesn't sink into the skin. The moisture comes from water within the skin; lotions simply prevent this from evaporating, so petroleum jelly is as effective as the most expensive creams.

A more common problem for teenagers is this one: "I've got freckles all over. Everyone calls me Spots, or Spotty Puss. What can I do to get rid of the hateful things? I tried getting tan, but it just made them worse." People with very fair skin, particularly those with red hair, are especially prone to freckling. Tanning does make it worse, for the sun is the cause, not the cure. Nothing makes them go away. Staying out of the sun, and most important, using a sunscreen lotion, is the only way to keep them from getting worse. Fair-skinned people should use a sunscreen with a sun protection factor of 15 (SPF 15) at all times. Even walking back and forth to the school bus or to the store can add up to enough exposure to the sun to make more freckles.

The effect of the sun on all white skin is to damage and age it. I doubt if parents can effectively persuade their daughters that they are going to deplore later the deep bronze tans they got in their teens. Squint lines, wrinkles, age spots, and eventually, cancerous skin growths beset older people who have had too much sun. Parents are fighting a fashion for the tanned "healthy look," but make sure your kids realize the consequences. Sun lamps, if not used with extreme caution, are just as bad, if not worse. And for Pete's sake don't let your teenager near those tanning parlors!

Make-up

"I'm thirteen and my mother won't let me wear lipstick." "I'm fourteen and my mother won't let me pierce my ears." "I'm fifteen and my mother won't let me wear eye make-up." There's no rule about the exact age at which make-up is permissible. It depends on family and community traditions. In general, when a girl goes to high school, I feel she is old enough to know what to wear, though some guidance may be needed. Before that, make-up is just one more factor in the rush to grow up too soon. Mothers can advise daughters that the object of make-up is to enhance their looks, not to be an object in itself. The cosmetic clerk of a reliable store can give a good lesson in how to use make-up well — but you'll have to resist the $75 worth of products some salespeople will want to sell you.

Using make-up for special purposes, such as covering a birthmark or disguising a large nose, should be encouraged for both sexes. A doctor or cosmetic clerk will usually have good advice for this. Thick purple eye shadow, heavy mascara, and bright scarlet lipstick look fake and are inappropriate in the classroom.

One health tip about make-up: It should be washed off thoroughly every night. A vigorous scrubbing can help promote a healthy complexion. Stale make-up, especially eye products, can cause irritation and even infection.

Girls usually wear make-up to appeal to boys, as well as to please themselves. They should realize that most males find a clean, healthy, and smiling face more attractive than one buried under layers of make-up. Boys frequently write to my column to complain that when they kissed their girl, they got "glop" all over their faces. And that goes for flavored lipstick, too.

Hair

"My hair is so greasy I can't stand it! I wash it every other day, at least, and it still looks terrible. — Oil Slick." Along with extra oil on the skin, puberty usually triggers extra oil in the hair. Regular shampooing is the only solution. Too much washing won't make your teenager's hair dry; if anything, it stimulates the oil glands to produce still more oil. Nevertheless, it is better for the hair to be clean than greasy, as oil collects dirt.

Whichever shampoo gets the best results is the one to use. Hair is dead. Nothing you put on it can change it once it has grown out from the hair follicle. Protein or balsam or any of the "new" conditioners don't get into the hair shaft. They coat the hair with a film, making it thicker, glossier, and easier to comb. This washes off in the next shampooing.

Hair styles are a matter of fad and personal taste, the former being most persuasive in early teenage. If your son or daughter persists in a hair style that is grossly unbecoming, a brief, tactful hint is about all you can make. Or you might suggest, and even pay for, a trip to a first-class hairdresser for advice on styling. The pressure at school to wear what's "in," whether it is suitable or not, is far greater than the pressure to please Mom and Dad, or even oneself, at this age. In fact, hair style is commonly used as a way to *not* please Mom and Dad. By the time children are in high school, they need to experiment with different looks. If they ask for your opinion, be tactfully honest. If they don't, save your comments for more critical matters. What they wear when with their peers is their own affair.

Dandruff is another problem that hits kids in puberty. It isn't easily cured, but can be satisfactorily controlled with frequent washing with dandruff shampoos. Different brands contain different chemicals, such as salicylic acid, sulfur, or selenium sulfide, and some work better than others. If nothing helps, there may be an underlying problem that will need the opinion of a dermatologist.

Feeling Ugly

To some extent, beauty is in the eye of the beholder, but each society has certain standards of good looks that kids will try to meet. Teenagers, who hold up critical mirrors, often find that their faces are not growing evenly. In puberty, the features are in flux, just like other parts of the body. Noses may seem too big, lips extra thick, the whole face out of balance. Parents need to reassure teens that maturity is going to bring great improvement, and help them keep an attractive self-image through this gawky stage.

Sometimes a self-conscious feeling arises when there's a need for braces or eyeglasses. Contact lenses are an excellent choice for many kids. Otherwise, glasses can be very fashionable if frames are chosen to enhance the appearance. Braces, on the other hand, have the virtue of being temporary. The main problem I hear from the girls who write is that boys don't want to kiss them, because they fear they'll get stuck in the wires! They won't.

Some adolescents face the grim realization that they have problems that are not going to be outgrown, such as oversized ears, a harelip, or receding chin. Parents should do everything they can to find what help is available. Plastic surgeons are doing more and more to correct misshapen or outsized features and scars. Health insurance will often pay for such surgery. Family support, with love and understanding for the handicapped child, will make the situation more bearable for everyone.

Adolescents with problems such as deafness or loss of a leg have written to me that parents who treat them as individuals with a handicap, rather than as handicapped people, have enabled them to accept their situation and go on from there. Parents can help such teenagers enhance other good features and develop other aspects of personality, especially good conversational ability, charm, and a keen interest in what others have to say, and can provide guidance in gaining fulfillment through developing talents and hobbies.

Name-calling and teasing by peers can create heartaches for an adolescent who is different in any way. Young children seldom ostracize a handicapped playmate, but young adolescents, with their desperate concern for peer approval, can do a fierce job of scapegoating. Parents can help their teenager hold on to good friends that will give him or her support against the crowd. Parents may also be able to show a child how to laugh off name-calling and ignore jeers with a jest.

It is important to keep close to the situation, but do so tactfully, so the teenager doesn't feel babied or embarrassed. The child may not let you in on what goes on at school, from shame, embarrassment, or pride. You may have to contact teachers to help you better understand the problem as well as help get the other students off your child's back. Scapegoating is harmful and if your child becomes seriously thwarted you may have to think of other solutions, such as changing schools or consulting a counselor.

Kids sometimes feel ugly, even when they clearly aren't. This is a dramatic example of poor self-image. The picture they see in their mirror is not what others see — it is of an inferior, inadequate and unattractive person. All teens feel down sometimes and find fault with their looks, but if yours seems to have a persistent lack of self-esteem, he or she quite possibly is in a real depression. (See Chapter 12.) Most teenagers, despite their woes about skin and hair, are resilient, healthy, and attractive people.

4. *Friends and Popularity*

During the school day, most adolescents travel in groups. Then, as soon as they get home, they rush to the phone and continue where they left off in school. Teenage socializing isn't just frivolous fun: Kids this age need each other's help as they try to become less dependent on their parents. They worry a lot about whether their development is proceeding normally and constantly compare themselves to others undergoing the same changes — their peers. Popularity becomes almost an obsession as they reach out to their friends for approval and support.

People need friends all their lives. Learning to pick suitable ones and to keep them is therefore a prime job in teenage and parents can help their kids learn how to be good friends, just as they can help them learn how to dress well and have good table manners.

Choosing Friends

Young teens may be very possessive about their best friends. Rivalry and jealousy can be almost as painful as a failed romance. Kids may "fall for" a new friend head over heels, and parents may have to point out how we often idealize new friends at first, thinking them perfect. Then we feel crushed when we discover they are like us, only human with a few weaknesses or traits we don't like much.

Sometimes parents feel concerned or even hurt because their children become so close to their best friends. If you find yourself feeling rejected, consider how this intimacy is helping your teenager learn about loyalty and sharing. Kids don't have to put up any front with good friends. They can tell their best friend things about themselves they're not proud of, knowing they won't be scorned. If they make a mistake, they know their pal will take their side.

Parents don't always like their children's friends. One wrote, "Our daughter, who used to be so happy and good-natured, now seems resentful and actually hateful toward us when her best friend is at our house. The last time she came they were so surly and rude I told my daughter not to bring her friend home anymore. Now she is furious with me." This girl may be using her friend to bolster her shaky independence from her parents by "ganging up" on the adults. Teenagers also may act churlish when their friends are around to show them that "My Mom can't boss me around!" In neither case is the rudeness really due to the friend's character. Parents can and should ask for more considerate behavior, but they will find the impertinence easier to bear if they understand the reasons for it.

A parent must have very good reasons to break up a teenage friendship. If your child's friend is from a different ethnic, racial, or even socioeconomic background, don't leap to the conclusion that he or she will have a negative influence. "My best friend comes from another part of town. My parents think she's too wise [sophisticated] and will get me in trouble. Neither of us even smoke. She is the only person who really understands me, and I'll just die if they won't let me see her anymore. — Child of Snobs." It's much more important to know the friend's character than pedigree. Children need to bump into other people who have different ideas, customs, and goals; it enriches their lives. This will mean kids from different backgrounds. Prejudice has no place in child-rearing. Remember the line in the song from *South Pacific*, "You've got to be taught to hate and fear."

Try not to judge your kids' friends from hearsay or to stereotype. Long hair and leather jackets don't automatically mean bad habits and crime any more than LaCoste shirts and perfect English necessarily denote an unblemished character. It's a mistake to blast your children's friends for superficial reasons. Save your judgment for more serious matters.

A way to understand people's character is to get to know them, and being hospitable to your kids' friends can help accomplish this. This means offering food, amusement, and open conversation about issues, friends, school, and even about values and goals. You are less likely to condemn your children's friends unfairly if you get to know them. Your condemnation can only make your children cling more closely to questionable friends.

Dealing with Troublesome Friendships

From time to time we attempt to blame our children's mistakes on their friends. We don't want to believe that our offspring can do wrong. And once in a while we may be right, for sometimes kids do hang out with clearly unsuitable companions. "Our son Kim has a new hero, who is a totally bad influence on him. This boy is a real hood. He's dropped back twice, and is two years older than Kim. He was arrested for car theft two years ago, but now he has his own jalopy, which he drives around with this group of hangers-on, like our son. I'm quite sure he provides alcohol, and probably other thrills, including ripping off stores. I've talked to Kim until I'm blue in the face. How can I get him out of this? — Desperate Dad."

It takes skill to make your child see that his or her friend has undesirable qualities without sounding prejudiced or narrow-minded. Point out to your children how their daily life would get messed up by failing in school, or getting arrested for shoplifting, drinking, drug peddling, or maybe even loan sharking. Your child is more likely to listen to you if you are rational and calm. If your teenager needs sterner advice, arrange for him or her to talk to a sympathetic lawyer, judge, policeman, or probation officer — one who will be informative without being too judgmental. You can also explore with your teenager the reasons why some kids get into delinquent behavior, and explain that it is kids who feel deprived who are driven to prove themselves by unlawful activities.

Some adolescents like the excitement of dangerous friendships. Sometimes they pick "wrong" friends on purpose, to get back at their parents for some reason. If your child hangs around with anyone who has a clearly corrupting influence, you may have to protect him or her forcibly. You can't prevent a teenager from seeing another student during school hours, but you can dissuade him or her from doing so afterward. At the same time, offer attractive alternatives: for instance, after-school activities, like a club, special lessons — for example, hang-gliding, wrestling, judo, or skiing — or a part-time job. If you get out-and-out disobedience, you will probably have to restrict activities or withdraw privileges to make the child obey. Meanwhile, try to find out what, if any, hidden message your child is trying to get across to you through this behavior. If your teenager feels you have been too rigid or restraining, some compromise on your part will make him or her feel more cooperative.

The Group

Teenagers are tribal; they like to stick together in groups because they are not sure of themselves. The group sets the rules about how to act, talk, dress, and with whom to associate. The group is the mutual-protective society; it justifies its members' actions: "But Mom, why can't I stay out until eleven? Everyone else can!"

Parents find their own influence waning as the group becomes the Supreme Court, Bible, and Emily Post all rolled into one. Kids this age love secrets and will whisper or carry the phone ostentatiously out of your earshot. Parents tend to assume the worst, fearing the group is plotting some nefarious action, but it's usually just the incessant teenage business of checking up, finding out "What's up?" "What's going on?" "What's happening?"

The peer group is the civilizing influence, the training ground for teenage social life. For instance, only certain boys are acceptable to one group of girls (or girls to a group of boys), and this pretty much dictates who goes with whom.

There is a definite status aspect to all this. Kids in the "in" group are automatically the most popular. Or there may be different groups, some of them straight, or conservative, others more sophisticated, or swinging. Kids may complain that members of a clique are snobbish, conceited, or wild, but yearn to be accepted as a member. "I'm not one of the popular kids. They all hang around together and hardly even talk to me, except one girl who is kind of friendly after school. How can I get in with the rest of the group? — Out of It."

It may not be noticeable to parents but there's an invisible organization chart in every school that is perfectly clear to the students. The students are stamped or not stamped with the in group's "seal of approval." Popular boys won't date unpopular girls. Unpopular boys don't get invited to the right parties. It all sounds a little like corporate adult America. A girl is afraid she'll be ridiculed if she goes with the wrong boy. "Why do boys all date the same girls?" one asks. "They may be pretty, but they have no personality. I could be a lot of fun, but they never even look at me. — Ignored."

Popularity

There is tremendous emphasis on being liked in our culture, and it is magnified in young teenagers. Budding adolescents' insecurity about their looks and behavior makes them acutely vulnerable to the opinions of others. Not to be accepted is a very traumatic experience in school. Everyone wants friends, but parents should put the emphasis on good friendships, not status-seeking. Otherwise kids may be willing to try anything to get into the right group, sacrificing ideals for popularity. The pay-off is not happiness but loss of self-respect.

I have discussed popularity-seeking with high school students, often, and they say it is not necessary to take up some new trick like smoking or drinking to win acceptance in a group. Kids lose respect for others who try to curry favor by acting contrary to their own nature. A better way to get accepted is to find out what classes or extracurricular activities members of the group are involved in, and join some of them. Genuine shared interests and time spent together usually create friendships. It is hard for kids to accept that some teens achieve top popularity through superficial means, like flashy clothes and cars or precocious social sophistication. Teenagers should realize that such success is transient and shallow. It may gain favorable attention but not for long. Loyal friendships develop through integrity and mutual sincerity. This advice won't make teenagers stop envying the most sought-after kids in their class, but it can help them recognize phony formulas for social success and encourage them to value individuality.

Being at the bottom of the heap is anguishing. "Nobody likes me! I'm not really ugly or fat, and I do okay in school, but most of the kids are either in the straight group or the popular one, and I'm neither of these. As for boyfriends, forget it! How can I make more friends? — The Lone Stranger." Parents can help this girl correct the problem she seems to have. Without adding to the pressure to be popular she already feels, they can check for sloppy or unusual dress or careless personal hygiene, which may be alienating her friends. Some kids are born with a natural social talent but others must learn how to make friends. Kids who have to work at making friends will have an easier time if given parental support and guidance.

On the other hand, a nagging parent doesn't help a child develop friends. "I keep begging June to bring her friends home after school, but she never does. We even planned a big birthday party for her with a band and everything, but she burst into tears and said nobody would come, and she wouldn't either. We were only trying to help." If June didn't already have a group of good friends, probably nobody *would* come. First you have to help the child make friends; then the socializing comes easy even without parties.

One consoling thought — although it may not help your teenager much now — is that kids who have to try hard, even be a little miserable in teenage, are going to be much more sensitive and understanding people later on. The kid to whom everything comes as if by magic doesn't have to develop very deep insights. Lots of wonderful adults have been unhappy as kids. There are some social skills you can help your child develop for use now.

Conversation is the keystone of social success. Many kids write me, "I like this girl and want to get to know her, but every time I get near enough to talk, I can't think of anything to say. Help! — Tongue-Tied." Boys have more difficulty with small talk than girls, who they seem to think talk some foreign language like Hitite or Urdu. Conversation doesn't have to be witty or clever. It is just a way to break the ice. This means finding common interests, such as school, friends, teachers, movies, and songs. Kids should ask the kind of questions that invite a real response, rather than start with something like "What's up?" or "How're ya doing?" This is friendly, but only gets a response of "Fine" or "All right," which leaves them right back at the starting gate. They should try something more detailed: "What do you think of Mr. Jones, the math teacher?" "What are our chances of beating the Rangers tomorrow?" Both boys and girls need to know that the point of small talk is to learn about the other person and to make conversation flow easily. Asking questions is the simplest way to get started.

A shy teenager should be encouraged to practice conversing with other relatives, the doctor, the clerk at the drugstore. Experience with older people will make it easier to talk to friends, even though the subject matter will be quite different. Urge shy kids into areas where they can shine, whether it's studies, sports, arts, music, or volunteer work. Dance and drama are especially good fields for gaining poise. Any class or team or club that develops its own sense of unity helps its members make friends and feel that they belong. If your child's school doesn't offer much along these lines, look into church youth groups, scouting, 4-H, the Y, or a Boys or Girls Club. Away from the established "pecking order" of the classroom, a student can often make a fresh start socially.

Some students are made the scapegoat by their classmates for no discernible reason, but the effect is devastating. Nothing is more destructive to self-worth than being pushed to the bottom of the heap by a bunch of jeering, taunting kids. Few fellow students dare to buck the class judgment by supporting the scapegoat. And as discussed in Chapter 3, without help, the victim may be permanently crippled emotionally. Parents and teachers must try to help such a child build confidence and gain a better social footing. If this doesn't work, it may be necessary to switch classrooms or even schools.

If you find that your own child is baiting or teasing others, you must try to make him or her see the havoc this causes. Ask your child to describe how he or she would feel if his or her sister or brother or girl or boyfriend was taunted in this way. Explain that only insecure people need to cut others down by jeering at them. Truly mature people can accept individual differences. They don't have to make anyone feel like an outsider to improve their own self-image.

Crushes

Almost every adolescent, popular or not, will develop a secret crush at some time as a teenager. First crushes are commonly on someone of the same sex, usually an older person, a relative, teacher, or hero of some kind. It is, in fact, a kind of hero worship.

Sometimes parents, and kids too, worry that such a crush is a sign of homosexuality. It usually isn't. Of course, some kids do grow up to be gay, but a same-sex crush at this stage of development is a normal phase of adolescence.

Another, usually later, kind of crush will be on the opposite sex. The object of this type of adolescent crush is usually a distant figure, some person they have no real chance with, such as a rock star, sports idol, or riding instructor, who is older, or famous or living far away. They can dream and yearn, collect pictures and keepsakes, but are never in danger of actual contact. They may think they want to meet the person, but actually a crush is an "impossible dream."

Wildly romantic fantasies are an adolescent specialty. Kids often run a sort of mental soap opera, in which they are the stars in sentimental love scenes, and later on, in sexual ones, too. Parents may get fed up when their teenagers play their idols' records over and over or paper the walls with their pictures. Even schoolwork may suffer for a while, but don't despair and don't ridicule. You can't legislate against fantasy and crushes are a wholesome and normal rehearsal for real romance later on.

The First Boy- or Girlfriend

Girls have a physiological head start, and mature faster socially than boys. "My mother treats me like a baby!" the distraught preteen writes. "I'm in sixth grade, and everybody else gets to go out except me." Or "I'm twelve, and my mother won't let me have a boyfriend. Can't she see that times have changed since she was a little girl?"

Young girls like to feel that they have a boyfriend and try to get a boy to say he likes them. Boys' first interest in girls is apt to take the form of teasing, bra-snapping, or threatening to peek into the girls' bathroom. Boy-girl parties are not apt to be very successful until the boys are at least thirteen or fourteen, and parents are wise to hold back on such gatherings and wait for a little more maturity to develop.

By junior high, parties and dances at school or home are a sensible way for teenagers to start socializing in supervised, safe surroundings where they can learn to cope socially under controlled circumstances. Young teenagers whose parents won't let them go to parties are at a disadvantage when they finally are allowed to date. They may become painfully shy and awkward because of the lack of exposure or they may become rebellious and overeager. Group activities provide a useful and safe training ground.

In seventh or eighth grade, there is usually much talk about who likes whom, but little real action. Kids may begin group dating, as three or four girls and a like number of boys go roller skating or bowling or dancing together, with lots of giggling, teasing, and shoving.

Mature-looking twelve- or thirteen-year-old girls who get asked out by older boys may find it hard to refuse, but parents should discourage it. A high percentage of young girls who have older boyfriends just aren't ready to handle the relationship, and the sad fact is many of them get pregnant.

Some young teenagers have no interest in dating or dances and write me complaining that their parents want to push them into it. There is already too much that draws adolescents into adult activities, not because they really want to but in order not to be ridiculed by their peers. Parents should try not to add to this pressure. If your teenagers want to wait until later to start dating, support them; it will help them grow in self-confidence.

The age at which a girl should start having a boyfriend is a big question in many families. "My Mom won't let me go anywhere because she's afraid I might look at a boy or something. I've already got a boyfriend at school, but she doesn't know it. How old do I have to be before she will let me go out with him?" Most parents worry because kids want to start dating too soon; others worry because their teenagers don't seem interested soon enough.

It is certainly a mistake to push young people at each other before they are ready. "My folks keep telling me I should go out with the girl who lives down the street. 'You look so cute together,' they say. Well, Sally's a nice girl, but I just don't want to go out with her, or anybody else. How can I get them off my back?" When teenagers hang back out of shyness, then it makes sense for parents to try to help. Otherwise, hands off. Let them grow up at their own speed.

Rules and Guidelines

Firm rules about supervision, transportation, and curfews help make social activities safe for teenagers. This is sticky. The kids feel that at last they are ready for grown-up social life, but it is courting disaster to turn them loose with no limits. Dances at school are chaparoned, but many problems arise today at parties in people's homes. Many kids write to me, "I was at this party. No adults were there and everyone was making out. Some kids were even going upstairs into bedrooms, and I just didn't know what to do." This kind of situation should never be allowed to happen. Young teenagers can't be expected to police their own parties, although they will cringe when their mothers ask if adults are going to be present at a friend's party.

Parents need to know about transportation, too. Kids interpret this as a strike against their independence, but it is purely a matter of their safety and should be explained to them this way. It is important to caution them about the dangers of hitchhiking.

One way to lessen young teenagers' embarrassment and keep them from feeling they are being discriminated against is to get community cooperation on guidelines for social activities. Parents can get together and agree on what kind of parties and dances will be approved, how much supervision is required, how the kids will get back and forth, and what time they must be home. If the kids themselves are involved in drawing up these guidelines, cooperation will be even better. It is much easier for a girl to say "We are not allowed to go there" or "We have to go home now" when all the other kids she knows have the same limits. Kids recognize the need for rules and they know, deep down, that these are a sign of their parents' love and concern.

Finding guidelines that are neither too strict nor too lenient isn't very easy, however. If your rules are much more restrictive than those of your child's other friends, they won't work because children who are overprotected don't learn to cope with social situations. If they feel the rules are unfair, they may rebel and resort to lying or sneaking to keep up with their less restricted friends.

Making too few rules isn't wise, either. One boy wrote, "Whenever I ask my parents if I should go to a certain place or do a certain thing, they always say, 'Just do what you think is best.' I don't *know* what is best! It's like they don't even care what happens to me." Children still need to feel loved and cared for, even while they protest that they can handle it. Good guidelines should be flexible and stretch to fit the teenager's growing good sense and self-control.

Parties can present problems for parents who want them to be fun but not get out of hand. One couple, who were hosts at a party of their daughter's ninth-grade friends dancing to records in the living room, were nervously listening from their bedroom. Presently the wife realized she couldn't hear any noise at all any more. Fearing the kids were making out, she said, "Go down and see what's going on." "I can't," said her husband, "Emily will be too embarrassed." "Well you've got to do something!" she urged. So he went to the stairs and called down, "Emily, whoop it up a little!"

Teenagers are mortified if their parents' supervision is too obvious. Vigilance should be low-key and unobtrusive. Precocious friends may try to sneak in beer, or uninvited older kids may crash the party. These situations need strong supervision. The mother of one girl having her first party was informed that "Everyone goes into bedrooms and makes out at parties." "Not in my house," the mother said sternly. "Well, don't say anything," the girl pleaded. To everyone's relief, the subject didn't come up, and undoubtedly, this was because the mother's attitude was clear to the kids. If no such authority is in evidence, however, you may get situations like these: "I was at this party and my boyfriend kept giving me beer. I got so bombed I was sick and made a complete fool of myself. Everybody dared me to do it, so I took off my shirt and danced topless. Now no one is speaking to me."

Junior high parties may involve kissing games, strip poker, playing "chicken" (seeing how far a couple will go on a dare). These games are a way for kids this age to satisfy their intense curiosity about the opposite sex. "Post office" seldom set a girl down the primrose path, but such games can lead to problems. Have a pragmatic discussion with young teenagers about the value of their personal reputation. A bad reputation can set a girl up for harassment because her friends may assume she is "easy" and try to get her to prove it. A boy's "rep" does not seem to be as fragile, but even a boy can lose standing in his group if he's too promiscuous.

Attracting the Opposite Sex

I get asked this question more than any other: "There is this certain boy. How can I get him to notice me?" Here are the suggestions I give to teenagers in my column: Find out where the boy you like spends his time, and figure out how to be there, too. Join his activities if this is suitable. If not, you might become an interested spectator. Both give you opportunities to be together and develop common interests. Pick out the things you admire most about him, and let him know, either in person or through the grapevine, that you feel this way. It is almost impossible for him not to like you if he finds out you admire him a lot. When you are together, talk. Don't try to act special — just try to open up and be friendly.

It isn't always easy for teenagers to reach out to others, especially to the ones they care most about. They're scared they might do the wrong thing and look foolish. Some kids feel they must try to assume a whole new personality to appeal to the person they are trying to attract, but this seldom works. It looks phony. It's better just to trust their friendly feelings.

"My sister flirts a real lot and she has lots of boyfriends. Isn't that kind of a hypocritical thing to do?" asked Ginny. The way most kids flirt is by teasing, which isn't really hypocritical. Both people know it is in good fun and that one person is getting interested in the other. Heavy flirting is insincere: It means using a lot of seductive body language to promise something the person doesn't intend to deliver. This usually earns the flirter a bum reputation.

Sometimes kids try too hard to get attention. A boy wrote "I have a lot of friends, and they think I am pretty humorous. Now I want to get a serious relationship with this girl, but she just laughs at me no matter what I say. How can I get over being considered the class clown?" A parent who senses a child is having this kind of trouble can sometimes drop a tactful hint by referring to another person who has a similar problem. This avoids personal confrontation and embarrassment.

"I've liked Harry for ages. Sometimes I catch him looking at me in class, but he never says anything. How can you tell if a boy likes you? — Dying for Love." A truly shy boy may act so reserved he appears angry at the girl he likes. Usually, though, if a boy keeps looking at a girl, he probably likes her. He will soon begin to pay her extra attention, seeking out her company, laughing at her jokes, listening to what she says. People also speak through a kind of body language, which is probably what people mean when they say they feel "vibes."

Teenagers believe today that it is okay for a girl to make the first move, in theory, but they seldom actually ask a boy out, except to a special girls'-invitation dance. Girls do feel more comfortable about calling boys up, and going dutch. Of course, girls have always found ways to help shy boys along, and perhaps this is still the best advice to give young teenagers right now: Be responsive to clues. Hint, if necessary. Some even ask, "Would you ever want to go someplace with me?" This breaks the ice.

Girls believe that boys have an easier time of it when it comes to going out, because they can speak to any girl they please, while girls are supposed to wait for the boy to make the first move. Little do they know how many fears the boys may be harboring: "What if she says no? What if she laughs at me? What if she tells all her friends I'm stupid?"

Boys phrase their dilemma in one of two ways when they write to my column. "I like this certain girl, but I don't have the nerve to speak to her" or "I want to talk to this girl, but I don't know what girls like to talk about, anyway." Boys want to appear cool and socially competent when approaching girls, but it's hard to do this until they have had experience. They worry a lot about being rejected, and may try to find out from friends whether the girl they are interested in likes them or not, before they put themselves on the line and ask her out. Boys seldom come to their parents with problems of the heart, but if you see your son agonizing, discuss the subject of girls with him in a general way. Point out that being turned down by one girl doesn't mean a person is unlikable. It just means things didn't work out with this particular girl, but they probably will with someone else. So try again. Virtually everyone winds up with a girl- or boyfriend eventually. And virtually everyone gets turned down, and usually more than once, along the way. Learning to cope with this is an important step in growing up.

Teaching About Relationships

Parents can help teenagers understand what good relationships are all about by the example they set with their own friendships and by discussing what friendship means. For instance, describe how it helps to express openly one's true feelings for other people without hurting them. Young teens can be insensitive and even cruel in their search for identity and popularity. They are warm and generous and true, too, but sometimes are blinded by the pressure for status or by their not-yet-fully-understood sexual desires. Consequently, parents need to stress vigorously the importance of honesty, compassion, and fair play.

Dating

When is a child old enough to go out on a single date? Twelve to thirteen is definitely too young, in my book, but between fourteen and sixteen most people can handle a dating situation. A young person's maturity and experience should be considered, as well as customs in the community. Though the prospects of dating will be thrilling to the child, it will probably be threatening to the parents. They have the tricky job of encouraging their teenager to leave the nest, to go out and have a good time, but at the same time, as parents, they are concerned with safety.

Rules about dating cause some of the worst friction in child-rearing, but they are necessary. Though limits must become broader as the teenager matures, there is still need for clearly understood rules about where it is safe to go, problems of transportation, and the necessity of curfews.

"My parents keep saying, 'We never did that when *we* were kids.' But this is *now!* How can I make them understand that things have changed since they were young?" wrote Silver Cord. A teenager is still the same kind of person, inexperienced and immature and in the same rush to grow up, that his or her parents were. The dangers of alcohol, drugs, and fast cars are greater than ever before, and rules for safety and well being should be emphasized with the reasoning behind them carefully discussed. Curfews are still needed even into high school and the rules should be determined more and more by the kids themselves as they mature.

When there are teenage drivers in the household, transportation is a major worry to parents. The accident rate for this age group is the highest in the nation. Some teenagers use cars as tools with which to test themselves. Parents need to discuss with sons — as well as with daughters, who are most often passengers — the hazards of driving with an irresponsible driver. It is especially hard for the teenage girl who has to stand up to an older driver, often a boy who likes taking risks or who has had too much to drink. Put in terms of valuing one's own safety, it's better to refuse a ride under these circumstances and lose a friend than to endanger your life.

You can regulate the time kids should be home and when they can borrow the car but what they do when they are out of your sight is not under your control. You will, of course, caution them about drinking and using drugs, about the dangers of city streets and what kinds of places to avoid and why. What they do with your advice is ultimately up to them.

Parents should still ask their children to bring their boy- and girlfriends home to meet them. You want to see what these friends are like as well as to let them know the guidelines you have for social activities. Make it as pleasant and easy as possible. "My boyfriends hate to come to the house before we go out, because my parents give them the third degree. I know this is because they love me, but I'm almost sixteen. Don't you think they should trust me by now? — Restrained." It is more a matter of courtesy than trust. Putting someone through the third degree sounds tactless, but young people value parental concern that is based on love. It is not asking too much of their friends to have a few minutes conversation with the parents.

How strict do rules have to be? Rules that are too restrictive do not teach mature behavior. "I'm fifteen and have a wonderful boyfriend who is seventeen. My parents even adore him, but they won't let me go out in a car driven by a teenager until I'm seventeen. That means I can't go anywhere! Unless they drive me. So I have to sneak, and I just hate it. — Prisoner." I think this is too restrictive. Instead of limiting Prisoner so severely, her parents should treat each friend on his own merits rather than his age. It is good when older brothers and sisters or friends can do the driving, but one simply cannot control every danger children face. Penning them up forces them to throw caution to the winds. Better to build confidence in their ability to choose by allowing them some freedom in helping make decisions. Instilling this confidence in your daughter will enable her to feel secure saying to a friend "Here, let me drive. You've had a few too many."

Stella's parents were afraid she would get too intimate. Her boyfriend wrote, "In the fifteen months Stella and I have been going together, we haven't been alone once. Her mother won't even let her go to basketball games unless she trails along too. And Stella is sixteen! I love her but I can't go on like this." Poor Stella may lose her boyfriend through no fault of her own. Kids who are so carefully watched, even though they have been docile and well-behaved, will often stage a full-scale rebellion in an attempt to break away from parents' authority. They question all their parents' rules, and may act out in extraordinarily wild and self-destructive ways. It is much wiser to allow some freedoms as soon as teenagers prove they can handle them.

Having too few rules is no answer either. High school age kids feel lost without any guidelines, even as they bitterly complain about them. There is too much at stake to let them simply flounder around until they figure it all out by trial and error. The pressures they feel may be relayed to you only as laments: "But you don't understand! Everyone else gets to stay out until one." You want to be reasonable. You might even investigate and find out if others really can stay out that late, and if it works out well for them.

But if you know your rules are right, don't cave in. When kids break the rules and do stay out late or go someplace they shouldn't, the punishment most parents use is to ground them. This is logical, so long as it isn't dragged out too long. Prompt discipline is important, but it also matters if the kids feel it is fair, otherwise they become resentful and sometimes rebellious.

The key to good guidelines is to make them flexible. When kids prove they can take responsibility for their own actions, the rules can be relaxed. For instance, it is common courtesy for all family members to leave word where they are going and when they are coming back in order to keep each other informed and relatively free of worry. When teenagers call up, voluntarily, to say their plans have changed and not to worry, then it's obvious they have developed responsibility and a spirit of cooperation with their family.

Dating is an essential part of growing up, and you want to help your teenagers do it well. Rules and discipline should keep this goal in mind. Treating dating as a privilege kids have to earn or a risky and suspicious business altogether gives adolescents a warped view of human relationships.

Unsuitable Boy- or Girlfriends

If you don't like your teenager's best friend it is unpleasant, but if you don't like a boy- or girlfriend it's a catastrophe. Sometimes parents find this person unacceptable because of age. "I'm thirteen, and Joe is seventeen. My Mom and Dad just don't understand how I feel about him. They say he's too old for me, but I love him. How can I give him up? — Heart Breaking in Two." These parents have good reason to be concerned. The gap between an eighth-grader and a junior or senior in high school is enormous. Girls are attracted to older boys because there's more status in being seen with them, but parents need to keep a careful eye on this. Some older boys are more considerate and understanding of an innocent younger girl than her own peers are. The younger boy's insistent developing sexuality may urge him to push her hard toward sexual experimentation. However, even some of the older boys are not much more patient, an unfortunate fact that contributes to a high percentage of accidental teenage pregnancies. The only answer is to take time to get to know every boy who wants to date your daughter.

Teenagers often complain to me that their parents don't like the one they go with because this person "is not up to our standards" or comes from "a financially unsound background" or is "the wrong type." Some young people do have accents, habits, and customs that differ from yours and their manners and ways of expression may not be those you have taught to your children, but be careful not to condemn them out of hand without getting to know what kind of people they really are. If you attack your teenagers' friends without personal knowledge, your fears may be unfounded. Your child will lose respect for your judgment and may not listen to you when a dangerous situation arises.

"My new boyfriend is Catholic. My parents forbid me to see him anymore, because we are Jewish. I have talked and pleaded and cried my eyes out, but they won't budge." Parents who have strong convictions about marrying outside their race or religion often feel that allowing their teens to "interdate" creates more opportunities for them to fall in love and intermarry. Actually very few high school romances go on to marriage. Interfaith teenaged couples very seldom become engaged. Strong opposition may have the wrong effect, as it often turns up the volume on what was originally a fairly casual dating arrangement.

Kids sometimes pick partners out of rebellion against bigotry, and rebellion is a very poor basis for romance, let alone marriage. Whatever differences exist usually become apparent if kids are allowed time together to become aware of them. Overreacting to unacceptable partners may create roadblocks, outright stubbornness, and ultimately, a poor decision. It's a part of normal testing and sorting out for adolescents to date people unlike themselves and important to their maturity that they are allowed to sort and test.

Your kids' friends should feel comfortable in your home, not only so you can get to know them better but so your teens can see how friends match up against the standards and customs of your own family. And kids do value these standards. They may head off in other directions for a time, but they generally come back to many of their parents' values before making permanent choices.

When young teens first start to go out, they may switch frequently from one boy- or girlfriend to another or go with several at one time. Some kids write me that they are being labelled as fickle, or two-timers. It's all right to have more than one partner, so long as both people are honest about it. Having multiple dates is a good idea. Young teens mostly go out just to be doing what everyone else does, but some fall deeply in love. Don't belittle their feelings by saying "It's only puppy love." Most often the feeling is temporary. This isn't the age for long-term, in-depth relationships.

"I don't want to go out with Stacey anymore. I still like her, but I think we're in a rut. How can I tell her without hurting her feelings? — Tied Down." When kids do break up it should be done in person, not over the phone or in a letter. It is hard to face the pain one is causing, but it's part of growing up to take responsibility for other people's feelings. Furthermore, by talking in person, your kids show how much they care about the other person's feelings, and the breakup will create less anger.

When your teens are on the other side of this situation, and being left behind by "that special friend," they should not interpret this as their fault. It is normal for kids to change partners, and therefore, it is normal to be the one who gets left, sometimes. Learning to cope with rejection helps kids cope with other rejections that are bound to occur along the way, such as not getting into a certain college or not getting that particular job. A teenager often assumes that rejection means he or she is not a lovable person. All it really means is that this friend has changed or has grown and doesn't want to continue this particular relationship anymore. It is not an indication of your teenager's inadequacy.

Going Steady

Many teenagers like to go steady. It's nice to know there is someone to go with to movies, parties, and dances. It feels good to have the status of a regular boy- or girlfriend, especially if that person is popular. And it is important to start developing more serious relationships as young people mature. There are negative aspects, however. Going with the same person all the time keeps one from getting to know a variety of different personalities. Young teenage is the time for exploring the field, developing the ability to get along with different types, and learning about oneself in relation to others.

To arrive at maturity with a severely limited dating background can be a handicap in adult relationships.

Another drawback to going steady too early is that it can lead to getting too serious. This is a legitimate concern. "My son and his Lucy have been going together all through eighth and ninth grades. They act like a little old married couple. Should I try to break them up?" a mother wrote me. Parents do need to watch such a relationship closely. In general, though, trying to interfere directly in this situation doesn't work well; it may heat up what had been a fairly casual friendship, just to prove the parents are wrong. Again, indirect action is better. For instance, get your child involved and interested in activities that foster personal growth and at the same time reduce opportunities for just hanging around with the boy- or girlfriend.

The trouble with worrying too much over the sexual possibilities of young couples is that it may blind parents to other real and maybe even more important problems kids can have. A great deal of what adolescents see and read today cheapens and sentimentalizes their concept of loving relationships. Parents can help them become aware of what is really needed in friendship by discussing qualities such as fondness and warmth, faithfulness and flexibility. How children get along with their parents and others in the family forms the basis of their future relationships, but parents still need to remind them that everything worthwhile, including love, involves hard work and even pain sometimes. Despite the pain, love is the most important thing in our lives.

5. *Sexual Relationships*

Falling in love for the first time is wonderful! One suddenly feels so excited and breathless, anxious yet confident. The world suddenly seems so vivid. This is infatuation, a heady mix of extravagant admiration, wonder, and passion. Adolescents shouldn't miss such an experience, yet you don't want them plunging headlong into sex, either.

The situation looks different to teenagers than it does to parents. Teenagers worry about issues like these: "I'm in love with Jim, but how can I keep him interested in me?" "I want to kiss Judy goodnight, but I'm afraid to ask her." "What do I do if Ben wants to French, and I don't know how?" "I want to touch Laurie, but I'm afraid she'll get mad at me."

Parents' worries are entirely different: "Will Judy's boyfriend try to get fresh with her?" "They aren't home yet. Are they up to something?" "I'm afraid Laurie may be fooling around. Should I ground her?" "I don't trust Jim's girlfriend at all, she looks much too sophisticated."

Limits and Guidelines

Few people talk comfortably about their sexual behavior. Certainly not many children can talk about their sex life to anyone as emotionally tied to them as their parents. Mothers and fathers don't want to discuss their own sex lives with their children, either. While such reserve is understandable, it sometimes doesn't help adolescents act sensibly when the time approaches for making decisions about sex.

Here is a four-point program to facilitate things:

1. Continue to set reasonable limits and guidelines for your teenagers' social behavior.
2. Talk about sexuality in impersonal ways, giving information and showing them that these topics are okay to talk about.
3. Give them permission to consult another adult if it would be easier to ask someone else about sexual matters.
4. Do not withdraw your love if your teenager's decisions about sex are not the same as yours.

"I used to be able to go places and do things with my friends. Now I'm thirteen, my mother won't let me go anywhere. I have to come home right after school, and as for going out with a boy, forget it!" Many young teenage girls complain to me that their parents don't seem to trust them anymore. It isn't so much a question of trust as of fear. To parents, young women need protection. Yet they also need to learn how to form closer relationships, and they have to start somewhere.

How much independence parents should allow depends on the age and maturity of each child.

By middle teens, young couples want and need some privacy, and guidelines still need to be discussed, but when teenagers go out on single dates, they are on their own. They can't take Mom or Dad along in the back seat — so you have to let go. The only aids left to the parents now are mutual trust and communication.

Talking with Teenagers About Sexual Relationships

Even though you have told your kids much about sex already, they will have to relearn many things now, with their new and more mature needs and desires. Parents will find out more about what kids think and believe if topics are brought up in a general way. A parent's role is not to pry and probe but to counsel and give information. Keep the discussion impersonal and avoid an atmosphere of direct examination. Ask about other kids and how they think and feel. This demonstrates your interest and concern.

Do not be judgmental. Conversation that is full of rights and wrongs falls on deaf ears. You have opinions and should make them clear, but you also need to show that you realize your child may hold different ones.

Good communication has to be two-way. Nothing improves communication better than acknowledging the equal right the other person has to his or her own opinion. Adolescents have been giving sexuality a lot of thought. They have things to say, and it's important to learn their views, as well as discover by listening to them what misconceptions they may have. Teenagers often write me that their parents don't listen. It may be that they themselves haven't said very much because they haven't been given a chance to be heard.

Good communication has to be honest. Teenagers have the world's most sensitive antennae for detecting hypocrisy. Opinions exchanged honestly and objectively will break the barrier between generations faster than anything else.

Wardell Pomeroy, coauthor of *The Kinsey Reports,* has written some good books for both parents and teenagers about sexuality (see Suggested Reading). He strongly emphasizes that communication is *the* key to successful parental guidance on sex. He suggests the family council as a way to open up the subject. In a family council, parents and children get together on a regular basis to discuss topics they feel need airing, including sex. One member is appointed chairman, on a rotating basis. The council works only if everyone, including parents, is willing to talk openly by confronting a variety of issues. Parents may have to face being accused of nagging or not spending enough time with their children, but they can't evade these issues and expect the kids to be forthright about sexuality. Furthermore, sexuality may have to be discussed in the presence of younger brothers and sisters, but this can help all the participants. The family that can talk openly together stands to gain, for solutions may be found to other family problems as well as those involving sex.

If your child needs more information about sex but won't discuss it with you, you will have to be the one to do all the talking. If the teenager is so embarrassed that he or she won't stay in the room when you talk, then write a note and with your explanation inject a note of concern and support.

Books are another way to get the facts across and there are many good ones, especially for adolescents. Make sure you find ones that match your teenager's reading level; aim for a level of sophistication that is a little higher than the one you believe your child has reached, for teenagers usually know more than their parents think they do. Your librarian and bookseller, of course, can be a big help to you if you can't decide what book is right.

Be subtle about giving the book to a shy teenager. You might say, "I have heard this is a good book, and I thought you might find something interesting in it." Then leave it in his or her room, so it can be looked over in private. A teenager can't help but have some curiosity about a book on sex, but a show of interest in front of parents may be embarrassing.

Sexual Advice from Outside the Family

Facts and information about sex are essential, but adolescents also need and often want someone to confide in and to talk to personally. If this person is not going to be you, don't feel hurt or guilty about it. Sex is such a sticky issue between parent and teenager that it seems almost impossible for most parents to fill this role. Find someone the teenager feels is unbiased and discreet, not just a spokesperson for parental authority.

It takes tact to suggest a substitute confidante. If you say, "Go talk to so-and-so about sex," it will turn your teenager off, for sure. So be offhand and casual. When a situation comes up that requires another opinion, you might mention people with whom your youngster feels at ease, particularly someone who knows something about the problem in question. Giving your children permission to seek outside advice shows that you are sensitive to their feelings. And it's best not to press them about whether they followed up on this or not. It could spoil things. Teenagers need to feel that it was all their idea and that the choice of an adviser is their own, not Mom's or Dad's.

Stay Loving, No Matter What

When you have done all you can, the chances are still good that your teenager will make some decisions about sex that are different from those you would prefer. It has probably always been thus. It is more "thus" now than ever.

If your worst fears are realized and your teenager is having intercourse, withdrawing your love or accusing your child of unacceptable behavior, saying he or she is bad, will not change the situation. It will only drive a wedge between you and the child that won't be easy to remove. More adolescents are having sexual relations than ever before. This situation raises problems that can be solved more satisfactorily if parents are willing to talk to their kids with respect and affection. This means don't close the door just when they may need you the most.

There are many aspects and angles of sexuality about which we wish our children to be forewarned. The rest of this chapter explores several issues that usually come up and suggests ways you may be able to discuss them with your teenager.

The Difference Between Sex and Love

When a person is infatuated, a large part of what he or she feels is sexual. A teenager who has never before experienced this sensation assumes it is love. "I love Peter, I really do. I've never felt like this about any boy before!" This is not the same thing as mature love, but if you say to an adolescent, "Oh, you're just infatuated," it downgrades your child's strong and passionate feelings. It isn't necessary to label those feelings.

Point out that sex certainly plays a large part in love, but there is a difference. A person can love with no sexual involvement, as a parent loves a child, a brother loves a sister, or a friend loves a friend. There is some sexual attraction in most affection, but we usually do not express this sensual component; it is not the binding force in these relationships.

There can be sex without love. Rape, for instance, is a sexual act, but there is no love involved; it is an expression of anger, rage, or hatred. But when intercourse is accompanied by feelings of tenderness and affection, it becomes an ultimate expression of love. Without such tender regard, sex is, at best, a temporary pleasure and a release from tensions; at worse, it can express dominance, dislike, manipulation, fear, and rebellion. Even by itself, sex is not necessarily "wrong," dangerous, or degrading. Children need to know that sexual feelings are normal and natural, and they should be assured that sex is not something shameful, dirty, or disgusting. These feelings are built into us, as they are into all animals, to insure the survival of the race, but human beings are unique among living things in that they have sexual relations for pleasure as well as for procreation.

There is another sexual difference between us and the animal world. We are subject to sexual desire at any time or place, and not just at certain seasonal times, as animals are. We can be aroused by seeing a person who attracts us, seeing a picture, reading about something sexual, or even just thinking about it. First of all, we have to make sure that our children recognize these feelings for what they are. And second, we should be sure they learn how to control the way they express these feelings.

Control is one of the most difficult tasks an adolescent faces. Keeping the lid on anything as powerful as sexual desire can be extremely difficult. "Why do we need so much control?" kids often ask. "Sex is natural, isn't it?" For one thing, sexual intimacy is just that — intimate, a very private thing. It would offend most of society if people "acted out" sexually, whenever the mood struck them. A more fundamental reason for control is society's need to manage how children are raised. Babies thrive best in settled situations where loving parents can look after them while they are helpless and dependent. Sexual taboos arose in the first place to prevent conception by women who were not in a position to raise a family this way.

Now birth control has removed the logic for this taboo, so sexual behavior has to be controlled by good sense. There are still plenty of situations in which sexual behavior is inappropriate: in a classroom, on the bus, on the dance floor. Desire may well arise in any of these places. A teenager has to learn from experience what is the right time, the right place, the right partner.

This all sounds very reasonable and easy, but it is not. A young adolescent has no way of knowing how powerful the force of sexual feelings can be. The hunger and yearning one feels can be a shocking experience when a person becomes infatuated for the first time. The craving to be with and close to the person one loves becomes the only important thing in life. Treating a lovesick teenager with understanding and respect instead of with ridicule or annoyance improves parents' chances of giving help in this crucial matter of self-control.

Psychological Closeness

In the past, parental advice about sex was almost entirely negative: "Don't do it." It is still a temptation to issue strong warnings about pregnancy and venereal disease. But, in the long run, it is more effective to start by talking about tender, affectionate, and loyal aspects of a relationship. Parents need to stress the very real pleasures people get from sharing fun and ideas, enthusiasms, hobbies, and all kinds of experiences, including sexual ones.

Teenagers need to know what else, besides sex, makes a close and abiding friendship; that is, what creates "psychological closeness." They need to understand about affection that is tender and caring, for it is out of these feelings that a true sense of commitment grows. This kind of affection is not the same as, though inextricably mixed up with, sexual attraction. And it is important to parents that kids understand about this kind of commitment, because truly committed people try never to hurt each other.

Without psychological closeness, two people are not nearly as concerned about each other's feelings, pleasure, desires. When the only bond tying them together is sex, they have little reason to care whether their partner is truly happy. With no commitment, they aren't involved in their partner's future. Their reason for having sex may be just curiosity or pleasure, which, though not generally harmful, seldom develops into a lasting relationship. However, teenagers should be aware that there are other motives for sex that are harmful — motives such as power, exploitation, rebellion, and anger — and usually bring pain to at least one of the partners.

Problems of Intercourse in Early Teenage

Many adolescents do not really believe that there is any moral issue about sex for sex's sake, so long as two people do not hurt each other. But there are some good reasons for not having sex too early, or having it with the wrong people, and the following arguments may help kids see that if they rush into sex, they only short change themselves.

Immature and inexperienced teenagers sometimes have sex in haste and in secret. It is hard for people to do anything well when they are hurried and scared about being discovered. They can't be very loving under these conditions. That means they can't feel much concern or responsibility for each other, so they can't care much for each other's pleasure and welfare. Fumbling with a nervous and inept partner does little to create ecstasy. Even if intercourse takes place in a house where the parents are away, guilt and worry about how to perform and ignorance about how the body works and what one is supposed to do can turn what should be a leisurely and loving experience into a hasty, awkward, if not downright painful, one.

Adolescents need to understand some requiremens for mutually satisfying coitus. The first requirement is *information:* A good basic knowledge of the human sex system is essential. Next, teenagers need to learn about *patience:* No two people, especially of the opposite sex, respond sexually at the same rate of speed. *Understanding,* to be able to sense what one's partner is feeling, is another requirement. *Self-confidence* is necessary in order to tell a partner about one's own feelings and desires. *Self-control* is needed to match one's sexual pace to that of one's partner.

Without these requirements, becoming sexually active at an early age can be overwhelming. It's like opening Pandora's box, and finding a storm of new emotions and feelings and thoughts that can take over the young person's whole life. A thirteen-year-old girl wrote, "I thought it was okay to make love. I know I'm young, but I've known the guy for four years. Now I crave sex all the time. I think I'm losing my mind." Boys and girls may get so wrapped up in their own urges they scarcely know who they are with. And being preoccupied with sex, they miss out on other important and interesting aspects of life.

Finally, there is a health issue. Many young people have no clear concept of the real dangers of pregnancy and sexually transmitted disease, and changing partners frequently creates greater susceptibility to diseases that are difficult to control and not easily curable.

A Gradual Approach to Physical Intimacy

It is normal and natural for teenagers who go out together to want to get closer and closer physically. "After I take my girl to a movie or out to eat, we usually park and make out a little. She lets me go to second base (fondling above the waist), but if I ever try anything heavier, she slaps me right down. Don't you think after three months, she ought to be willing to go a little further?" Kissing and necking, petting and making out — whatever you call it — have probably been the human method of courting since the Iron Age. And this is a good thing. By approaching sexual activity gradually, young people learn their own sexual reactions and those of their partner. They learn to trust each other, and discover what gives pleasure to them and how to give pleasure to others.

Making out is probably much more satisfactory than intercourse to young people, girls especially. It is safer and more acceptable. The female sex drive is not so specific as that of the male, at least at the start of sexual behavior. A male is programmed, either by nature or society, and probably both, to "go for it." One of the great cries of protest in the early stages of the women's movement was that men did not perform very expertly as lovers. They were in a hurry. They didn't know how to stimulate their partners. All that foreplay is, really, is making out. So it *can* be good for teenagers to hug and kiss, and even pet, in appropriate situations. They need to experience some feelings of moderate sexual excitement before being confronted with the full blast of sexual arousal.

Parents can help kids to see that there is no need to push so hard for "going all the way." Having sexual feelings doesn't have to mean getting into action. Contrary to legend, such feelings can be controlled, just as we learn to deal with moments of anger. Most of us don't hit people every time we get mad at them.

In her book *Sex with Love,* sex educator and counselor Eleanor

Hamilton goes into great detail about how teenagers can postpone intercourse. This is a good book for teenagers who are struggling with the decision of whether to have intercourse or not. Some parents may have trouble with the idea that they should accept, even condone, their adolescents' making out, but as a matter of fact, parents have been allowing this for generations. Back in the seventeenth century, when beds were scarce, young unmarrieds sometimes wound up sharing a bed. Parents put a division called a "bundling board" down the middle and just hoped the young people wouldn't slip over it during the night. Even our grandparents gave tacit approval to "courting" out on the veranda, allowing a decent interval before they finally called their daughter in by flicking the porch light on and off.

Some people protest that sexual difficulties in adulthood arise when adolescents are urged to control their feelings too rigidly. There are ways to relieve sexual tension other than coitus. Counselors and sex therapists now believe that one can defer intercourse without becoming inhibited or sexually dysfunctional through masturbation or even mutual petting to climax.

Pressures on the Young to Have Sex

Throughout history it has been understood, if not actually stated, that young couples would eventually embrace. And no one supposes that today's teenagers are any less eager to get together. They get a tremendous bombardment about sex from all sides: Radio, TV, books, magazines, movies, songs, and newspapers all feature sexual topics. Censorship is almost passé, as practically all aspects of sexuality now pass the one remaining standard, "having redeeming artistic value." With all this pressure, kids become sexually aware at an ever younger age.

Advertisers use sex-related images to sell everything from Cadillacs to manhole covers. Point this out, and it might help your kids understand how much these images may be influencing them. Ask them to analyze the ads in a magazine, and see how many of the pictures and settings promoting liquor or vacation spots, furniture, or even trucks use frankly sexy themes. Acknowledge the irony of a nation professing strong taboos about sex on one hand while the other hand busily paints these seductive pictures in order to sell products.

Kids, too, pressure each other to make love. Peer pressure is one of the strongest pressures of all, and very tough to resist. A little book by Sol Gordon, called *You Would If You Loved Me,* lists the lines that kids use to try to talk each other into bed; it is a gold mine of information on teenagers' ploys to pressure each other: "Come on. The way to prove you love me is by having sex." Or "If you don't give, I'll have to find a girl who will." And "What, you're still a virgin? You must be frigid or something." And "Don't say no — *everybody* is doing it."

Teenagers need to understand what a line is. It's what one person says to try to talk another into doing something against her or his will. If you make sure that the most common lines are already known to your daughter, she will be able to recognize them for what they are — coercion. And coercion spells trouble. Kids need to see a red flag when they hear lines such as "We could make beautiful music together." "You can't tease me and leave me." "Having sex is a natural result of our growing and deepening relationship."

In letters to me, teenagers reveal incredible misconceptions about sex, and some of these come up in lines boys use to try to seduce young girls: "He said I couldn't get pregnant the very first time." "He said 'You can't get pregnant, it's not that time of the month.' " "He promised me he could pull out in time." These letters came from unwarned girls, who believed what they heard and became pregnant.

Boys are under different pressures to become sexually active. Their sexual feelings are physically more specific and more intense. Though increased equality and freedom may lessen the difference between the genders, most teenage boys feel a strong urge toward sexual release, while most girls are more concerned with affection in their relationships.

On top of this physical drive, boys get strong messages from their peers. "Having intercourse proves you're a real man," goes the macho myth, "and the more you score, the better man you are." What young male doesn't want to appear to be a "real man" to his friends? So the pressure to make it on each date is heavy indeed.

Many, probably most, teenage boys are nervous and fearful about petting and intercourse. They worry about how to begin, what their dates will think, and what friends will say if they fail to get some action. With few wiser, more experienced, people telling them it isn't necessary to go all out for sex, boys naturally assume they are supposed to score frequently and often. If someone they trust and respect can talk with them about this, help them see that sex doesn't really prove these myths, and that there's no hurry, many boys would probably heave a sigh of relief.

So would their girlfriends. A large percentage of the girls who have intercourse do so because of a mistaken idea that it will make the boys love them. Many girls think it is worth the risk to their consciences and reputations, even their health, to trade sex for affection. It doesn't work. A boy who is trying to prove something to himself will not fall in love just because a girl gives him what he wants.

On the other hand, not all teenagers get into sexual activity by coercion, by any means. This is the age when sex drive and natural curiosity are at their peak, and anything as mysterious and hush-hush as sex is bound to be attractive.

Sometimes a girl persuades herself that she is in love in order to make intercourse "all right." And this can surely be a disappointment if she discovers that her feelings for her partner and his for her are not deep after all. If she allows herself to be talked into something she doesn't really approve of or isn't yet ready for, she may end up not liking him very much and herself even less.

Still, other teenagers want sex for sex's sake. "What is wrong with sex without commitment?" they ask. Perhaps nothing. I have yet to talk to a psychiatrist who has found proof that sexual experiment damages a young person's psyche; that is, if it is nonexploitative, considerate, and responsible sexual activity that does not result in venereal disease or pregnancy.

Promiscuity

Many factors combine to propel young children into intercourse: the lowering of the age of onset of puberty; the invention of effective, easy birth control; the sexual revolution; and sex therapy, clinics, and manuals. When you consider all these factors, it is surprising that every teenager isn't promiscuous, but most are not. It is the younger teenagers, not yet mature enough for relationships of depth and durability, who are most apt to flit from partner to partner. Girls as well as boys may believe that having many sexual encounters proves they are mature and attractive. These are the teenagers, girls especially, who are most at risk of pregnancy, venereal disease, and unhappy emotional experiences.

What should you do if you discover your own teenager is "sleeping around"? The usual reaction is to ground the youngster, and try to halt all social life. Like the chastity belt of medieval times, this may limit a girl's opportunity for sex, but it does not deal with her motives for it. In my experience, most girls who are promiscuous are trying to buy attention in exchange for sexual favors. It brings attention all right, but not the kind they really want. They need to be shown that it is impossible to buy love with sex. If a boy doesn't respect a girl, he can't love her, and most teenagers do not respect a person who will have sex with practically anybody. A promiscuous girl gets a bad reputation. She will be called a slut or a sleaze. Boys who specialize in "one-night stands" are not respected either, but the old double standard still prevails — promiscuous boys are not subjected to as much scorn as girls. Their motives, too, are somewhat different.

What the poor girl who is looking for popularity really needs is not grounding, but building up. Parents can help by finding other ways in which she can be successful. Is she appealing, in terms of her clothes, hair, skin, and figure, from her classmates' point of view? Work with her to improve her appearance. Of course, beauty is only skin deep, but that skin is important at this age. Looks matter so much in adolescence that if a girl feels she looks okay, her self-image is likely to improve.

It doesn't usually help an unhappy kid to be locked up to brood. Of course, you don't want a teenager who is abusing sex to lead an unmonitored social life, but no social life at all is not good either. Try to fill such a teenager's time with activities other than one-on-one dates. You can't go out and corral a "nice young man." You may not be able to interest the now-sophisticated young person in more innocent pursuits, but it is worth trying to help such a child actively explore other ways to develop skills and talents that will raise her, or his, sense of competency and worth.

Not all adolescents who act out sexually are looking for popularity. Some are looking for love. Children who feel deprived of love, either from parents or peers, may try to fill this void through sexual intercourse, but it seldom brings love and certainly not the kind they have been missing. If your teenager is in this predicament, try to provide more demonstrable affection at home. Find ways to show you care. Take time and interest in your child's activities. Be appreciative, give compliments, and openly express your love.

Some promiscuous behavior is beyond a parent's ability to help. A teenager who is compulsive about sex, the nymphomaniac or Don Juan who tries partner after partner but never forms any satisfactory relationships, has deep-seated anxieties about sexuality and needs professional help.

A vast majority of teenagers just drift into sex because they haven't thought out what is the right thing for them to do. Some, mainly boys perhaps, get into physical relationships because they are shy. Believe it or not, it is easier for them to make out than to make conversation.

Many girls want to say no, but they don't know how. "My boyfriend started making out with me at a party last night. Then he took me upstairs to the bedroom. He was all over me, and I didn't dare say no because I knew he would call me a baby. He's seventeen and I'm only fourteen." Teenagers hate to be thought of as immature or childish. They hate to be termed a prude. Some boys who want to take advantage of this will label a virgin frigid because she chooses not to have intercourse. Try to help your kids see that it's really quite mature to be able to say no. I got this letter from a twenty-three-year-old woman: "I have been taken advantage of, felt used, angry, and guilty. Only now, after endless hours of self-examination and the help of a competent psychiatrist, have I finally acquired the courage and will power to say no . . . What a relief."

Both the shy boy and the timid girl lack self-confidence. This isn't something a parent can remedy overnight, but you can certainly help your child feel wanted and valued. When adolescents find success, whether at home, at school, or at work, it raises their self-image.

Making a Conscious Decision About Intercourse

The crux of the adolescent sexuality issue for parents is to help young people make wise decisions for themselves. The time will probably come when your adolescent feels mature enough and enough in love to have intercourse. "I have been going with Jim for almost two years," a girl writes. "We feel closer and closer in every way. He is not putting any pressure on me to have sex, but I feel we are going to want to do this soon. How will I know when the time is right?"

Here are the important questions to which anyone contemplating intercourse ought to be able to answer yes.

- Are you really grown up physically? Teenagers go through puberty by age fourteen or fifteen and can perform the act of intercourse far earlier than that. True physical maturation, however, isn't usually reached until seventeen, eighteen, or even later.
- Are you really mature emotionally? It takes patience, self-control, and understanding for two people to have mutually enjoyable sexual relations.
- Are you really knowledgeable about sexuality, and how it works for both males and females? The psychological and sexual consequences of first intercourse are far more important and longer lasting than other "first impressions."
- Do you have enough confidence in yourself to be able to share your most inner self with someone else? It is not easy to surrender one's individuality for the mutual intimacy of intercourse.
- Do you know about reliable birth control measures and are you definitely going to use them?
- Do you accept the responsibility for possible consequences, either accidental pregnancy or venereal disease? This means having both the information and the courage to get help in case either should occur.
- Do you and your partner have a committed, mutually kind and understanding relationship, so that you will give each other consideration and pleasure, not pain?
- Are your motives for intercourse pleasure, fun, and closeness?

Wanting sex to please your partner, keep up your status with peers, prove you are grown up, or "get over" virginity are not good enough reasons.

• Are you really looking for intimacy and affection? You may find it in addition to sex, but sex can also be an empty, physical exercise.

• Do you have a safe and comfortable environment, so you won't be hasty and furtive in your lovemaking?

• Do you honestly approve of this for yourself morally? Lingering guilt is still the one thing most likely to sour an early sexual experience. Again, it takes considerable maturity to search your mind and know truthfully what you believe.

This is a stiff test to pass. Not all adults could pass it all the time. However, people who can will seldom have any ill effects from sexual relations.

How can you get your teenager to consider such a list of questions? You don't want to present it like a math quiz. If you can talk about sexuality comfortably, it should be easy to bring up. If not, you may have to refer to this book, or perhaps copy the questions for your teenagers, suggesting that they see what a complex decision this is and how many factors there are to consider.

A person who makes an educated decision about intercourse will avoid the type of thinking that went into this letter. "I have met a boy who is everything I could ever want. I know it's not just puppy love and that we could have a meaningful and *fun* relationship. He is the boy I would like to release me from my virginity." There is something wrong with thinking that virginity is a state of bondage. Other girls speak of virginity as something to be gotten over, like a common cold. This is an offshoot of the modern dehumanization of sex. Sex has been used in recent years for all the wrong purposes, for getting riches, fame, and power, things that have nothing to do with love. Sex has become so commercialized that many young people no longer look forward to their first experience of coitus as an important and expressive moment in their lives. It is something to get over and done with. How sad.

Not that there weren't problems in previous eras. The women's liberation movement has freed females from thinking that their only role in sex is to please the male. Now women are free to please themselves as well. But in the process, we have placed ourselves in a performance contest. Romance has disappeared. We need to reemphasize romance in talking with our teengers. We want them to realize that sex becomes the ultimate communication of love when it caps a closeness between two people already sharing psychological intimacy in many rich and different ways. Then sex is loving, not just experimenting or performing.

Homosexual Relationships

It is hard for many adults to realize that a significant portion of the population is homosexual; the idea of being attracted to someone of the same sex is so tinged with guilt and sin that they find it unthinkable. Yet many of the people we come in contact with every day — the supermarket clerk, the mailman, the radio announcer, doctor, or lawyer — may be gay, and we never realize it. So, too, many teenagers are gay, but it is undetectable unless they choose to reveal it.

If your child is having a homosexual relationship, you will probably be the last to know. Children know how strongly most parents oppose homosexuality and don't dare tell them, or "come out" to them. They are afraid this will make their parents stop loving them, a dreaded possibility for a child. This is not totally unrealistic of gay teenagers. It is almost impossible for parents not to feel overwhelmed with fear and guilt, berating themselves for what they did wrong, and as a result, becoming very angry at the teenager. Many parents find the situation so unbearable they refuse to see the child anymore, or at least until such time as they learn to tolerate the truth. This alienation only creates greater guilt and unhappiness for both parent and child. Some parents can accept the reality, but often cannot talk about it.

The life of a gay adolescent can be one of harsh loneliness. Parents who rise above their anger and guilt can provide enormous support, because a gay teenager usually finds it virtually impossible to get help from others. "All the kids in my class talk about is their boyfriends and girlfriends, and the parties they go to and how they make out. I make up stories like them, but the problem is, I know I'm gay. I've taken girls out, but it's not what I want. Sometimes I want to scream out the truth, but I've heard how they talk about other boys they call 'faggots' or 'queers,' and I know what would happen if I did come out. What can I do? — 17 and All Alone."

Homosexuality is a delicate matter to talk about with a teenager. As previously discussed, if you see your son having problems with girls, for instance, there could be a number of explanations and to accuse him right away of having homosexual tendencies is not a solution. If the accusation isn't true, it could crush a teenager who is already self-conscious and insecure. If his homosexuality is a fact, find a way to respond with sympathy. The same considerations should apply to your daughter. Let your child know you are capable of understanding and your attitude is such that he or she can approach you without facing certain rejection. Of course you first must be sure your attitude *is* one of acceptance. You don't have to approve, but you need to be sure you can face the reality which may be more complicated than you anticipated.

Gay teenagers certainly can use parental help. It's difficult for them to find loving companions. If they come out to a straight friend who can't accept them, they may become totally ostracized in school as well as in their social surroundings. They're too young to go to gay bars, and you wouldn't want them there in the first place. Undoubtedly, one of the major reasons many gays have trouble forming long-term relationships is that they don't get the usual dating experience that straight kids do, gradually learning to develop the loyalty and mutual-support system of a heterosexual partnership. Society's disapproval still makes it difficult for teenage gays to date.

Everyone needs a close, loving relationship with another person; without this we don't thrive. It may be too contrary to your values to encourage this in your gay child. It's important, then, for parents of gays to seek outside help, both for themselves and their child, through organizations being formed, many within the homosexual community, to help gay adolescents. Straight psychiatrists and therapists occasionally advise clients to avoid these groups, fearing that gay adults would advocate the homosexual life to teenagers. While this is sometimes true, most gays do not promote the gay lifestyle. Living life as a homosexual can be difficult and harsh. The burdens can be lightened, however, if the parents understand that the key to success for their child is their continued love, respect, and support.

Sexuality and the Handicapped

Handicaps can put roadblocks in the way of normal sexual relationships. Certain disabilities, such as paralysis, cerebral palsy, or mental retardation, affect normal sex life, a fact seldom mentioned in books about sexuality for adolescents. All young teenagers have sexual desires, however, whether handicapped or not, and if they are bound to have extra problems coping, they need special help.

Adolescents can be harsh on anyone who is "different," as this teenager has found: "I am a sixteen-year-old boy who is deaf, and a hearing aid can't help me. I read lips very well and can talk with kids who will speak right to my face, but too many kids turn away or speak too quickly. That's not why I'm writing, though. It's about girls. They are okay to me, but won't ever go out with me. I had a girlfriend when we went to the Islands on vacation summer before last, and so I know I can get along great with someone who just takes the trouble to speak so I can 'hear'! Why do all the other girls ignore me? — Unwilling Monk."

Kids who are lame or disfigured in any way may have just as much difficulty as Unwilling Monk in finding a boy- or girlfriend. It causes great unhappiness, and you can't just ignore it at home. Parents' concern, however, shouldn't add pressure to an already discouraged teenager. Your aim is to get other kids to see that your teenager's problem in no way prevents him or her from being a delightful social companion. Work to find areas in which your child can shine. A sympathetic teacher may be able to find legitimate ways in which such students can "strut their stuff" both in class and in extracurricular activities. Perhaps a teacher can also work with other students to arrange escorts for handicapped kids; not romances, just someone who will go to a dance or party with them, so they can have a good time and be seen by other kids as capable of being in the social swing.

If a child has a handicap that really interferes with sexuality, such as paralysis, you have to explore ways to help this child find the best accommodation. You can't just assume that all sexual drive has been blotted out. The movie *Coming Home* showed how the paraplegic war veteran (played by Jon Voight) was able to derive pleasure from satisfying his girlfriend (Jane Fonda). This would be a very difficult area for most parents to tackle on their own. A pediatrician might be able to help, but be sure it is an issue he or she is both knowledgeable about and comfortable with. Many doctors receive no training in sexuality. And it might be wiser to discuss the problem with a sex therapist.

Most rehabilitation hospitals have someone on the staff who is trained to help with problems concerning sexuality and could refer parents of handicapped children. Or you could write to the Sex Information and Education Council of the United States (SIECUS), 84 Fifth Avenue, New York, NY 10011. Their library is the best clearing-house for information about sexuality in this country.

Beginning Adult Relationships

Teenaged couples are much more likely now than in the past to progress rapidly from a sexual relationship to setting up housekeeping together. This reflects the speeded-up tempo of our times and the breakdown of social barriers. Cohabitation presents many problems teenagers are too immature and inexperienced to foresee. Parents will want to help them explore these issues beforehand, but, as parents are seldom consulted first, they can only offer tactful advice as soon as feasible.

Living Together

The phenomenon of young couples living together without getting married increased eightfold between 1960 and 1975, and continues to grow. Most of these young people were of college age or older, though some set up housekeeping at seventeen, eighteen, or even earlier. With the abolition of parietal rules and the advent of coed dorms in most colleges, the distinction between sharing an apartment and being roommates in a dorm has become negligible. "My girlfriend and I and another boy and girl have rented a little house near the campus," explains a university junior. "My parents say we are 'living in sin,' but we don't see it that way at all. I love Christine, and it seems as right to be together in a house as in that great crowd in the dorm."

It is hard for parents to understand how behavior that was considered so wrong in their teenage has now become so commonplace. Part of the explanation is the loosening of restrictions about sex in general, so that the old taboos have lost their force for young people. Kids see that many marriages are unhappy and end in divorce, and they want to avoid such mistakes. It is easier to separate if there are no legal ties. These facts superimposed on teenagers' natural urge to learn about intimacy and close relationships and their need to become independent mean kids simply feel few compunctions about moving in with each other today.

Parents don't see why kids can't wait. Even when parents accept that some kids are living together without a marriage license, they wish their children would wait to take on the burdens of such a complicated relationship until they finish their education, and get started in careers. Kids don't see things this way anymore: It takes too long now to get launched on a career. They aren't willing to wait.

Some parents are growing more comfortable with live-in arrangements, but many are deeply troubled, especially when a teenager brings his or her partner home to visit. Do you put them in the same bedroom or not? This is entirely up to you. If you feel acutely unhappy at the prospect, don't do it. It is your house. Just be honest and say, "I am giving you separate rooms; I will be too uncomfortable otherwise." One mother who couldn't even bring herself to discuss it simply told her son, "I have put Polly in the guest room and you in your old room." Another parent said, "I made up a clean bed in your room and one in the spare room because I didn't know where you want to sleep," and turned the decision over to the young couple.

Parents may be particularly disturbed about sleeping arrangements if there are younger children at home. It does set a clear example about what parents will or will not permit. If the older couple has been living together for some time, however, the younger siblings are likely to be aware of it anyway.

When children are old enough to go off to college or start

working, they are generally old enough to run their own lives. You can't interfere with their living habits, except when they are in your home. All you can do is state your own point of view clearly and try to help them see what the implications of such a close relationship are. If you have close communication with your son or daughter, you can raise some constructive questions, though it is very delicate work if they haven't asked for your advice. The key to whether living together is a good idea or not is their motivation. A genuine attempt to develop a serious and mutually respectful and responsible relationship is healthy and promising. Other motives, such as playing house, rebelling against parents or other authority, trying to get away from a boring home or school life, escaping an unsatisfactory social life, or simply shifting dependency from parents to a partner, are very poor reasons for any union.

A parent's view of the situation may be very different from the child's. One father told his daughter that what bothered him most about her living with her college classmate in an apartment instead of the dorm was that she was taking on the boring burdens of housework unnecessarily early. But she disagreed. "Dorm life is unbearable to me. There is no privacy. My roommate always had boyfriends in our room, and other kids came in and out with their incessant gossip. Stereos thump all hours down the hall. I love Jim and I love to cook and we are very happy. Just wait until you see my report card, you'll see!"

Another worry parents have is that a breakup is harder for a couple living together than for a couple in an old-fashioned, just "going steady" relationship. Maybe so, but it is also less complex than the divorce of a married couple, which so often disintegrates into spiteful and vindictive negotiations. In the old days, some young people got married to legitimize sex, and in the end it seldom worked very well. Today, kids who live together just to avoid the commitment of marriage will not forge strong relationships, but those who are involved in genuine trial marriages may do quite well.

It used to be thought that trial marriages might help winnow out mistakes in picking a lifetime mate, but the climbing divorce rate shows that this doesn't seem to be happening. Nevertheless, 93 percent of Americans still get married. So the answer for parents may be this: If you see serious problems in your child's live-in relationship, try to offer him or her some advice; if things seem to be going well, don't interfere.

Teenage Marriage

The divorce rate of couples who marry before age twenty is very high. When these marriages are motivated by a pregnancy, the prognosis is especially poor. In one year, 50 percent of all the teenage brides in the state of California were pregnant at the altar. Fortunately, this is not so often the cause of marriage now. The marriage rate for fifteen- to seventeen-year-olds is going down — perhaps because teens realize that the desire to give babies "a good name" seldom gives them a good home.

Teenage marriages so often fail because adolescents are still growing and changing. Students in high school share a remarkable number of interests, such as friends, classes, sports, recreation, music, and lifestyle. As they mature, however, even the most loving and committed couple may grow in different directions and find that their values, tastes, hopes, and goals have grown so far apart that they no longer have enough in common to enjoy life together.

If your teenager is considering marriage, ask the same hard questions about motives that came up in regard to living together, adding that pregnancy alone is not a good reason to get married. In addition, the whole question of what a person expects out of marriage has to be thoroughly explored. Teenagers tend to believe that fairy-tale ending "they lived happily ever after," which leads young people to grow up believing that if they just find the perfect mate, all their problems will be solved. False expectations of marriage are among the most prevalent reasons couples are disappointed in marriage partners. They expect that all their spiritual and emotional as well as sexual needs will be met by this one miraculous person.

Such expectations are difficult to fulfill. Kids who have known each other only by going out and having fun at dances and parties, perhaps sharing an exciting sex life but few hardships or pain, have little idea what happens when it comes down to the two of them, face to face with the very "daily-ness" of married life. For one thing, they have left their support group, their crowd of classmates, behind.

They may be lonely, in addition to having to work out how they will handle the multitude of issues every couple must face — money, housing, leisure time, careers, friends, family (especially in-laws), religion, rituals and customs, and sexual relationships, which may be quite different after the wedding ceremony is over. Fitting into the new role of husband or wife was always difficult, but has become a critical problem just now because our whole society is in transition. We are no longer locked into the traditional sex roles, in which the husband made certain decisions and the wife others. Marriage is tending more and more toward a partnership of equals. Finally, adolescent couples are still facing their own maturing processes, such as their relationships to their parents, which could be one of the most troublesome aspects of their marriage.

A good marriage establishes a working pattern and is flexible enough to allow partners to change and grow in competency, self-sufficiency, and self-esteem. There will be some suffering, loneliness, and fear, and even some fights. They can, however, learn to fight constructively. People don't give up their personal struggles just because they are married, but loving mates can help each other endure travail and haggling differences. One problem many people have with matrimony today is the belief that if everything isn't perfect, they should get rid of the marriage. Yet, if the truth be known, it is normal to have some unhappiness in marriage. At times, people who love each other can hate each other, too. People don't have to look for a new mate when the old one doesn't fill some immediate need, and certainly divorce isn't the only solution. People can work on their inner feelings and their relationship to each other for answers that sometimes help bypass divorce. In other words a marriage that allows for some discomfort and discontent, requiring patience from both partners, can succeed.

It well may be of intrinsic value for schools to adopt course studies in human relationships, child development, and family life, if the rate of divorce and troubled families continues to rise. The media, too, could help by presenting marriage in a real way instead of as a fairy tale. As it is, children who have been brought up to make their own decisions in a healthy, constructive way will be able to cope best, but even these kids are not ready for marriage in adolescence.

Parents should discourage early marriage as strongly as possible for reasons of age as well as for the many, many other issues marriage brings up.

After they are of age, even if you think your kids are making a mistake, you can't control or pressure them. All you can do is be a guide when possible and a consultant when asked. You really should not interfere unless there is serious trouble, such as when a child is being seriously abused or exploited and unable to extricate himself or herself. Otherwise, you should just keep in touch. Listen. Don't prejudge. Be available, but don't become a crying towel for a string of complaints. Encourage honest evaluation and honest communication between the partners. A marriage in serious trouble needs the help of a professional, not that of a mother or mother-in-law.

6. Sexual Health

We try to teach children to brush their teeth and get plenty of sleep and take care of cuts and scrapes so they don't get infected. We want them to learn to take on responsibility, gradually and sensibly, for all aspects of their health. When it comes to sexual health, however, parents often are so reticent that they can barely bring themselves to mention something like venereal disease or birth control or breast examination. It may help to think in terms of generating a positive attitude toward sex in your kids, rather than a series of negative and painful confrontations.

Girls' Exams

The first pelvic exam can be a terrifying prospect for a teenaged girl. "I am almost sixteen, and my mother is taking me to the doctor because I haven't menstruated yet. What will happen? I am scared silly, but it would help a lot if I knew what to expect. — Annie Hall." Failure to start menstruating by age seventeen, highly irregular periods, vaginal infections, birth control, or having a mother who took DES during pregnancy are some of the reasons a girl may need her first pelvic exam. Any girl having sexual relations, and all women by age eighteen or twenty, ought to have this exam regularly. And Annie Hall is right. It will be far more comfortable if the procedure has been thoroughly explained in advance.

A young girl ready for a pelvic examination should know about the special table with stirrups and how it enables the doctor or nurse practitioner to examine the genital area. The speculum, which looks scary, is just to help see into the vaginal opening, and a special smaller instrument can be used for girls who have smaller openings in their hymens. This should not be particularly unpleasant, if the woman is relaxed, and she should not hesitate to tell the doctor if there is discomfort or if she has any questions about anything she doesn't understand. She might even want to make up a list of written questions ahead of time to be sure of answers.

The Pap test (or Pap smear) is essential for all women, all their lives, to check for early warning signals of cancer. It's an important test for women who are having intercourse, particularly if they have different partners, because they are more exposed to sexually transmitted infections.

Another procedure included in most pelvic exams is the "bimanual" exam, which involves the doctor putting one or two fingers in the vagina or rectum. This is the normal way the doctor feels for any unusual swelling or position of the uterus or other organs.

While undergoing a pelvic exam, a young girl should be taught to examine her breasts for lumps. Breast cancer is practically unknown in girls this age, but self-inspection is an important method of early detection, so it's good to get into the habit while young. Older girls may have developed an attitude that it's not right to touch themselves, but the lifelong practice of self-examination can save lives.

Boys' Exams

Males are not usually given a regular genital exam in the same way girls are. If there is a question of lumps or discharges, the doctor would feel the testes and scrotum and ask about possible problems.

In some cases, as with girls, a doctor might do a rectal bimanual exam on a boy, to test for lumps, swelling, or other obstructions of the prostate and accessory glands. Although one testicle is normally somewhat larger than the other, a big difference might indicate a hydrocele, a benign watery cyst. Undescended testicles are usually discovered long before puberty.

Cancer is rare in teenagers, but boys need to know of its possibility, and should get into the habit of examining genitals regularly, the way women do regular breast exams. Boys whose mothers took DES would benefit from genital exams.

Birth Control

I have to say right here that I am in favor of contraception. It is much healthier for teenaged girls not to get pregnant and for teenaged boys not to be fathers. Pregnancy has high risks for women under age nineteen, both to their health and to their future lives. Birth control is an emotional issue for most parents, but the best chance of preventing teenage pregnancy is to tell kids all the facts about it.

Information alone is not enough, however. Many adolescents today know something about birth control, but don't use it for a number of reasons. All in all, nearly two thirds of unwed teenage women report that they never practice contraception or that they use a method only inconsistently. One factor that makes a critical difference in kids' use of contraception is whether or not their parents talk to them about it. The fact that parents discuss it at all matters more than what they actually say. When an issue is discussed, it becomes an issue that can be thought about and acted upon. When it's not discussed, kids tend to use no judgment about birth control.

If you simply can't bring yourself to talk about contraception, give your kids books with all the facts, and do it early. Accidental pregnancy usually occurs soon after intercourse has begun. One out of five pregnancies occurs in the very first month; half within the first six months. Sexual activity can start at fifteen, fourteen, thirteen, or even younger, and you should arm your children with knowledge about birth control before puberty, not afterward.

"My daughter has her first really serious boyfriend. She is a freshman in high school, and he's a junior. I don't think they make love, but I know some of her friends do. Should I get birth control for her, just to be on the safe side?" Parents should make sure a girl or boy knows what good birth control practice is, and where to get it. But the adolescent should do the actual getting. Sex is a serious, grown-up activity that takes grown-up responsibility. An important aspect of sexual maturity is caring about one's own welfare and one's partner's, too. If Mother or Father provides that safeguard, it reduces intercourse to a childish level, as well as shifting the decision about sex on to the parent.

If your religion opposes birth control, then it is a matter of personal conscience. It's unrealistic, however, not to allow your children to learn the facts and make their own decision. Since church law often lags behind human behavior, there is a difference between most religious dogma and actual practice. In an ABC/Washington Post poll in June 1981, 91 percent of Catholic respondents believed that the Catholic church should "approve the use of artificial birth control."

Contraceptive Methods

Contraception is not just an issue for your daughters. It used to be considered the male's responsibility, but since the development of the pill, it has shifted almost entirely to females. Parents need to teach sons that pregnancy is their concern as well, since it takes both partners to accomplish it.

Abstinence

This is not a joke. Abstinence is the only 100-percent-safe method. Young people can be in love without having intercourse. They did so for years before the sexual revolution. As discussed in Chapter 5, there are other, very satisfying, ways to be physically as well as emotionally close.

Condoms

This is an excellent contraceptive for adolescents. It gets the boy involved. It has a good safety record, especially when the girl also uses contraceptive foam. It can be bought easily, inexpensively, and without prescription and is the best prophylactic against sexually transmitted disease. There are no side effects.

To be effective a condom has to be properly used. Both boys and girls should know that it must be worn with a space at the tip in which semen can collect, otherwise it might burst. Also the boy must withdraw his penis before he loses the erection, or risk the condom slipping off too soon. Some males complain that condoms spoil their enjoyment, but a properly placed and well-lubricated condom is almost undetectable. Caution kids against using petroleum jelly, such as Vaseline, as a lubricant, though, because it destroys the rubber. They should also be warned against leaving a condom in a place that gets too hot, such as the dashboard of a car, or where it can get holes rubbed in it, such as in a wallet. Condoms should never be reused. Girls should question whether a boy who refuses to use a condom is a thoughtful, caring, or responsible partner.

Contraceptive foam

By itself, foam has a poor safety record — one in five accidental pregnancies — but used in combination with condoms, it is very effective. Foam can be bought without prescription, and it also acts as a barrier against sexually transmitted disease.

The disadvantages are that girls sometimes don't use enough (two applicators full are recommended if the boy is not using a condom), and some don't insert it far enough into the vagina, or insert it too far in advance of intercourse. It should not be used more than half an hour ahead of time.

Oral contraceptives

The pill is 99 percent effective when used according to directions. There is nothing to be carried around, or to be remembered at the last minute. It is not difficult to get into the habit of taking a pill at a regular time every day and even if one pill is forgotten, the chance of pregnancy is still small. The pill also regulates the menstrual cycle and usually reduces cramps and premenstrual tension as well. Some women worry that the pill promotes cancer.

In August 1982, the Center for Disease Control reported on major studies that showed that oral contraceptives reduce the rate of cancer of the ovaries and the lining of the uterus, and of arthritis as well. Users of the pill run one-fourteenth the risk of benign ovarian cysts, and the risk of Pelvic Inflammatory Disease is cut in half. Incidences of benign breast disease, anemia, and ectopic pregnancies are also reduced. However, the report also reported that women over 35 who smoke and take the pill have a higher risk of heart disease and stroke. For nonsmokers, the benefits of the pill far outweigh the risks.

There are disadvantages. Oral contraceptives must be used only under a doctor's supervision, and many girls find it hard to go to a doctor or clinic unless their mothers consent.

The pill is not recommended for those who have not had periods regularly for at least a year, because their hormones are not yet "tuned up" to menstrual cycles. Many doctors and clinics will not prescribe contraceptives to girls under sixteen, or sometimes eighteen, without parental consent. The laws are not very clear, and the political climate is changing from state to state.

The pill's less harmful side effects, weight gain and breast enlargement, affect teenagers as well as adults. But weight gain is usually temporary; breast enlargement may be welcome. The increased chance of blood clotting is negligible for most women under thirty, and practically unheard of for women under twenty. Teenagers are at far more risk from pregnancy than they are from the pill. However, most doctors will not prescribe oral contraceptives for women of any age who smoke or have certain inherited diseases.

Parents should make certain their daughters know that the pill offers no protection against sexually transmitted disease. Quite the contrary, the pill makes the vaginal climate more receptive to certain infections.

Most young women have intercourse only seldom and may prefer not putting extra chemicals into their bodies for just occasional need.

Diaphragm

The diaphragm involves no chemicals, and there are no side effects. When correctly used, with spermicidal jelly or foam, the diaphragm is 95 to 98 percent effective and reduces exposure to sexually transmitted diseases. Why, then, isn't it the perfect contraceptive for young women? It must be used *every* time, which means a girl must carry it with her whenever she needs it.

Because the diaphragm must be fitted by a doctor, or health-care professional at a clinic, it also raises the issue of parental consent.

The argument that males object to this device because they can feel it is not valid; if properly inserted, a diaphragm is not uncomfortable.

Cervical cap

This smaller version of the diaphragm fits tightly over the cervix and can be left in place for several days at a time. It has not been well researched as yet, though, and the failure rate is still high. Since it is hard to fit, insert, and remove, it would not be recommended for teenagers anyway.

IUD

It was hoped that the intrauterine device would be perfect for adolescent girls, as it eliminates the need for last-minute preparations and uses no chemicals. Once installed, an IUD needs no care except for occasionally checking the string to make sure it is still in place. The safety rate for those who can use it is 97 to 98 percent.

Girls who have never been pregnant have lots of trouble with this device, however, due to bleeding, cramps, and spontaneous expulsion. Some gynecologists do not recommend the IUD for adolescents, though some girls have used it successfully.

Other disadvantages of the IUD are the necessity of going to a doctor or clinic for insertion; the expense, which ranges from $35 to $75 or more; the need to return for checkups; the danger of infection when anything is inserted into the body; and the suspicion that an IUD increases susceptibility to sexually transmitted diseases, since germs can make their way up the string. Studies have clearly shown that women who use the IUD have a much greater likelihood of getting PID (pelvic inflammatory disease). These infections of the reproductive organs can and do lead to sterility. The IUD seems to dislodge the mucus plug, which normally fills the cervix opening and forms a natural barrier to bacteria.

Another possibly serious side effect of the IUD is perforation of the uterus, or the imbedding of the device into the uterine wall. If pregnancy does happen, the IUD must be removed, which may cause a miscarriage, but nonremoval risks a serious infection. Furthermore, with the IUD there is a higher rate of ectopic pregnancy (pregnancy outside the uterus, generally in the Fallopian tubes), which is dangerous. While this happens rarely, it must be taken into consideration.

Rhythm method

This has the advantage of being the one method of birth control sanctioned by the Catholic church. It is harmless and needs no medical prescription. What it does require is a regular menstrual cycle and meticulous attention to the calendar, and as neither of these are strong points in adolescence, the failure rate is very very high.

Still, this is the method likely to be attempted by many girls, so it is important for them to know the facts about fertility, and how to learn their own menstrual cycle by keeping a chart. The method of figuring "safe" days is quite complicated, and young girls should be given a good book on reproduction, or consult a family planning clinic.

More complete rhythm methods, such as the Sympto-Thermal and Billings methods, also take into account changes in the body temperature and cervical mucus at the time of ovulation. This makes them somewhat more effective, but is a demanding process, and needs to be learned at a special clinic. Few doctors recommend it for teenagers, whose motivation often isn't strong enough to follow complicated procedures faithfully. Furthermore, there is some question of whether these methods can predict ovulation far enough in advance to be practical. What they really tell is when ovulation has already taken place.

Withdrawal

This is the method most often used by young couples first starting to have sexual relations. It is better than nothing, but not much. Boys should know that the main reason for failure is that a few drops of semen almost always leak out before ejaculation. This is totally outside a boy's control or even his awareness. Girls should be warned not to believe a boy who says, "Don't worry, I'll pull out in time"; there is no such thing as "in time." It demands herculean control, anyway, to pull out when the whole body is yelling "go." Teenage boys are not noted for this kind of self-awareness and control.

Both boys and girls should be persuaded that it is really dumb to rely on such an ineffective method. Too many pregnancies are happening, every day, as a result of withdrawal.

Pregnancy without penetration
While on the subject of ejaculation, there is another fact that boys and girls need to learn about conception. "I have heard that girls can get pregnant from very heavy petting, even if they don't have intercourse. This isn't true, is it? Or is it?? — Worried." It is true that a few women have conceived when their partner ejaculated at the entrance to the vagina. Some sperm, relentless in its determination to reach and fertilize the ovum, has made its way to the vagina and through the cervix into the Fallopian tubes. It happens rarely but enough so that both boys and girls need to know it is possible.

Douching
Many girls try to wash sperm out of their vaginas with all variety of substances, from coke and vinegar to Clorox and antifreeze. This does practically nothing to prevent pregnancy. At the least, it may even serve to push sperm farther into the reproductive system; at the worst, such strong solutions can do great harm to the internal organs. It is no contraceptive measure at all.

Telling Kids Where to Get Birth Control

I believe parents should make sure their kids know where they can obtain contraceptives. Clinics are the places most teenagers prefer to go. They are cheaper and more attuned to adolescent clients. They are not connected to the family the way a doctor may be. If you are giving your consent, though, teenagers may feel comfortable about turning to the family physician.

Instill the idea that once a decision to have sex is made, contraception is a necessity. You can say you would rather your child deferred sex, but if this isn't happening, then a birth control method is the next best thing. As things stand now, most kids do not use anything until an accidental pregnancy or the scare of one has jolted them into seeking prevention.

Two thirds of sexually active adolescents never use contraception or use it only inconsistently. According to the Alan Gutmacher Institute report of March 1981, 51 percent thought they could never get pregnant. The rest said they didn't know about contraception, or couldn't get it when they needed it.

Sadly, those adolescents with the least knowledge about birth control are apt to be the ones who are most active sexually. I even get letters from college students showing some astounding ignorance about conception. "I think he is about to ask me to make love, and I don't know exactly what is the safe time of the month," wrote a Stanford sophomore. A boy at Harvard wrote, "I thought it was safe so long as we never came at the same time."

Some young people shun contraceptive devices because they think they take the spontaneity out of sex. "I don't think using a rubber or a pill seems natural," they write to me. Or "I don't want anything to come between me and my girl." Kids who have this notion need to be helped to look ahead and see how pregnancy would affect their lives.

Young couples are seldom comfortable enough with each other to discuss birth control, especially if they have never even been able to discuss it with their parents. It takes a lot of confidence for a girl to insist on protection in the face of all the moral confusion, plus the excitement of the moment, and few boys have the sophistication of a John Travolta, who asked his girl in *Saturday Night Fever* "You have got a 'C.O.D.' or something, haven't you?"

In the end, your influence in persuading kids to take precautions against pregnancy is most effective when your relationship with your children is strong. If it is warm and approving, the young people will have the confidence to take your advice and the will to take good care of themselves. If they have neither, the risks are enormous.

Pregnancy

Many parents fear the calamity of their child's unwanted pregnancy almost more than anything else, for it is a crippling event in a young person's life. Today, it happens too young and too often. "I am thirteen. This seventeen-year-old boy asked me out, and I went, because all the girls are crazy about him. He kept after me to have sex, and practically forced me to, and now I'm pregnant. Help!! — Premature."

A small number of young girls become pregnant on purpose. It is hard to believe that any fourteen-, fifteen-, or sixteen-year-old could bring this on herself, but some of them seek pregnancy as a way out of a boring or rigid or unpleasant home or school life. Girls who fail repeatedly in school and personal life may feel "the only thing I can do right is to have a baby." Some get pregnant to prove they are grown up. "I'll show 'em I'm a woman now." Some rebel against parents or other authority they feel is hostile and get pregnant for revenge, and others try to bind their boyfriend to them through parenthood. The heartbreaker of the group is the girl who feels deprived of love and expects her baby to give it to her.

Boys, too, may deliberately impregnate a girl to prove they are a man or to "get back at" overly domineering parents. In all these cases, pregnancy is a cry for help. If parents heed the message in time, the pregnancy could be avoided.

Most adolescent pregnancies aren't wanted and are calamities to the families. Teenagers represent only 18 percent of the fertile women in this country, but they have 46 percent of the out-of-wedlock births, and 31 percent of all abortions. According to the 1981 Alan Gutmacher Institute report, the U.S. teenage birth rate was among the highest in the world!

Risk to Adolescent Mothers and Their Babies

Parents are right to consider adolescent pregnancy a heartbreaker. Girls under age twenty are at far higher risk of complications in pregnancy than adults because immature bodies are more susceptible to toxemia and anemia. Girls aged fifteen to nineteen are twice as likely as older women to die from hemorrhage or miscarriage. The death rate from such complications in pregnancy and delivery is 60 percent higher for girls under fifteen. The health risk to their infants is greater, too. Babies whose mothers are under twenty are two to three times as likely to die in the first year. They are more often premature or of low birth weight, a major cause of infant mortality and birth defects, such as mental retardation. Most pregnant girls leave school. Pregnancy is now the leading cause for dropping out.

This means preparation for life, job training, social development, are all curtailed. Motherhood is a severely limiting experience for a teenager. Schoolage mothers are doomed to less economic and social success and face a far greater risk of unemployment and welfare dependency than other women.

The cost to society is high. Over 8 billion dollars a year goes for Aid for Dependent Children. Almost three quarters of teenage mothers are on welfare, and the younger a woman is when she gives birth, the more likely her family is to remain poor.

Helping Pregnant Girls

"I'm fourteen and I'm pretty sure I'm pregnant. How can I ever tell my Mom? She'd kill me!" This is what most girls under sixteen ask — How can I tell my mother? If you suspect your daughter might be pregnant, don't push the thought under the rug. Frightening as the prospect may be, the sooner the situation is faced, the more options are available. Although teenaged girls are desperately afraid of what their parents will think of them, they are also desperately in need of parental support. They may be dropping clues, hoping you will come to their rescue. You, in turn, can drop hints that you are available if needed, being careful not to make false accusations. Casually mention, maybe, that a certain clinic gives free pregnancy tests or that "a lot of girls are getting pregnant nowadays. I hope you never do mistakenly, but if it should happen, I would want to help you." And you *do* want to help.

The first thing needed is a pregnancy test. Worry over a pregnancy can itself delay menstruation. The only way to be sure is to get the test. According to gynecologists, home-testing kits are not very satisfactory for young girls, because results can so easily be spoiled through nervousness and haste. A test done at a family clinic is cheaper and more reliable. Planned Parenthood can also be called for referral. One of the tragedies of teenage conception is fear of discovery, which compels a girl to put off getting tested.

Making a decision about pregnancy is an extremely tricky business for a girl and her parents. "I am seventeen and just discovered I am pregnant. My boyfriend loves me and will marry me if I want. I did not plan for this to happen, but since it has, do you think we should try to make it on our own, or should I not have the baby, or should I give it up? — Undecided." This is a life-shaking kind of choice. Some parents may want to influence their daughter's decision. Some flatly state what a girl must do, while others believe she should make up her own mind. And a very few still would banish a pregnant girl from their home.

Confused, scared, with no experience to fall back on, a girl is under a terrible strain and certainly needs help at this time. She doesn't know what raising a child is like and parents need to provide some guidance here. Above all, it's important not to insist on adoption or abortion against the girl's will; it can create grave emotional problems for her.

Since making a decision about pregnancy is serious and long lasting for the girl as well as the parents, it's best to consult a professional. Doctors or nurse practitioners who work with pregnant teenagers can see all sides of the issue. It is not true that they would press for abortion. They know the complexities involved, the moral and other questions, and what the consequences are apt to be. Since they have no emotional involvement with your daughter, they can help her come to an informed decision that best suits her and everyone else involved.

There is no "perfect" choice. Each solution brings problems to a teenaged mother, but with proper counseling, and the assurance that her decision is the best one under the circumstances, a girl can accept and live with it most satisfactorily. The four choices are:

Abortion

"I got pregnant last year and my parents forced me to have an abortion. I'm fifteen, and they said I could never raise a baby, so I did what they wanted, and now I'm so unhappy. Every time I see a baby, I start crying. I know it was wrong, and I'll never forgive them. Never!" Legally, parents cannot force a child to have an abortion, but they can put on so much pressure that a young girl cannot stand up to them. It may not be the wrong choice, if the girl's moral values can accept it, but it is certainly the wrong way to go about it. A woman has to feel she made the decision willingly.

The following is not any better: "I am pregnant, and have thought out what I want to do very carefully. I have decided on an abortion, but my parents won't give their consent. 'Don't let me hear you talk about it. It's murder!' my mother says. But what about me? I'm sixteen, and it will be murder for me to raise a child, and I can't just give it away — Same Old Story."

Those who feel that abortion is murder cannot condone it, of course, though I feel each female is entitled to make this decision for herself. In either of the above cases, adoption would have been a good alternative.

In some states, girls whose parents refuse to consent to abortion can go to court and ask for judicial consent. In a confidential hearing, the judge will determine whether the girl is mature enough to make an informed decision on her own, or if it is clearly in her best interest to have an abortion, anyway. This is something younger teenagers may not be confident enough to do. What they may try, however, is to seek an illegal abortion. We all know how dangerous this is. Some even try to abort themselves, inserting sharp objects or strong solutions like Clorox or antifreeze into their bodies. Too often the result is infection, sterility, or even death.

There is very little danger from legal abortions performed in the first trimester of pregnancy. They are fourteen times safer than giving birth, and probably double that for young girls. The advantage of giving parental consent is that a girl can then consult the best doctors or clinics and will receive good counseling before, during, and after the operation. Abortion is an extremely emotional experience. It is, as it should be, a very hard choice to make. Girls who receive continuing support from their parents will be able to make a good adjustment, and get on with their lives more intelligently.

Adoption

This has a bad name among teenagers today, unfortunately. Adults who ardently want to adopt a child are usually in a much better position to raise it than an immature teenager would be. Though it is an agonizing decision to give up a baby at any age, skilled counseling will help a girl understand that her baby is being given *to* someone loving, not just being given *away* . It is an altruistic decision and the young mother has the satisfaction of knowing that her child will have more opportunities for a better future. Adoption also gives the girl back her childhood, which makes it especially appealing to parents. This option should be fully explored.

Foster care

Many girls who cannot bring themselves to give up their baby are placing the infant in a temporary foster home. Others who find they can't cope when their babies get a little older also turn to foster care. The courts place children in foster homes when they see they are not getting proper care from adolescent mothers.

Temporary care is necessary in these cases, but the increased use of foster homes on an in-and-out basis is a frightening prospect. Nothing is more devastating to babies than not having a permanent home with a constant, loving parent, whether biological, adoptive, or foster. While many foster homes provide excellent care, some do not. Even with good foster parents, a lot of switching around is emotionally traumatic to children. Parents should make their daughters aware of what a foster child faces.

Keeping the baby

It is now more acceptable for unmarried mothers to keep their babies. Since 1980, upward of 94 percent of teenaged girls who carried their pregnancies to term kept their babies. It is a decision fraught with problems for both mother and infant. If a girl is considering raising her baby, her parents should put some very serious questions to her:

1. Does she realize she will be raising a child, not a baby? Most adolescents are ignorant of child development. A little baby-sitting experience doesn't teach them what the total dependency of a nursing baby or the constant demands of a self-willed two-and-a-half-year-old are really like.
2. Does she really believe a teenager can have the maturity, knowledge, patience, money, sense of responsibility, and so on, to tend to a child twenty-four hours a day?
3. Does she realize how severely baby care will limit her life? Parenthood stymies a young person at the time of most rapid expansion of personality. She should be exploring her new self, her rela-

tionships with peers, her career ideas, but she can't while sitting home with bottles and diapers.

4. Can she stand the loneliness of not being with the other kids at school, at parties, on dates? Polls of adolescent mothers show that isolation is their biggest complaint, one that increasingly results in alcoholism, drug abuse, and child abuse among teenage parents.

5. Does she realize that having to spend so much time with a baby will curtail her education and training for a future career? Statistics show that teenage parents earn less money and don't rise as far up the employment ladder as other young people do.

6. Does she know how much it will cost to raise a baby? How will she pay? How can she leave her child if she has to go to work? Will this be good for the baby?

It is hard to see how becoming a mother is a good choice for either the school-age mother or the baby. Parents of a daughter considering this should have her visit some teenaged mothers who are coping with all these problems.

Another question arises for parents of a teenaged mother. *Should parents help?* Wanting so much for their daughter to finish her education, parents may feel compelled to step in and help. Often it is the only way a girl can go back to school. An offer of such help will certainly influence her decision. A few women may genuinely welcome the job of raising a grandchild. Most women in their forties or fifties have worked out a new kind of life for themselves, however, and may not want to go back to baby care.

There are other problems besides the time and money required. "When I come home from school, I take care of Johnny," a sixteen-year-old mother writes. "Mom is cool, and tries to stay out of my way, but every time he falls and hurts himself, he runs to Granny. It makes me feel so bad. And it's hard for him to have two Moms." This girl will have a better future, but it still won't be easy, for her or for Johnny. We don't want the babies punished for their parents' choices.

Should parents offer money to help out? If they cannot or do not want to raise their grandchild — and they should not feel they must — they may want to offer their daughter money to help her out. Here again, the offer can't help but affect the girl's decision. Any girl who plans to raise her child must consider whether she can do it on her own. It sounds heartless, but it is better for both the young mother and her child if the parents do nothing that enables her to keep the baby. Often a teenage girl assumes that just having the baby is enough to make her an adult. It is not.

If the expectant mother is determined to make it on her own, there are support programs that can provide medical and nutritional care, child development training, parenting skills, and employment help. No one agency is a panacea, but they do give help. Information about such an agency can be obtained from National Clearing House for Family Planning Information, P.O. Box 2225, Rockville, MD 20852.

Boy's Role in Pregnancy

The boy is as responsible for creating a life as the girl. Usually he feels frightened and guilty when the discovery is made that he's fathered a child. And he's not likely to run to a parent with this information, but if he does or if his parents find out some other way, blame should not be heaped on the girl.

Boys in high schools have said to me "If a girl gets pregnant it's her problem. She got herself into it — let her get herself out of it." Washing their hands of their responsibility reflects the old double standard: She sinned, she must pay. We know she didn't sin all by herself and we know it's the baby who pays most.

Parents who raise a son to be concerned and understanding will find that he's not blithely going to run out on his responsibility. Many boys do try to help. "My girl is fourteen. She's pregnant, but her parents won't let me see her or even talk to her on the phone. She told me she would never have an abortion, but I'm afraid they will make her. It's my baby too! Don't fathers have any rights in this?" One can understand the wrath a girl's parents feel toward the boy who got their girl into this situation, especially when she is so young, but this is not the best way to handle it. A boy does not have any legal rights to stop an abortion, but he should not be denied his role in the pregnancy. The ultimate decision is up to the girl, but it helps her if the boy acknowledges his part. In this situation, parents should urge a boy to support his girlfriend. If she doesn't want to see him anymore, that's her choice, but he is entitled to hear this from her. She needs to wind up their relationship honestly.

A boy who acknowledges his paternity does have legal rights after the baby is born. In some states, unless he voluntarily surrenders his rights as the father, he must give his consent before the baby can be adopted or put in a foster home. If the mother is raising the child, and they do not marry, he must contribute to Aid for Dependent Children (AFDC). Teenaged fathers have even won the right to raise their own children, when the young mother wouldn't or couldn't do it. This can be an almost impossible task, without tremendous help from the boy's parents.

Sexually Transmitted Disease

The rise in sexual activity has caused an increase in venereal disease, now more commonly called sexually transmitted disease, or STD. VD was taken to mean mostly gonorrhea or syphilis, but now many sexually related infections such as pubic lice, venereal warts, trichomoniasis, are on the rise, so the more general term STD is commonly used. The most menacing of the new STD's are herpes simplex II, or genital herpes, and nongonococcal urethritis, or NGU.

Genital herpes is a virus that causes red and very painful sores, often weeping blisters, on the genitals. No treatment has yet been found to cure it. Though the symptoms clear up by themselves after a couple of weeks, they will usually reappear from time to time, for once a person has contracted this virus, it never goes away. There is now a new drug called Acyclovir that relieves symptoms of primary infections and may shorten the contagious period. It is only helpful in the first episode. There is a possible link between herpes simplex II and cervical cancer in women. As females may have the herpes virus with no symptoms, it is important to have regular Pap smears.

Nongonococcal urethritis is a sexually transmitted inflammation of the urethra. It produces the same symptoms as gonorrhea, discharge and painful urination, and like gonorrhea, women in particular and sometimes men can have the disease with no symptoms at all. It is caused by bacteria different from gonorrhea, however, called *Chlamydia trachomatis,* and it must be treated differently. Chlamydia are not killed by the penicillin used to treat gonorrhea; they respond to tetracycline. If untreated, NGU may cause permanent damage to the reproductive organs, of both sexes. Women may develop pelvic inflammatory disease, a serious inflammation of the organs, especially the Fallopian tubes, that may result in ectopic pregnancies and/or sterility. NGU in boys may result in inflammation of the testes and possible sterility. Both sexes may suffer urinary problems from scarring of the urethra, which can also lead to difficulty in male ejaculation.

Sexually transmitted diseases are not an easy subject of conversation between parents and teenagers. "I have reason to believe I have got a venereal disease. Will you please tell me how I can find out? I couldn't possibly discuss this with my mother, or our doctor either. — Is My Face Red." In the past, even doctors have not been very objective about this subject, and patients would get a stern lecture, a VD test, and treatment. This did not deter young people from having sexual relations: it just stopped them from going to the doctor. Now that, by law, doctors cannot inform parents, teenagers feel it's safer to seek medical help.

At last, the rates of gonorrhea and syphilis are decreasing; however, the incidence of other STD's are rising dramatically. In 1980, the number of new cases per year of STD was estimated at: 3,000,000 for trichomoniasis, 2,700,000 for gonorrhea, 2,500,000 for NGU, 81,000 for syphilis, 300,000 for genital herpes, and 300,000 for pubic lice.

Except for herpes, all these diseases are curable. If kids all knew about the threat of infection and how to prevent it, the symptoms, and the fact they can be tested and cured for free and in total confidence, STD's could be wiped out. Herpes is not curable, but there are promising new developments for treating this. Another incurable STD is the newly isolated AIDS, or Acquired Immune Deficiency Syndrome. Though few cases have been reported, it is increasing and deadly, a compelling reason to avoid casual sex and promiscuity.

Parents need to make kids aware that people can have these diseases with no symptoms they can see or feel. Adolescents are prone to be ostrichlike, and believe that what they can't see doesn't exist. They are apt to become "carriers," people who have an STD and don't know it, so they go on infecting others.

Preteens are quite likely to ask about venereal disease. They might, for instance, hear a slang term such as "the clap" or "a dose" for gonorrhea, and want to know what it means. It's important to tell them the salient facts about STD's at this age, and it is a good time to try to get across the principle that mature and self-respecting people take care of their sexual health and get treatment if they need it.

After puberty, the most sensible way for kids to get all the facts is probably through books and pamphlets on the subject, sources that describe the symptoms of various diseases, how they are transmitted and effectively treated, and dispel the old myth that they can be picked up in locker rooms. "My girlfriend must have lied to me. I just found out she gave me gonorrhea and she's the only girl I ever slept with. She insists she was a virgin and must have got it off a toilet seat, but I heard this isn't possible. — Burned." It really isn't possible, and "nice girls" can and do get STD's; so do kings, duchesses, prime ministers, musicians, politicians, and even some clergymen.

Avoiding infection is not always easy. "I read that you are supposed to make sure a guy doesn't have VD before you sleep with him, but how can you tell? You can't very well say 'Er, by the way, you don't have the clap or anything, do you?' It would kill the whole thing." One really should know and trust one's partner well enough to be candid before becoming this intimate. Kids need to understand that this is by far the best way to prevent infection. The worst way is to have casual sex with lots of partners.

Embarrassment and self-consciousness are the main problems for adolescents. Few of them dare mention the topic even when they know each other well. If parents discuss STD's with them in a matter-of-fact way, kids will have an easier time broaching the subject with each other. Parents may also instill in their children the idea that long-term health is much more important than a brief moment of embarrassment.

Kids today should know how to guard against infection. The most practical safeguard is to use condoms and foam. Washing oneself with soap and water or douching right after intercourse may help a little, but can't match the prophylactic effect of condoms. Many people mistakenly believe that the pill protects them from STD's, which is just not true.

After prevention, the second most important thing for parents to stress is how easy it is to get treatment. Find an opportunity, perhaps in response to a story in the newspaper or on TV, to say something like this: "If people only realized that anybody, of any age, could get tested at a clinic, this VD epidemic could be licked. It's such a shame kids don't know that they can get tests and treatment for a small fee, and without even having to tell their parents." When you say this, kids not only learn where help is available, but also that they have tacit permission to get it if they need it.

If you can't find out where the nearest clinic is, or have any other questions about STD's, there are at least two national VD hotlines: Operation Venus, 1-800-523-1855 (everywhere except Pennsylvania), and the National VD Hotline, 1-800-227-8922 (everywhere except California).

The danger of failing to get treatment for many of these diseases is that the infection can cause scarring of the reproductive organs, leading to sterility. Because of this, it is important to teach young women and men to be seen by doctors, nurses, or clinicians for complaints of discharge, pain, or abnormal bleeding.

Three last points for parents to make to kids: First, mention how important it is to have follow-ups after treatment for STD's. The symptoms probably will be gone after the first treatment but not the infection. Second, treatment does not create immunity. Anyone can get an STD again, and again, and have more than one disease at the same time. Third, home treatments don't work. They may alleviate the symptoms but will not kill off the bacteria, and partial cures are worse than none because the remaining bacteria become increasingly resistant to the antibiotics.

Infections That Are Not STD's

Vaginal discharge scares many girls. Sometimes it is normal, sometimes not. "I have this awful itch down there, and some stuff that looks like cottage cheese. I know this must be VD, but how could I possibly have that? I'm only thirteen, I've never even looked at a boy. (Well, just looked.) Help me, please!!" This poor girl has probably got candidiasis, a yeast infection that can be but was not in her case sexually transmitted. Wearing synthetic underpants, which keep out air, or taking tetracycline for acne, may create a vaginal climate that fosters the growth of normal bacteria and yeast to abnormal proportions. It is not VD, but needs to be treated by a doctor.

When a girl first starts to menstruate, it is a good time to tell her that most women have a little vaginal discharge at times, some more than others. So long as it doesn't smell or itch, there's no problem. If it does change in color, consistency, or odor, your daughter should tell you or the doctor. The right treatment can cure such vaginitis, but it has to be diagnosed first, as there is more than one kind.

Jock Itch

Boys sometimes get a fungus infection called jock itch, or jock rot. As with candidiasis in girls, it comes from wearing underpants that don't breathe or from wearing a jock strap for long periods of time. Jock itch causes itching and redness in the genital area and is cleared up by keeping the skin clean, dry and chafe free, and by dusting with cornstarch or a medicated powder that you can get at the drugstore.

Cancer of the Sex Organs

Cancer is a big fear among people of all ages today. It is very rare in adolescents, but I get many letters from kids who are worried about it. "One of my breasts is a littler larger than the other. I'm so afraid I have cancer!" or "I have these funny bumps on my penis. Could it be cancer?" Breast cancer is very rare among young women, but changes in the breasts during the menstrual cycle may produce a lumpy feeling. Girls need to be assured that this is normal and encouraged to start breast self-exams early so they can learn what these normal changes feel like.

Cancer of the cervix is also extremely rare. It has been found that girls who start sex earlier and have more sexual partners have a slightly higher tendency to develop cervical cancer later on. It may be linked to the genital herpes virus.

Cancer of the testes, while also extremely rare in teenage, does occur occasionally, so boys should form the habit of examining their testicles, just as females do their breasts. Any lumps are likely to be cysts, which generally go away by themselves but should be seen by the doctor. Cancer takes the form of a painless swelling of the testicle, so any unusual enlargement should also be checked by a doctor immediately.

Cancer of the penis is almost unknown at this age. The lumps and bumps that frighten boys are most often minor skin irritations, unless they have contracted some venereal infection, so their fears about cancer are almost always groundless.

DES (diethyl stilbestrol) is a synthetic estrogen that was given to mothers during pregnancy between 1940 and 1970 as a means of preventing miscarriages. A few (probably 1 in 10,000) daughters of these women developed cancer of the vagina and cervix. Up to as many as two-thirds of DES daughters may show normal cells in abnormal places. It is most important for young women who were exposed in utero to DES to start yearly exams within one year of beginning to menstruate, or by age fourteen. Any DES-exposed daughters should be seen for abnormal bleeding, and their choice of contraceptives should be discussed with their doctor.

A few sons of DES mothers have also been found to have abnormalities in the genitals and lower urinary tract, such as undescended testicles, low sperm counts, and benign cysts. Mothers who know or suspect they were given DES during pregnancy should make sure that their sons as well as daughters get special medical checkups. To find out more about this, write to DES Action National, Long Island Jewish-Hillside Medical Center, New Hyde Park, NY 11040, or call the National Cancer Information hotline (1-800-638-6694), which will put you in touch with your local cancer communications network for DES information.

"One of my testicles is *much* larger than the other. I know this is abnormal, but I'm afraid to go to the doctor. Do you think it could be cancer?" Cancer of the genitals is rare, but not unheard of in adolescents. This boy may very likely have the hydrocele, which is discussed in Chapter 1, but still should be diagnosed by a doctor. Kids, like adults, sometimes hang back because they fear being told "the worst," but early diagnosis of most all diseases often means a complete cure is possible, whereas delay may have tragic results. Raise your children to turn to the doctor right away whenever they have worries about their health — sexual or otherwise.

Sex is one of life's blessings, free to rich and poor, young and old alike. When all is right with our sex lives, all is usually bright with our world. So keeping well sexually, emotionally, and physically is vital to our well being.

7. *Sexual Offenses*

Some problems connected with sexuality have an enormous effect on emotional health. One of these is sexual harassment, which may consist of a suggestive remark, indecent gesture, or frankly improper advances. It is particularly difficult for children to resist such harassment by adults because they are raised to be polite to grownups. As soon as children are old enough to walk to school or visit friends alone, parents need to talk to them about the fact that seductive suggestions are sometimes made by unscrupulous adults. One need not scare them unduly, only make them aware that strangers, or even friends, may possibly get too friendly. Children should trust their own "vibes" and not be afraid to be firm and negative if an older person gets fresh.

Make clear to your children that you always want them to tell you if they feel harassed, or threatened with harassment, no matter if the threat comes from an adult friend or relative, such as an uncle or stepparent, or a baby-sitter, employer, or teacher. Assure them that your first loyalty is to your children, and that you will cope with the situation in an adult way, which is next to impossible for a minor to do.

"I'm a boy, fourteen, and I am so worried. This man in our neighborhood has followed me home from the bus twice. He called to me, but I ran. — Chicken." This boy is no chicken. He should run, right to his parents, or the police if necessary. He is being harassed.

I get quite a few letters like this one: "Our science teacher is young and so good-looking. I used to like him a lot, but now he makes me nervous. He keeps trying to look down my blouse, and gives me these little pats. I don't want to get him in trouble. He might flunk me. What should I do? — Stacked." She is being sexually harassed and should tell her parents immediately. Attractive, maturing high school students can be very appealing to young teachers, and while most teachers don't step out of line, some of them do. Parents may confront the teacher if they feel confident this will end the harassment. Otherwise, they will have to speak to the principal or superintendent, making sure the girl is not penalized for the incident.

Instill in your kids the idea that their own protection comes first. It is far more important than marks. They don't have to put up with harassment from teachers, bosses, counselors, or anybody, but they need to be firm and prompt in turning off would-be exploiters. It's better even to make a mistake about someone's intentions than to let an exploitative situation develop out of timidity. Scared, self-conscious, and obedient children may be so bashful they appear to acquiesce. It might be a good idea to play-act a situation at home to give children practice in saying no, loud and clear, and in walking away from harassing situations, even in the classroom.

Rape

Technically, rape is the act of forcing a woman to have sexual intercourse, but I include boys being forced to engage in sex against their will, too. Most acts of rape are performed by men, and frequently against younger people. There are persistent myths that make it hard for the victims to report the act. Although the idea is fading, some people still believe that women invite rape, because they secretly enjoy it. Because many victims do not report being raped statistics about rape have been inadequate. Rape is now one of the fastest growing violent crimes in the country, and the figures are probably much higher than actually reported. "Dating rape," where a girl is forced to have sex by a boyfriend, is seldom reported, for instance.

We want to warn our kids about the fact that rape happens, but we don't want to scare them so much they become too timid to go anywhere. What works best is to tell them about high-risk situations, so they can avoid them. It is folly, for instance, to walk alone in city parks, on dark or lonely streets, especially at night, or to ever hitch-hike alone. From a very young age children must be taught not to accept candy or rides from people they don't know. They should never let strangers into their house, as most rapes occur in the victim's own home. Young children should never be left alone, but if they must be, they should know how to keep doors locked and what to do if they sense trouble and are frightened.

Most rapists are known to the victim, however, so it is not enough just to warn kids about strangers. It is important to teach them to trust any warning signals they may get from others. One school in Minneapolis tries to show children in grades one through six the difference between affectionate and exploitative behavior.

Recent studies are finding out more about what kind of people become victims of rape and mugging. Those who are weak and timid in appearance, or vacillating, needy, and vulnerable are most likely to be assaulted. Kids should know how to walk confidently, with long and purposeful strides, and to carry an umbrella or some other item of defense if ever they must be in risky places.

"I met this cool-looking boy at the skating rink, and he asked me to go to the movies. He took me to this creepy place and parked and tried to get really fresh. I finally got out of the car and ran away. Luckily I found a place where I could call home." Sometimes rapists meet their victims and set them up for rape ahead of time. This is an excellent reason to urge kids never to go out with casual "pick ups" or go anywhere with anyone whose background or friends are totally unknown to them or to the parent, and never to answer "blind" newspaper ads.

It is imperative for every person, young or old, to think out ahead of time what strategies to use in case of rape. It is important to have several strategies on hand to implement the one that seems best at the time: running away; yelling "fire" (so people won't be afraid to help you); trying to talk the rapist out of it — he may be less likely to hurt you if you can make him see that you, too, are an individual with feelings; fighting back; or finally, submitting, to save your life.

Self-defense measures, such as judo or karate, are good if they are taught in a way that simulates a rape situation. It must be taken into account that the victim will be terribly frightened. The best thing about self-defense may be that it gives a boy or girl self-confidence, which in itself is a deterrent to rape.

Young people of both sexes need to know that it is critically important to get help if they should ever be raped. Victims of any age need an immediate medical checkup to prevent STD, to cope with pregnancy in the case of girls, and to find evidence that could be used if the rapist is found and arrested. Boys, too, may find it hard to seek help, but need it fully as much as girls. Homosexual rape may leave an unwarranted stigma that the victim is gay, and this must be countered. Counseling is essential. Any victim is bound to feel terrified, furious, and guilty. These emotions must be talked out through wise counseling or they will affect the victim's future adjustment.

There are rape crisis centers or hotlines staffed by people who are ready to help at any time and kids should know about them. Most police and hospital staffs now have trained personnel to help rape victims, who need emotional care as much as they do physical treatment.

The parents' reaction makes a big difference in how a young rape victim adjusts. Some parents act as if it were an offense against themselves. While their fury is understandable, it is better to remember that the main goal is the child's mental and sexual adjustment even more than punishment of the crime.

Incest

Public awareness of child abuse has uncovered a far greater amount of sexual mistreatment than anyone ever dreamed existed. Most incest occurs between father or stepfather and daughter, some between uncles and nieces. Mothers and sons and fathers and sons are less often involved, though this, too, is more common than once imagined. It is seldom heard of because boys are more reluctant to seek help. Incest happens in every income bracket and social class.

Most parents are openly and physically affectionate with their kids, hugging and kissing them, which is good for children. Psychiatrists would say there is some sexual involvement in all affection, but it is not apparent in most parents' feelings for their kids. It is not bad for fathers to flirt a bit with their teenaged daughters, and mothers with sons, as it makes the kids feel attractive and helps them learn how to react with their boy- and girlfriends. However, it has to be absolutely clear to both sides that this is part of parental affection and only that.

Some parents have difficulty distinguishing between parental and sexual affection since it's hard to differentiate between tender feelings and sexual feelings. Those who feel sexual desire with their children and cannot control their impulses are usually parents who have trouble with their own sex lives. When incest does take place, it is devastating and traumatic to the child. Even very young children know there's something wrong. They become frightened and angry, but they can't refuse or fight the person they love the most. Incest is very destructive to family relationships and disrupts the normal parent/child distinctions, confusing love with authority and sex with discipline. Children who are victims of incest feel guilty as well as afraid.

Parents who feel sexually attracted to a child and have to fight the temptation to go further than just cuddling and hugging can get help before the impulse is acted out.

Recent public attention has been focused on all kinds of child abuse, making people aware that incest is not something that just occurs in oppressed and disadvantaged families. I get letters daily from girls, and occasionally boys, who are being exploited by their fathers, uncles, and sometimes even mothers, as well as other adults. Any parent who feels confused about impulses toward his or her own children, or who suspects that his or her mate is involved in genital play with a child, can get help. Call Parents Anonymous national hotline, 800-421-0353 (in Massachusetts, 800-822-5200), for referral and counseling.

Incest does not occur when parents themselves have a good relationship. Most incest occurs between fathers, stepfathers, or sometimes a mother's boyfriend and daughters. Treatment that strengthens the mother's position in the family will help her protect her children. Competent abuse treatment centers help the whole family back to emotional health.

The impact incest has on a child's later life depends on the way the trauma is handled. Children who are allowed full expression of their fears and anger and guilt can get rid of much of the emotional aftereffects. If they are well counseled, and convinced that most men and women do not victimize each other, they may go on to develop satisfying sexual relationships. If the reaction to their experience is negative or punitive, or if they don't get the pertinent help in making an adjustment, they are bound to have enormous problems with relationships as lovers and spouses in later life.

Incest between brother and sister is not nearly as damaging, but it isn't very healthy either. One girl wrote, "I'm thirteen and my older brother baby-sits me. When my parents go out, he gets in my bed and wants to do this funny stuff with me. He says if I tell, he'll kill me. — Hates Brother." This girl is being exploited by her brother and it is bad for both of them. Sometimes a brother and sister are tempted into sexual activity out of mutual curiosity, or because they lack boy- and girlfriends of their own. While this may not be psychically damaging, it should be firmly discouraged. An incestuous relationship will not further healthy social growth for these children. And if a pregnancy occurs, it would be disastrous socially, and perhaps genetically.

Parents who find such experimenting going on should keep a level head. Explain why incest is wrong, and put most of your energy into finding out why these kids are not having successful social lives with their peers. This doesn't even mean sexual relationships, which can certainly be deferred. Teenagers who have enough friends and companions and who go on to develop psychological closeness with others seldom feel a need for such a sexual outlet.

Sex is the second most powerful drive we have, after hunger, so the potential for its misuse is great. Lumping all the sexual offenses together in one chapter, however, tends to promote the misconception that children face constant danger from sexual assault, and this is not the case. If we raise our children to have a wholesome attitude and to take sensible precautions, happy and loving sex is the kind they are most likely to find.

8. *Rights, Privileges, Duties, and Discipline*

In order to develop self-confidence and a sense of responsibility, adolescents need to learn to do their share of work around the house. They may complain when asked to work, but don't back down; they need to accomplish things, and to learn to get work done on their own.

It does create a lot of wrangling, though. Kids write, "I'm practically the maid around here. I clean my room and wash all the dishes, and on weekends I have to vacuum the whole house. My brothers do nothing. I don't get paid. All I get is 'you forgot to dust. You didn't sweep under the bed.' They just use me! — Cinderella." Parents write, "My kids disappear when there is work to be done. If I don't stand over them, the lawn never gets mowed, the garage swept or the table set. My sixteen-year-old washes the car because he uses it, but as for the rest it's a constant battle. I wonder, is it worth it?" It is, but there are three things that make it a considerable effort. First, rights and duties almost always become a big issue in the struggle over control that goes on between parents and adolescents. Second, the methods of discipline that were used in childhood have been outgrown, and there is uncertainty about what is appropriate now. And finally, authority is breaking down in our society as a whole, making a parent's job doubly difficult.

The struggle over control is intense. You want your kids to become self-regulated, to remember to do their work and do it well, and to take on more adult responsibility for themselves in general. Often they forget, or are too busy, or do a sloppy job. It shows they are still immature and need control. You call your routine guidelines; they call it tyranny. They feel if you just gave them more freedom, everything would be okay. So bickering and nagging prevail. You may feel like clamping down, or throwing in the towel, but neither method is very good!

Discipline can be a real puzzle to parents at this time. The old techniques don't work; you can't lock a daughter in her room, or slap a son who's now as tall as you are. As a result, parents usually punish kids by restricting their freedom, but this is the time when kids need more freedom to test their new strengths and develop new controls. It will help if you think of discipline as teaching, rather than as punishment. Try to choose methods by asking yourself: Will this process show my child how to do this thing better in the future?

Parents can't expect instant obedience from children. One can't expect unquestioned obedience nowadays from anyone, except perhaps the Marines. Many people now feel that we should try to return to a more structured society, and the "back to basics" movement is trying to counter some of the obvious failures of permissiveness. Even while they protest, teenagers do feel more secure when they have clear rules and limits, but it won't work to go back to overly strict and rigid rules. Demanding blind obedience from children produces automatons who won't be able to function intelligently in our highly complex, technological world. Kids today need to be resourceful and self-reliant, which means they must have more, not fewer, opportunities to test themselves. Parents have to find that delicate line between giving enough freedom for exploration and giving enough discipline to create self-control. It means setting reasonable limits — a hard job when much in the cultural stream still seems to be going the other way.

Growing children should have a hand in how rules, duties, and punishments are worked out. If they get some choice in the matter, they will feel more cooperative. Don't offer them the choice to do or not to do anything, but let them pick the lesser of two evils or rotate unappealing chores. A family council, in which regular meetings are held to talk issues out, works well for some families. Then there can be open discussion until everyone is in agreement about what work is expected, and what action should be taken if agreements are broken. Duties might include meal planning, shopping, putting away groceries, cooking, cleaning, maintaining appliances, cutting wood, and tending houseplants, gardens, lawns, and cars. You should be flexible enough to cover special situations, but do impose penalties for unexcused failures. Of course, parents have to bend a little and not insist on their own agenda, but many parents are surprised at how much kids will offer to do when they are given their say. With others present, family meetings may lessen the tug-of-war over control between one parent and one child.

Some parents simply lay down the law, and this may be necessary in certain cases. It is essential no matter what methods are used that both you and your children really agree on what the rules are. Their understanding may be quite different. Be direct. Give reasons. Speak calmly, not in anger. Listen to the kids' point of view. And finally, if there are questions, put the rules down in writing. This makes matters official and not subject to later misunderstandings.

Avoid making rules that won't be followed. You can encourage obedience in young teenagers by letting them know you are flexible and will modify the rules as they grow and demonstrate they can assume more responsibility for themselves.

Punishment

When a child fails to do a chore, makes a mess, comes in late, or just plain disobeys, parents get mad. The failure makes extra work for you, perhaps, or is just disappointing. It may have caused inconvenience, given you a bad scare or questioned your authority, and naturally you respond with anger. However, anger isn't the best emotion to use in disciplining intelligently. Failure teaches its own lesson and punishment on top of it causes resentment instead of learning. More often, kids will be mad at themselves for getting into trouble in the first place. A bawling out will conveniently turn their anger on to you. It would be better to say something simple such as "Well, that didn't work," and make a suggestion for a better alternative.

Some failures do not provide obvious lessons to children. If there is a good relationship of mutual respect, your disapproval and genuine disappointment will speak for itself. This may be enough. Most kids don't like to upset their parents. If the message obviously isn't getting across, however, then you have to show them why their behavior isn't permissible.

In general, methods of punishment are imperfect. If one method fails, you try another, and it's never too late to try again. You do have the right not to be caused thoughtless worry, and some form of punishment is in order. You might insist that your child come in early or do extra work to pay you back. It's an important lesson: Youngsters who don't learn to be considerate of others ultimately have problems in adulthood.

Face-saving is important at any age, and giving teenagers leeway when following orders keeps self-esteem intact. It's especially effective to let them feel they are acting on their own volition, not Mom's or Dad's. And never punish them in front of their friends. This creates an unbearable loss of face and embarrassment.

As for spanking, parents should first ask themselves if it will really teach the child to do what they wish — say, to make their bed or stop swatting a little sister. No child, of any age, should be hit with a paddle or stick or even a hairbrush. All this teaches is violence. People who are beaten as children will use violence themselves to handle problems in later life. In fact, they are most likely to beat their own children when they become parents.

Teenagers can be masters of the sassy retort and the wounding remark, and it does make you want to slap them sometimes. Kids have to learn that rudeness arouses anger, and everyone has a limit beyond which he or she shouldn't be pushed. Adolescents go through a "regressive period," acting out childish behavior from their past, trying to sort out which responses are now appropriate and which aren't and they may well behave in outrageously childish ways. Happily, these periods are short-lived. While they last, parents should remember that children learn most by example, and hitting other people is not an example one wants to set.

Parents often criticize a lot as they try to shape their kids' behavior. Try to keep the ratio of your comments 70 percent favorable to 30 percent unfavorable. While it is often assumed that criticism must be negative, it really can be positive as well, which does a lot more good than the negative kind. A complimentary remark makes a person feel good and invites a more cooperative attitude. Try to pepper your conversation with pleasant little comments like "You look great today" or "I like the way you fixed that" and "That shirt looks nice with those pants."

Be chary with negative criticism. Adolescents are their own most severe critics anyway. They may act cool to cover it up, but their letters to me show how sensitive they are: "I try so hard, but I make a mess of everything I do!" "Why can't I look as neat and chic as Alice? I look like the Salvation Army dresses me!" "I'm so dumb, why can't I ever think of good things to talk about?" When you do have to rebuke kids, don't wound and don't be mean to get their attention.

Anger is often involved with discipline, and it is important that parents show children how to deal with it. This may be hard. Many people don't know how to express anger sensibly. The trick is to get angry at the situation or event that caused the problem, not at the person. Limit your remarks to what has upset you. Suppose your teenager carelessly drops his dinner on the floor. Say it made a terrible mess and you hate messes. Put all the anger into it that you need but don't say: "You're such a slob!" Just don't let yourself lapse into name-calling. When you label someone a slob, he or she takes it to heart and files it away with other hurts. This evaluation is most destructive to self-esteem.

Kids should be allowed to get angry the same way as parents do, by channeling their anger at things rather than at people. Parents often enforce rules the young don't like or believe are fair. Encourage them to talk, even to yell about how badly they feel, then listen. Be sympathetic to their feelings, even if you can't give them what they want, and this will usually be enough. If they don't vent their feelings, a sense of resentment may develop that later becomes explosive.

"I was working on my bike and broke one of Dad's tools. I said I'd buy a new one, but he hit the roof and won't let me use his shop for a month. I'm usually real careful, but he makes me so nervous yelling about how to do this or that, I can't think. I don't think he's fair. — Not a Stumblebum." If a teenager errs and is genuinely aware of it, he or she should be given a second chance. Your faith that he or she can do better is much more productive than skepticism that it won't work. Most of all, avoid "I told you so!" Who wants to hear that?

"I promised Mom I would never smoke, but she found cigarettes in my purse. I'm not hooked, and I made a vow not to smoke anymore, which I know I'll keep. But she doesn't believe me. How can I get her to trust me again?" Kids constantly ask me about trust. Parental faith surely gets severely shaken sometimes, but the way to develop trustworthy kids is to show that you do trust them. Avoid asking the impossible of kids, such as "Prove you can be trusted" or "Promise you'll never think about a boy again." Set a tangible way they can regain your trust, or set an arbitrary, short, time limit on the "purgatory."

Failure to receive sufficient discipline is not good for children. When parents take the easy way out, it teaches kids to take the easy way too, and may lead them to believe their parents don't care about them. Kids themselves have surprisingly stern standards for discipline. Here are a few suggestions some eighth-graders gave for parents: "Give children some freedom, but have certain rules and stick to them. Just let kids do what they want *some*times." "Don't tell your kids you'll let them do something, and then not." "Set ground rules you wish kids to follow, and when they start to get older, make the rules a little less harsh, but never let the rules be too lenient." "Forgive kids who make mistakes."

A good final note on discipline: Remember to be forgiving, even if the act itself is unforgivable. Failure to heal the breach quickly is detrimental. When parents continue to treat children with scorn, even after punishing them, repentance turns to anger. Prolonging mistrust is also a mistake. It makes children less trustworthy; they feel they might as well go and do what you no longer trust them *not* to do. Furthermore, if you are not forgiving, kids won't be able to come to you and admit their failures. You may not hear about the trouble they are in until it's too late, and this can be dangerous. If you judge deeds and misdeeds firmly and fairly, your teenagers develop high standards. If you show love, sympathy, and encouragement, they develop confidence, courage, and optimism, which helps them believe that they can accomplish almost anything they want.

Chores

The very word *chore* implies an unpleasant duty. In today's well-applianced household, it is hard to find challenging work for kids to do. Yet it's important that teenagers be depended on to help out and to show they can handle responsibility. It takes imagination and tolerance on the part of parents to turn over jobs that they can do better themselves, but it pays off.

Kids need a chance to prove they are reaching adult status. Instead of just asking them to set the table and wash dishes, suggest they take turns planning meals — and buying and cooking the food — on certain days. Instead of just having them wash the car, let them learn to tune it up and keep it running well. They can't weave and spin anymore, but kids can paint and paper walls, make curtains, do cement work, repair plumbing, change fuses, and do all kinds of useful things. Your goal is to give them responsibility for the whole job, not just the picking up afterward.

"I love to cook, but my mother won't let me. She says I make too much mess in the kitchen. She says she can do it better herself. I can cook at my friend's house, but never at home. — Frustrated." It's true, kids often do make messes, and probably can't work as efficiently as their parents, but is it worth saving a few minutes time at the expense of your kids' self-confidence? Teach them to be more efficient and show them why being neater is more practical, as they'll find out when they clean up after themselves. If you can't stand the way they do things, go into another room, but do let them try. Working parents who have to rely on their children more find it is paying off in self-reliance and camaraderie.

Our society needs to reestablish the sense of pleasure in working, the satisfaction of a job well done and gratification from doing a job for its own sake, not just for money or praise. The way to do this is to provide work for kids that has results they like, such as a tasty meal, a smooth-running car, a freshly decorated room. Kids can't usually observe parents working at their careers anymore, so they need to see the pleasure in work by the way you tackle jobs at home. It is important, therefore, to show some enthusiasm instead of groaning and bemoaning. Set a good standard of performance, but not so much perfectionism that kids feel defeated before they even start.

Demonstrate that "a job worth doing is worth doing well." Sometimes you will have to prod kids, probably many times, but it should be done with encouragement, humor, praise, and appreciation.

Consult the kids themselves about which jobs they are going to be responsible for. If their ideas are unrealistic, you may have to negotiate, but give them the chance to test and try to prove their new capabilities. Everyone may be happily surprised. You can't treat all children the same — different ages, talents, and strengths will dictate certain chores — but the more input the kids have, the more cooperative they'll be.

Assigning chores according to sex is now pretty much out of date. Let boys cook and girls fix tires and change fuses. Work discrimination by gender is destructive to good relationships. If boys and girls in your house are treated as equals, it will make them better friends, better mates, and eventually better parents.

In a single-parent family, kids' input in running the house is necessary. This can be a big benefit to growing teenagers if it doesn't interfere with their own work and social life. On the other hand, guard against depending on children too much, lest they turn into little parents themselves.

Schoolwork becomes more demanding and time-consuming in teenage years, and extracurricular activities are important to growth and experience. This can make friction at home. "I am a single mother with girls aged thirteen and seventeen. They used to be so helpful to me, but now all we seem to do is argue. I come home later than they do, and they used to get supper started, put the laundry away, empty the dishwasher, etc. Now they don't have time. They say I constantly nag, and they would do the jobs if only I didn't bug them. But they don't. — Harassed Mother." It's time for this mother to renegotiate. The girls probably have more to do at school, and dinner needs to be later. Perhaps it will have to be "TV dinners" for a while. Most situations can be worked out if both parents and kids listen to each other, rather than present fixed positions that can't be budged.

Post a sign on your wall that says BE FLEXIBLE. This isn't the time to tighten the reins. "My parents are too tight in controlling me. If I come home late by five minutes, or miss emptying the garbage just one morning, I'm punished. I'm grounded so much I never get to go out with the guys. How can I get them off my back a little?" I have said kids need lots of work, and parents need to set high standards, but be adaptable. Does it matter if the garbage goes out in the evening instead of the morning? Nagging doesn't do much good and it is better to forget details that aren't essential. If kids don't make beds well and you can't stand the mess, shut the bedroom door. Save your breath for the things that really matter to you. If kids let you down seriously, clamp down. If the "crime" was a willful disregard of duty and you feel some punishment is needed, make the punishment fit the crime. Grounding for not vacuuming the living room doesn't prove very much. Fining for not mowing the lawn isn't relevant. Neglected chores make extra work for you, so it makes sense to demand extra work from the kids.

"I was late getting home from a play rehearsal, and couldn't help Mom with dinner. Dad was very angry, and I guess I used a few unladylike words. Anyhow, he marched me upstairs and turned me over his knee and paddled me with my own hairbrush. I was really sorry I was late and spoke as I did, until he spanked me. Now I'm just mad and want to get even! — Hurt Two Ways." This girl's response shows why getting angry at her and then using corporal punishment doesn't teach the right lesson. A more creative punishment, involving some extra kitchen help, would have been more effective for all concerned.

Here's a letter that provides a bit of hope: "My daughter's room used to be such a mess! Oh, she'd clean it up if I got really adamant about it, but then you'd open her closet door, and it all fell out on your head. I kept a neat house and didn't fuss at her *too* much. Now she's grown and married, and her whole house is like a dream. It is nice to see that she has followed my example. — Mrs. O'G." Things don't *always* work out this way, but often they do.

Parents ask me if they should pay their children for doing chores, and the answer must vary from household to household, but all kids ought to do their fair share of household maintenance without pay. After all, mothers and fathers don't get money for doing dishes and making beds. Money could be offered for extra work, if the family can afford it, but there's too much emphasis on money in our society. We want to make sure our kids learn that many things in life are worth doing for their own sake, or someone else's sake, and not just for pay.

Human beings are born curious, inventive, inquiring, and playful: It is our nature to like to work at things. When children don't want to do work anymore it may mean they have been taught *not* to. Their tasks have been dull and meaningless, and the only thing that rewards them anymore is money, love, or power. Kids will work like beavers at anything they feel is worth doing, such as learning to get a ball through a basket, making a jalopy run, or sewing a skirt for a special party. Chores will never have that level of interest, as they are by nature routine, but if you expand your teenagers' involvement through adding responsibility, they will have more at stake and the work will be more interesting to them. If they learn to take pride in skills and careful work, the attitude will stick.

Money

It's no secret that money is power in our society. All of us are concerned with how to earn it, spend it, and save it. Those who earn a great deal are honored and envied. The "teenage market" is flagrantly courted by big business, in its ads and commercials. We don't want our children's values to be corrupted by money, yet through rewarding and punishing, bribing and withholding, parents, too, use money to control their kids, further emphasizing the importance of money.

In our affluent society many parents have tended to overindulge their children. Parents who grew up during the Depression often try to provide their children with the things they missed. They shower them with goods, and the kids grow up having no respect for money. Buying kids everything they want deprives them of the deep satisfaction of working hard for something on their own. Children who have everything handed to them on a platter don't develop a sense of competence and self-respect because they know the things they have are not a result of their own skills or effort.

"My parents are divorced, and when I visit Dad on weekends, he keeps buying me all this stuff. I know he loves me, but I feel like he's trying to make up to me. I can't tell him I don't need things without hurting his feelings." Children can quickly see through attempts to buy their affection.

The present economic pinch may eliminate the problems of affluence for many. Certainly it is more important than ever to teach children "the value of a dollar." Kids learn this best when they have some control over their own spending money, which usually means an allowance. Children should be given some pocket money as soon as they start going to school. By adolescence, they should be responsible for as many of their needs as possible.

"How much money should a teenager get for allowance? I asked for $10 a week, and got laughed out of the house. My girlfriend gets $25 every two weeks. I need just as much money for my clothes and to pay for stuff like bowling and skating and books. My folks pay for these things anyway when I need them, so why won't they let me have the money and pay for myself? — Desperate for Dollars." This teenager makes the point. If the parents are going to provide certain things, it makes sense for the teenager to do the purchasing via an allowance.

How much to give depends on the family income, the age and ability of the child, and what the allowance is intended to cover. It should first be worked out on a temporary basis. Ask your child to keep a careful record (a good idea in any case), and then the amount can be reevaluated after a few weeks and revised up or down as needed. Giving too little means the allowance isn't worth much, and not much is learned from it. Too much is also a mistake, as nobody values things that come too easily.

As soon as possible, try to make your teenager responsible for some substantial, seasonal payments, such as schoolbooks or a winter parka. This teaches how to budget and plan ahead.

Almost more important than the amount of the allowance is dependability. "I couldn't do all my chores last week. Well, once I forgot, but the other time I was kept after school. My Dad took my allowance away, and now I can't pay for the tickets to the dance. He says, 'Well, you should have thought of that when you shirked your work.' I never know how much they are going to give me! — Unfair."

If an allowance is to teach fiscal responsibility, it can't be used as a punishment or reward. Unfair is right. How can kids learn to budget if they can't count on a fixed amount of money each week or month?

Parents ask if they should loan money to kids who get short-handed. I think that's fine. Adults get loans from a bank. Just make sure it is absolutely clear when and how the money is to be paid back. If borrowing happens too often, reexamine the amount of the allowance, and how it is being spent. Your child may get an object lesson on why it is important to keep records.

Teenagers often want to get jobs after school or in summer. It is useful for them to learn to earn money; to explore different kinds of work; to find the pleasure of acquiring skills, the joy of creativity, and the deep satisfaction of watching things happen under their own hands. Jobs provide new experiences, new responsibilities, which may help put adolescents on a more equal footing with adults. For instance, a live-in baby-sitting job over summer vacation can give valuable insights into the way another household is run, enabling young people to reevaluate their own homes. The benefits from having a job are many, but parents should not overemphasize its importance. Recent studies reveal that teenagers who become engrossed in after-school jobs often become overly money conscious and acquisitive, and their interest in schoolwork suffers.

"I have a part-time job after school at the supermarket. I have to give all I earn to my parents, and then they give me some back when I need it. We aren't rich, but we aren't that poor either. Don't I have the right to have some control over my own earnings? — Breadless." Kids can certainly be expected to contribute, but it would be much more rewarding if Breadless were allowed to give his parents his own contribution, rather than their taking it from him.

Older high school students can manage a bank account, and it is wise for them to learn as early as possible how to cope with checks, deposits, and monthly statements. If they have a monthly or quarterly allowance, they will have to map out their financial needs in advance. It gives them more freedom over their spending. And although they will undoubtedly make a few miscalculations, try not to give them so little they are predestined to fail.

Kids sometimes get a distorted idea about money when their parents are unwilling to tell them how much the family income is.

Some parents fear it will seem to be too much, and their kids will ask for more, or become lazy or spendthrifts. Other parents are afraid it isn't enough, and their kids will stop looking up to them, or that they will tell the neighbors. None of these things is likely to happen. Children are usually loyal to the family, especially if parents are honest with them. They will have a far more rational attitude toward money if they know the facts. "I never knew how much money my Dad made until I had to fill out application forms for a college loan. I was amazed. I wish he had told me before, because I am ashamed of how I kept begging for so much all through high school."

One divorced woman not only made no secret of her income, she even had her sixteen-year-old son make out checks for the family bills every month. She had to sign the checks, of course, but this saved her some work, and it gave him a whole new attitude toward finances. "Before he kept bugging me for cash for records or gadgets for his car. Now he knows we may need that money for food or new shoes."

Money is important, but not in and of itself. We want to raise kids to be sensible, to provide for themselves, and not to be afraid of accounts, receipts, and statements. But we don't want to raise them to put dollar signs on everything they do or think or have.

School

Unlike allowances or household chores, your children's education is not directly under your control. Most parents feel strongly about what their kids are learning in school, and how well they are doing, and want to be involved in some way. Teachers say that students whose parents cooperate with the school and show concern have fewer problems than students whose parents pay no attention to what goes on in school. It is possible to care too much, however, and put undue pressure on kids to succeed. Those who see their children's success as their own success — "*My* boy is on the honor roll!" — can cause trouble for the student.

Sometimes the developmental processes adolescents are going through create some troubles at school. "I'm in eighth grade, and my teachers keep calling me down for being 'inattentive and uncooperative.' I know I'm not doing as well as I did last year. I try sometimes, but other times it just doesn't seem as important, and I daydream a lot." Lack of attention is common at this time of life. With the advent of puberty, teenagers are distracted by their own physical and emotional changes and daydreaming is endemic at this age. High school freshmen are often anxious about the prospect of more difficult work and a more sophisticated environment. Some respond by trying very hard in school. Some flounder. By sophomore year there is such a common falling off of effort that teachers call it "the sophomore slump." School just seems irrelevant. "I don't know what's the matter with me," a sophomore writes. "I used to like school, but now I can hardly force myself to go every day. I keep telling myself to try harder, and finish all my assignments, but then something comes up, and I let them slip. I can't make myself feel it matters."

It is not only puberty that causes teenagers to have problems with school. Young adolescents still haven't developed the ability to see far ahead. They can't visualize themselves three or four years hence, at college or at work, therefore they don't see why they should have to study things like fractions or chemistry. This is one reason students of the seventies said education was irrelevant and certainly many schools can do a better job of showing students why such courses will be important to their future. Parents can also help their children understand how certain knowledge and skills may make a big difference to them later on.

By junior year, students who are heading for higher education are able to understand the need to buckle down. While the competition for getting into college has diminished somewhat from what it was during the years that the postwar baby boom generation passed through college, the world economic situation is creating new pressures on kids to do well academically. It still takes a very good scholastic record to get into the more prestigious colleges, and a good degree is still impressive in the job market.

Although most education systems try to do a good job, we know there are schools that are boring; teachers that are dull, uninspiring, or unfair; and curricula that are bland and deadening. Consequently, some of the troubles facing kids in school are the fault of the schools themselves, not the students. Parents should evaluate their local schools by visiting and talking with school authorities and other parents. Most schools will cooperate with concerned parents, valuing their involvement and support. If your child is at serious odds with a teacher, you may want to investigate the reasons and ask for a change. If the whole school falls short of your expectations, it may be best to change schools. If this isn't possible, try to see that your child doesn't feel squashed by the experience. Students who do poorly usually assume it is their fault, even if they don't admit it. Poor teaching, therefore, results in students who feel guilty, frustrated, and mad at themselves, even though the problem is with a teacher's inability to teach. These children need reassurance and help in finding ways to succeed outside the classroom, lest their self-esteem be damaged by repeated failures. Bored, frustrated, and defeated, kids either turn their anger on others, through vandalism and other rebellious behavior, or turn it on themselves in equally destructive ways.

Teenagers complain a lot about school, even when their school is all right. "Whenever I come home and tell Mom that my teacher bawled me out for something, she always says, 'Oh, no. What have you gone and done now?' Sometimes I have been sloppy or something, but sometimes I haven't. Just once I wish she'd take my side! — Ninth-Grader." Many times students' complaints are just blowing off steam. They want their parents to listen to them and sympathize with how they feel. Even if what happens is their fault and they annoy the teacher some way and get a reprimand they deserve, it still makes them feel badly and they want someone to share this feeling. They don't need more criticism — the teacher has chastised them already. Instead of leaping to the teacher's defense, do a little creative listening. Usually all your children want is a sounding board, and they can work out their own problems if you lend a sympathetic ear.

School pressure becomes increasingly intense in the upper grades: pressure to keep up classwork, social standing in the crowd, and performance in extracurricular activities as well. Athletes, especially, have a lot of stress. Some schools put heavy emphasis on sports. So do some parents. Most students find sports a great outlet, relishing the physical activity and challenge to compete. They get satisfaction from bettering their own performance as well as from beating other kids or other teams. But, alas, many schools stress winning instead of teamwork and sportsmanship. The star of the ball team is looked up to by everyone, while the athletic lubber feels inadequate and ashamed. A fine athletic record deserves community recognition and approval but it is unfortunate to overstress its importance. It may help kids get into college, it's true, but athletic prowess is not, after all, a very big factor in most adult lives.

Parents need to find out how much stress is put on athletic education in their children's schools, particularly if their children are not especially gifted athletes. If your kids are being turned off, not on, by the prevailing attitude at school, you may have to come to their defense. Even the nonathlete needs some kind of physical outlet, and parents will have to help their kids find it if the school can't or won't. Individual sports such as biking, running, swimming, or skiing may fill the bill, or your community may have a baseball league, tennis or golf club, or ski team that can provide group and competitive opportunities.

The arena in which teenagers and parents usually become most involved is homework. "My parents bug me constantly about homework. They won't believe me if I say I did it at school, and never let me go out with my friends. This makes me feel like not doing it, just to get back at them. — Nagged a Lot." Overinvolvement in your child's schoolwork is a mistake, but so is a completely hands-off approach, such as the following: "My Dad will never help me with my homework. If I come to him with a problem, he just says to do the best I can, or ask the teacher at school. My friend's Dad practically does his homework for him every night. Who's right? — Eighth-Grade Neglect." Parents obviously should never do the homework. They can make suggestions about how to figure things out, but the point of the work is for the student to practice something, not just to get a good mark. Dad is right to suggest that his son ask his teacher about work he really doesn't understand, but at the same time, a more supportive attitude would better benefit his son.

Students' two biggest problems with homework are to find time to do it and to concentrate on it when they do. Parents' main responsibility is to provide a quiet, undisturbed place where kids can work at home. Is it okay to let kids play the radio or stereo while studying? If not played too loudly, music often helps concentration by blocking out other distracting noise. Watching TV while trying to do homework is ridiculous and parents need to ration TV if it interferes with schoolwork. Effective budgeting of time for homework won't happen automatically for most kids, but constant nagging won't help it along either. It's better to let the student find out what happens when work doesn't get done, and take responsibility for changing his or her schedule. If a real problem develops, and work is consistently left undone, or done poorly, parents should set up a three-way conference with the teacher and the student to find out what is going on. When a child does improve, acknowledge it! While academic work ought to be done for the student's sake, not the parents', a kind word can lend effective support.

Grades are often a bone of contention. They are the most obvious measure of the student's success, and parents often worry more about marks than about learning. The two are not always synonymous. It is possible to get good marks without being very interested in the material. Some kids learn to take exams more easily than others. Parents need to pay attention to a student's command of the subject matter as a whole, not just to his or her grade, to determine how much is learned.

Parents want to encourage their children to do well but shouldn't get too involved. "I hate to bring my report card home. I usually get B's and a few A's, but sometimes I get a C, and then my Dad gets so mad I can't stand it." It is disappointing when a child doesn't do as well as you know she or he can but anger doesn't help anybody learn. A calm discussion of whether the student is disappointed in his or her own performance and how it might be improved, with suggestions and/or offers of help from the parents, is much more encouraging.

If there is a consistent gap between what grades you think your child ought to be getting, and the ones on the report card, meeting with the student and the teacher will establish a reasonable expectation of that child's performance. The teacher may have helpful advice about study habits, test-taking, and independent work, like term papers, etc. The student may discover that he or she really doesn't understand some areas of the work. The parent may find out that C is a very good mark for this particular child in this particular subject. Be careful not to embarrass the child in front of the teacher. At the same time, take advantage of the situation to ask what, if any, parental help would be useful. Your child may respond differently in the teacher's presence and away from the emotional entanglements of the home scene.

"My parents ground me whenever I get a mark below an A. This means I am grounded all the time. I just can't live like a prisoner anymore. My work is getting worse, not better, because of this. — Ground Hog." Rewards and punishments have nothing to do with marks. Too much emphasis on scores may be harmful. The pressure to score high and get into college has brought cheating to epidemic proportions in many schools, corrupting the very purpose of education. Don't harp on report cards, direct your attention to the content of what goes on in the classroom. Even praising kids a lot for good marks can be a trap. It is certainly fine to tell kids they've done a good job and that they deserve to be proud of themselves, but overreacting to good report cards makes some children think they are only valued for their high scores; they feel they have to keep slaving for high grades or they'll lose their parents' approval.

We hear more and more about students cutting classes or skipping school entirely. It comes as a shock to see your teenagers start off on the school bus, only to learn their destination has been some other place. The school may say the problem starts in the home and parents may, in turn, blame the school. A coordinated effort is needed on the part of both teachers and parents to consult and determine the underlying causes of the truant's behavior. This is the most direct way to make changes.

The Car

A struggle for rights and privileges often takes place over teenagers' use of the family car. Getting a driver's license is the closest thing our society has to a "rite of passage." Kids assume that as soon as they have the legal document, they are entitled to unlimited use of the car. Parents worry. They feel that adolescents don't fully appreciate what a dangerous machine a car is. Even if they have taken driver education, youngsters don't have enough experience for safe driving in heavy traffic, on a high-speed highway, on a wet, dark night, or with a car full of peers urging, "Don't be chicken — floor it!"

Parents should make sure their teenager is capable of handling a car under all these conditions, which means finding ways to get hours and miles of training with a mature driver. It's tedious, but let your kids chauffeur as often as possible after they have learning permits. Get them into rush-hour traffic and onto interstate highways as soon as they can handle it. The experience and practice may put a damper on reckless joy-riding and help to reduce the appalling accident rate.

One of the reasons getting a license is so important to kids is that it is a huge step in severing dependence on their parents. They can go where they like so long as they can get the car keys. Most of the trouble, however, comes when kids can't resist the pressure to show off this new power. Before turning teenagers loose on the road, you have every right to insist they show you they are not easily swayed into reckless behavior behind the wheel, as well as in other areas such as drugs, drinking, smoking, staying out too late, and generally breaking the family rules. Talk over the rules of the road, about driving recklessly or competitively and the tragedies that can result.

Once kids have shown they know how to drive in different circumstances, they do have some right to the car. "I asked for the car to take Wendy out three times this month, and my parents say 'kids your age don't need cars. Why don't you walk the way we did?' No girl will go out with me if I make her walk three miles to the movies!" Life in our society is built on the premise that people drive. Cities and towns are laid out for cars; there is no public transportation in many suburbs. Bikes are cold in winter, and sometimes even dangerous, and it is unreasonable to say that kids don't need to drive at all.

A good way to get teenagers to pay attention to safety is through their wallets. Have them pay their share, not only for gasoline but for upkeep and insurance. You may have to increase their allowance, or they may have to earn extra money, but if they have to pay out, they will pay more attention. Drivers who know they are going to be held accountable financially for dented fenders will take far fewer risks. Suggest they learn to do maintenance themselves, which will save money and is also a valuable skill for both boys and girls.

Though traffic violations are punished by fines and other legal restrictions, these are sometimes not sufficient to make kids slow down or be more careful. If your teenager is cavalier about the rules of the road, you may need to add some restrictions of your own. It pays to be very strict about compliance with the law. This means you have to be strict with yourself. Parents who boast about getting away with high speeds or parking illegally and never getting caught can expect their children to follow their example and bend the rules to suit themselves, maybe fatally. "I got pinched for speeding, and had to pay $50. My Dad always goes twelve miles over the speed limit, and brags he never gets caught. Now he's burned up at me and won't let me have the car again for six weeks. I got tagged because I'm a kid. — Unwheeled." This boy's father seems to be punishing him for getting caught, and this is not a smart way to view the law. His six-week restriction is an "add-on" penalty. The boy has already received a big enough fine to impress him with the lesson of good driving. Grounding him may make him drive like fury when he gets his hands on the car again, to "show 'em."

Fast driving is certainly a problem. Speed is *the* great highway killer. The need to find challenges, test nerve, and get kicks out of speed and power, as well as alcohol, are all major causes of teenage traffic accidents.

A less-well-known but powerful contributor to highway accidents is anger. Kids need to be informed about this, because it is seldom mentioned. People often rely on the automobile as an emotional outlet, especially to take out anger and frustration. These emotions are particularly common in adolescence, as teenagers are often thwarted in their reach for more control over their own lives. The resulting fury leads many a teenager to drive recklessly and too often wind up wrapped around a tree. It may be assumed that he or she had been drinking, when the fact is that strong emotion can warp a driver's judgment just as badly. Your teenager should walk, instead of drive, when feeling irate or deeply depressed, and should be patiently dissuaded from getting behind the wheel during the cool-down period.

Summing Up

It is hard to find just the right balance between too much and not enough discipline, and as a parent, you will probably make mistakes along the way, but this won't matter much if it is always clear that your intentions are in the best interests of the child. Don't be afraid to say no. Frequently kids are relieved. The very shrillness of teenagers' insistence on getting their way is often a measure of their lack of confidence. Growing up is hard work. Kids are under strong pressure to do things they aren't sure they can handle, and shouldn't have to handle. They are often secretly pleased when you take them off the hook.

Above all, be fair, and don't be afraid to change your mind. Issues have to be reevaluated constantly, based on your child's past performance and growing evidence of maturity. By age sixteen or so, most kids can be depended on to run the basics of their lives pretty well. And they thrive under your dependence on them — so long as you are prepared for a magnificent foul-up now and then.

9. *Challenge, Danger, and Lawbreaking*

We expect, even permit, a certain amount of boisterousness in teenagers. "Boys will be boys," and girls will be too, more and more. Serious excesses should not be condoned, but peer pressure may challenge kids to dangerous extremes. Sometimes teenagers are more afraid of being called a coward than they are of bodily harm. Some kids confront dangers deliberately to overcome their fear. This can be positive, but it can also lead to trouble. There has been a dramatic rise in juvenile crime in the last few decades: nineteen-year-olds have the highest rate of arrests and sixteen-year-olds are in second place.

The parent's role is to help their teenagers find adventure and challenge and even risk, while guiding them along reasonably safe and sane paths. It doesn't work if you only allow kids freedom to do what you want them to do. Kids who feel that their every move has been programmed by Mom or Dad are unable to explore and develop their full potential. Urging teenagers in a certain direction without killing their enthusiasm is a delicate business, because they know it is your idea, not theirs. Here's the way one father did it. "I admired Joe's interest in the cornet. I found out when the band tryouts were, and happened to mention a couple of kids he likes who were going out for band. I particularly noted a certain girl. Then I bit my tongue. Joe went off to school with his cornet case, and my wife winked at me. At dinner that night, Joe let drop a remark about some music the band was rehearsing. 'Oh, you're in the band now?' I casually inquired. 'Yup.' We were all extremely cool, but I could see he was really pleased. Me too."

You seldom succeed by pushing, but you can find out what is available, both in and out of school. Sports don't have to be varsity football or basketball. There is community baseball, bike racing, canoeing, hockey, running, nature study, cross-country skiing. Scouts can be very challenging, as can 4-H and other clubs. Volunteer jobs afford excellent opportunities for kids to test their social skills and responsibilities. So do certain jobs and summer camps, especially those that pit child against nature, and ultimately her- or himself. Outward Bound provides such an experience.

To keep kids' challenges within the law, parents have to show visible and consistent standards themselves. If you brag about fooling customs, bilking customers, fudging on your income tax, or passing children off at half fare, it will be hard to demand that your children obey the rules.

One of the most effective ways parents influence teenagers' behavior is through fair, consistent, and loving discipline. Some parents abdicate all responsibility as soon as their teenagers begin to push for more freedom. Setting no limits, no time to be home, no insistence on work or chores, sets teenagers up to go overboard. Kids feel guilty when they misbehave, and if they aren't stopped, may act even worse, to force parents to step in. When children start testing you, that's the time to stand firm. They can't learn what their limits are if you don't set some.

Some parents react in the opposite way, and clamp down violently at the first sign of testing-out behavior, their discipline becoming rigid, punitive, retaliatory, even vindictive. This creates even more rebelliousness in teenagers. You need discipline, but keep it as light as you can. You want to teach caution and good sense, not stamp out all attempts to explore and try new things.

Adolescents need parents who act mature, dignified, and true to their adult values. Some parents try to act and dress like teenagers, either because they can't face getting older or because they sincerely believe that acting like one of the kids will put them in better communication with their teenagers. It doesn't work. Adolescents are made exquisitely uncomfortable by parents who act like teenagers.

They need parents, not pals. Kids are trying to establish their separateness from parents by creating their own styles in clothing and language, so don't invade their turf: it blurs the lines, and may drive the kids to more outlandish, even dangerous, rituals.

Teenagers still need their parents to "be there" for them. This means making the time you have with your kids highly personal, paying close attention to each child's individual needs, thoughts, and feelings. Offer information and suggestions when needed, but mainly just be there to listen, with your full attention.

Lack of parental support and approval can also make kids defiant. It's great to have high expectations for your kids, but they must be backed up with visible approval and support. Otherwise when they reach adolescence, children bitterly resent parents who pushed them so hard without any reward and they sometimes turn to stealing, vandalizing, and running away.

Many aspects of modern life make it harder than ever for parents to keep children in line. Recent social upheavals upset traditions, and there is widespread mistrust of authority, in what has been called the Watergate Mentality. Divorce and breakdown of the family structure, as well as unemployment, leave many adolescents idle and more likely to get into trouble. The loss of a sense of community and neighborliness means that kids aren't watched over by as many adults, and also that they have fewer compunctions about acting maliciously against others because they are strangers.

Our educational system must take some of the blame for teenage delinquency. Many students who feel bored, alienated, and isolated form gangs right in school that bully and intimidate not only the weak and vulnerable students but teachers as well. Some people believe we should go back to smaller schools, others think our whole philosophy of education needs reexamination.

Urie Bronfenbrenner, a professor of Human Development and Family Studies at Cornell University, thinks that junior high schools are one of the most destructive influences on young peoples' development, because they give students no challenge, no real responsibility. "We don't let kids do anything important. They have no experiences in being responsible for other human beings. Kids need to learn how to care by taking care." One suggestion he makes is that schools have day care centers and include working in them in the curriculum. It would teach the students, benefit the smaller children, and help working mothers as well. This is an example of the kinds of things enlightened education could provide.

Parents need to find out what is really going on in their children's schools so they can pick up the slack and help find outside opportunities for their kids to meet challenges and gain responsibility.

Today's complex technological careers require long training. Education is thus stretched out, prolonging the time before young people can enter the adult work force. In the old days, a spirited boy might seek adventure by going West or going to sea, as early as age fourteen, and girls of that age often got married. Now fourteen-year-olds are just entering high school, with four, eight, even ten or twelve, years of training ahead. Those who are not good students or not well motivated may chafe and rebel in unfortunate ways.

There are certain signs that can indicate to a parent that a teenager is getting into some undesirable behavior, even though he or she has not been caught in the act. Here are some suspicious signs parents should watch for: flagrant disobedience at home or school; repeated truancy; bullying of smaller kids or cruelty to animals; late hours; unexplained cuts or bruises; untidy appearance; secretiveness about friends or possessions; keeping weapons. Many of these signs could indicate alcohol or drug abuse as well as delinquent behavior, but whatever the cause, they are indications that some kind of anger or frustration is building to dangerous levels and that the child needs the advice and attention of a professional counselor.

Even the best of kids skips school once in a while. It is "playing hooky" if it happens only occasionally, and parents may not even know about it. Often the reason is nothing more serious than a student's worry about a test, pique at a certain teacher, a dare from other kids, or spring fever. Prolonged or frequent absence is another story and parents need to consult with the school to find out what's wrong. Few parents want to resort to labeling their child incorrigible and stubborn and turning him or her over to the authorities. It's important to seek help from a therapist or child guidance clinic before a minor offense becomes a serious crime.

Lawbreaking

Kids from comfortably well-off families who break laws do not do so out of economic necessity. A few commit crimes for neurotic reasons, such as a deep depression or guilt, but most kids who break the law are retaliating against an adult world they find boring or neglectful.

Most children don't have enough to do after school. Often there is nobody home to steer them into useful activities, and even when there is, kids want to do something more challenging than chores, homework, or the menial kind of jobs usually available to them, such as mowing lawns or baby-sitting. They look for thrills, and pretty soon someone cooks up an idea for a little excitement — throwing rocks at a passing train, setting a little fire, or breaking into an empty house. These are crimes of opportunity that can lead to vandalism, shoplifting, drinking, or even assault.

Junior-high-school-age kids are especially tribal. They like to hang around in groups, which can easily create a "we against them" mentality. A few bored or angry kids seeking excitement or taking out their bad feelings against family neglect can entice the whole bunch into destructive behavior and acts they would not normally dream of but do just because they want to be one of the gang.

Most kids in these gangs know better than to break laws. They would probably jump at the chance to partake of more acceptable activities if any were offered them that were interesting, challenging, and useful. But even wealthy suburbs, which have public tennis courts, playing fields, swimming pools and meeting places, need something more. They need some kind of organized youth activity agency or teen center with a good leader, one who can attract adolescents. This isn't easy to set up, but it's not impossible. And the cost for such an effort is a tiny fraction of what it costs a community to repair the damage of young vandals.

True Delinquency

A "true delinquent" is a minor for whom criminal activity is a way of life, and most often he or she is the product of poverty. There certainly are chronic offenders from middle- and upper-class families, but the common denominator for most true delinquents is poverty. When families are impoverished both socially and economically, the children may turn to street gangs for acceptance from a group already adept at stealing and burglarizing.

The classic study of juvenile delinquents as a group made by sociologists Eleanor and Sheldon Glueck showed that delinquent children were the victims of broken and unstable homes. They were most affected by overstrict or erratic discipline by the father, unsuitable supervision by the mother, indifferent affection or actual hostility on the part of either parent, and lack of cohesion in the family. These findings by the Gluecks suggest some tips for all parents in helping their kids stay out of trouble. Parents should avoid overly harsh discipline, and make sure children are not on their own too much. Parents need to know what their kids are up to, and with whom they hang around. They should discipline in ways that let children know that under the sternness there is affection and respect, clearly reflecting parental love and admiration. And finally, while it is all right to change your mind, and change your tactics occasionally, make sure that in back of everything is a consistent and loving pattern of standards and guidelines that your children can rely on.

Challenges Gone Out of Control

Shoplifting

This crime is high on the list of teenage lawbreaking. It has increased enormously in the last few years, among all age groups. Some kids shoplift because they need things they can't afford; others have money, but have little self-control and can't resist taking something they covet when they think they can get away with it. Many kids swipe things not so much to get the goods as to "put one over on the authorities," in this case the store owners. Among the better-off kids it's sort of an initiation rite. In an exclusive prep school, a group of kids may demand that all members "prove themselves" by stealing something from a store. One such group labeled themselves the K.K.'s, which stood for Klepto Kids.

Real kleptomania is a neurotic compulsion to steal, even when there is no economic reason to do so. There are other neurotic problems that may lead to shoplifting. For instance, a girl whose mother refuses to let her grow up may resort to shoplifting to get herself the lipstick, earrings, or perfume that she sees as signs of womanhood, but that her mother won't let her have. The girl's motives are subconscious, and she and her mother both need counseling.

Far and away the most common juvenile shoplifter is not neurotic but is a teenager with a weak sense of right and wrong, who is acting rebellious or acting out a "teenage rite" at the urging of friends. Such kids, if caught in the act, will usually mend their ways if better challenges are provided.

It is hard for parents to know when their kids shoplift. If your daughter brings home a suspicious number of new clothes, jewelry, or toilet articles, don't scream accusations you cannot prove, even if you are pretty sure the things were stolen. Some kids honestly don't realize that shoplifting is the same as stealing. They think of store owners as some vague "them" who have all these goods and won't miss a few. Talk about the issue. Explain how this attitude has magnified shoplifting into a billion-dollar problem. It makes salespeople suspicious and sometimes unpleasant to customers. It necessitates those huge metal tags on merchandise, and the closed-circuit-TV "eyes" watching from all corners of the stores. But most distressing, it is forcing sky-high the price of goods as stores compensate for the millions of dollars they lose every day. Ask your teenagers how they would feel if their lunch money were stolen every day — it is really the same thing.

If you know something has been stolen, or your child admits it, call the store manager and say, "This is Mrs. Jones. We are returning something taken from your store." Accompany your teenager, both for support and to make sure the ordeal is followed through. Often a manager will be very decent when you are being so honest as to bring the item back, especially if it is a first offense. Hopefully, he or she will give your teenager an impressive description of the problems shoplifting causes, and why it *does* matter, very much indeed.

Store owners sometimes call the parent of a teenager who is caught stealing. This is the time to have a hard talk about ethics, and how they aren't just for other people but apply to every person, old and young. One mother was so overcome that she could say nothing to her son when she was asked to come and pick him up. She simply wept all the time she was driving him home. Since she was a person who seldom cried, this was extremely painful to him, and he never again had the faintest urge to steal. Crying wouldn't always work, but in this case it served very well to show a child how disappointed his mother was that he failed to live up to the family's standards of behavior. And kids basically do want to live up to your code of ethics.

Shoplifting has become so widespread that most stores now prosecute anyone they catch stealing, first offense or not. Your first awareness that your child has lifted something may be a call from the police.

Kids steal from schools and libraries, garages and amusement places. Some even commit burglaries, which means breaking and entering, though this is less common, and car theft is a national catastrophe.

Vandalism

Kids have always found it hard to resist throwing a rock through the window of an empty house, but the senseless destruction of property by rich, poor, and middle-class kids alike steadily climbs. It isn't just windows in empty houses that get broken. Mailboxes are smashed, tires slashed, buildings set on fire. Schools, of course, are a popular target. Students in one well-to-do community put all but two of the toilets in their school out of commission with cherry bombs. In another, the science lab was reduced to broken glass and shattered equipment by a couple of disgruntled teenagers.

What is behind this wanton destruction? Again, it is bored kids, looking for thrills and excitement; it is the challenge of showing off to peers; it is alcohol; and it is anger that drives some kids to drugs and other destructive behavior. As our communities and schools get more crowded, people become more and more impersonal. Children don't know the neighbors in any personal sense. The postman, store owner, even the principal may scarcely be known by name and there is rarely any real communion with them. Kids do not feel connected to other people and they have fewer compunctions about vandalizing their property.

"We have had a lot of vandalism in our town lately, and my daughter told me that she knows the boys who are bragging about what they call 'trashing.' Two of them are brothers who come from a terrible home; the father is alcoholic and the mother sick half the time. They are well-to-do, but nobody looks after the boys. Martha says I mustn't tell anyone, or they will beat her up. What can I do about this? — Alarmed." Here again is a case of kids going wrong because they have been deprived of love, attention, and respect. They are lashing out to call attention to their suffering. Martha's mother would be justified in notifying the police or other town officials, not only to stop the vandalism but to get this family some badly needed help. If the case is properly handled the boys will be relieved, and in any case, it is unlikely they would know which of their peers told on them.

The following experiment shows that vandalism, especially in the schools, can sometimes be controlled. A suburban junior high school has been allotting to each class the money that is normally spent to repair vandalized property in school. At the end of the year, the class gets to keep any unused portion of the money for whatever fun they want to have with it. The students have turned into regular campus cops. With an eagle eye, they monitor classmates to make sure nothing gets broken and cuts down their "fun money," which proves that teenagers can be mature and sensible.

Violent crimes

Even more alarming than vandalism is the fact that more teenagers are now committing crimes of violence. The FBI reports that violent crime by all age groups increased 353 percent in the period between 1960 and 1980; 45 percent of those arrested for murder in 1980 were twenty-five or younger.

Even kids from the most advantaged families may be involved in crimes of violence, as for instance, the young man who shot President Reagan. In California a sixteen-year-old boy murdered a fourteen-year-old girl and took his classmates on trips to view the body for two days before anyone reported it. Some of this may be the result of the lack of connection many kids feel to other people, but it could also be the result of the television violence most kids grew up with. Teenagers who seem unable to understand or care very much if they inflict suffering are teenagers who have seen terrorists kill Israeli athletes in the Olympic village in Munich, hijackings, assassinations, and Americans held hostage in Iran. If there's a lack of humane understanding in our youth, we can put some blame on a violent world they can see by merely turning a knob. Recent studies indicate a strong link between violence on the screen and an increase of violence in children's behavior. This is another good reason, in addition to the sexual messages on TV, for parents to monitor their children's television watching. They might want to complain to the networks about irresponsible programming, as well.

Running Away and Hitchhiking

Most teenage misadventures are not violent, but may still get a child into trouble. Running away, for instance, is as American as Huck Finn. Who hasn't dreamed of floating away from tiresome responsibilities, including nagging parents? We don't usually think of running away as a criminal act, but it is a "status offense" — the legal term for certain actions, such as running away or truancy, that are illegal only for minors. Running away from home became a national phenomenon in the late sixties and early seventies. The Flower Children tried to set up hassle-free worlds for young people in various cities, such as San Francisco and Boston, and many teenagers from the suburbs ventured forth to see what was going on.

Some runaways are fleeing from unbearable hardships at home, such as abusive or alcoholic parents, incest, or physical or psychological neglect. Some children run because they are failing in school, about to be busted for drugs, or pregnant and they fear their parents' reaction. Others leave home because they resent the rules their parents have set and are unable to find the freedom they need to develop independence. A few kids still run for the promise of fun and a carefree life, adventure, and challenge.

The typical runaway today is a girl of about fourteen. Her experience on her own depends a great deal on her motive for leaving. If she's off for adventure, she may hang out with friends for a few days or weeks or months, or take a hitchhiking trip for a long distance. Most of these kids stay less than a couple of months and come home unscathed.

Teenagers who leave home out of desperation are more vulnerable. Pimps and pushers watch the bus stops and parks, on the lookout for kids who are wandering aimlessly. Some needy kids respond quickly to offers of food, a place to stay, indeed any kind of attention. Typically, runaways become very attached to their "saviors," and it is hard for them to break out of this pattern. Unless they get in real trouble with the police, they go unnoticed.

Most runaways are not in such a desperate situation. If your teenager gets miffed and leaves home, he or she is more than likely to hole up with a close friend. However, you can't expect friends to betray a confidence, so you have to be circumspect about questioning them. Here's how one father handled it: "My wife and I had a terrible blowup with our fourteen-year-old daughter, Jessie, about staying out late after school. All kinds of bad things were said on both sides, which I regret very much, and Jessie flounced out of the house. When she didn't come back all night, I called her friend Lori and something about the haste with which Lori denied seeing Jessie made me pretty sure Jessie was at her house. Jessie didn't show up that night or at school the next day, and by the second night, we were nearly crazy. I called Lori again and said, 'If you see Jessie, tell her we are truly sorry for what we said. We want to reopen the issue — no yelling and no punishment.' Two hours later Jessie appeared back home, to our heartfelt relief!" If you are certain your child is in the neighborhood, get word to him or her that you are willing to listen to the case, which may do the trick. You might also leave such a message with a trusted teacher, one about whom your child has good feelings.

Many kids stay away one night, knowing how much anguish this causes. If your child does not return after twenty-four hours, you may want to call the police — the incident will not go on their records as a truant. Check the drop-in centers that have been established in many cities to shelter kids who are out on the street. Some cities have specific runaway houses to protect kids from pimps and other exploitative adults. Local police, mental health centers, or local children's service agencies can tell you about these shelters.

There are two national hotlines that relay messages between parents and runaways. The hotlines will not reveal the whereabouts of the teenagers, otherwise the kids would never call. However, after the agony of wondering how a child is faring, just hearing that he or she is okay is most important. The number for Peace of Mind is 800-231-6946; The National Runaway Switchboard is 800-621-4000.

When a runaway does return home, no matter how long the absence, parents should greet him or her with love and gladness and not with "How could you do this to us?" Of course you were worried, and kids should know this, but if you lay on the guilt, it won't help you find out why they ran. Perhaps you think your child was acting like a spoiled brat to scare you into making concessions, since your child has all the love and advantage any child could want. Still, your love may seem stifling and overpowering, and this youngster had to run and find more room in which to become an individual. Some children find their parents' expectations so high that they can never live up to them, or the rules are so hopelessly rigid that they feel helpless.

Sometimes the dramatic act of running away will force a new level of communication and the problem will get solved, or it may take a third person to help mediate and clear the air.

Like running away, hitchhiking may also put a child in danger but it is not usually a sign of emotional trouble, just a convenient method of transportation. "My mother heard that I have been hitchhiking over to my friend's and she made me promise not to, or else stay home. What am I going to do? There's no bus or anything in our town, and my girlfriend lives three miles away. Mom isn't home to take me, and if I go on the schoolbus, I can't get home without thumbing. I'm sneaking but she'll catch me for sure. — Hog-Tied." This is a common complaint. There is no public transportation in most areas, so kids hitch rides.

Kids should know about the real dangers of hitchhiking and how they can easily become the victims of robbery, molestation, rape, and even murder.

Hitchhiking should be vigorously discouraged, either through car-pooling with friends or neighbors or maybe the purchase of a good bicycle. If all this isn't possible, the cost of a taxi is a small price for a parent to pay given the present-day grim statistics of hitchhiking problems.

Promise your kids that if they get into a dangerous situation and can get to a phone to call you, you will pick them up with no questions asked. If they can't reach you, they should be encouraged to call a taxi and you will be glad to pay for it.

Parents' Role in Arrest

Parents may sometime discover that their teenager has got into serious trouble. This they learn by way of a summons, a call from the police, or a call from the child. The parent's first reaction may be denial. "It can't be my Jim [Harriet]!" But it can. Almost any parent can have this experience. It is the time to swallow pride and stand by your teenager. You may feel like saying "You're no child of mine!" and washing your hands of the whole affair, but in such a predicament, kids need their parents' support and love. It is to the advantage of both parent and child to understand the laws that affect young people and to know that minors have the same rights as adults and that these rights are explained to them at the time of arrest. Kids will be better off if they are already familiar with the legal process.

When a minor is given a citation, say for speeding, the court will issue him or her a summons and a copy is sent to the parents. The summons gives the date for the court appearance, and a copy of the complaint. It is wise to get a lawyer at this point.

If minors are arrested away from home, they are taken to the police station to be booked and then allowed to call their parents or the family lawyer if there is one.

The teenager should know that he or she is obligated to give the officer a correct name and address but no other information until the attorney has been consulted. Sometimes arresting officers will try to persuade minors to talk about the charges against them, and it can be hard for young people to resist such pressure from an adult — especially one in uniform. Teenagers should understand that it is all right for them to say "I can't speak about this until I get my lawyer's permission."

When arrested, teenagers should not resist being searched or fingerprinted. The only time one can legally resist search is at home when the police have no warrant. If those under arrest are dangerous or acting suspiciously, the police have the right to search.

Arraignment is the process of being formally charged with a crime, and if the arrest is made early enough in the day, arraignment can take place right away. The defendant must stand before the court and enter a plea of guilty or not guilty, or delinquent or not delinquent, to the charge, and the date of the trial or hearing is set. If the arrest is made late in the day, arraignment is usually the next day, and the defendant may be released on "personal recognizance" (his or her own word that he or she will return for arraignment), if the offense is small and the court knows the family reputation is reliable. Otherwise, the teenager or the parents, lawyer, or friends can post bail. The amount will depend on the severity of the offense and the background of the defendant. The amount is small for most misdemeanors. If the parents cannot post bond for the amount, a bondsman will arrange it for about $25 or $30 for most minor offenses. The police will provide information about bondsmen.

If the family has no lawyer and no ready reference for one, the nearest bar association or Legal Aid Society can provide a list of attorneys. The lawyer's fee can be anywhere from $50 to $100 an hour or more depending on the complexity of the case. The fee is often in the range of $300 to $600. A minor may waive legal help, or the court may appoint an attorney if the defendant has none and wants one. The quality of court-appointed attorneys varies greatly, depending on case load, experience, motivation, and environment.

Arraignment takes place in a juvenile court or a special session in a regular or district court. Some states have a special form of court with jurisdiction over minors.

Juvenile hearings are closed to the public and are more informal than regular court. This informality is designed to provide quick and beneficent justice for children. A wise and experienced judge can use the juvenile court system to try to reeducate defendants. The judge, or referee in some states, may make use of psychiatrists and social workers to learn about the juvenile's family, background, previous experience, and attitude before making a decision. A judge who does not like juvenile court work may not be prepared to deal with the complex social and economic issues that surface in such cases. This can sometimes lead to infringement of the minor's rights, which is why the advice of a good lawyer is important.

After arraignment and while the case is being prepared, the "dispositional phase," is an extremely important time. Both the teenage defendant and the parents should cooperate fully with the lawyer who must have the youngster's honesty and unvarnished facts to allow him or her to prepare the case. Confidentiality is a highly protected right of the legal profession, and attorneys can do the best job of defense only when they know all the facts, even if evidence seems incriminating to the defendant. The attorney-client relationship is privileged for juveniles, too, so teenagers' evidence is confidential even to the parents, though the lawyer will want to confer with parents and get their view of things as well.

The dispositional phase is an important time for parents to prepare to demonstrate their concern to the judge. School counselors, teachers, therapists, ministers, and so on can be asked to present information toward developing a treatment plan for the defendant. Mitigating circumstances can be brought to the judge's attention. Fair and equitable restitution can be discussed. It is a time for creativity and imagination, both to help the individual teenager and to confront a community problem. In many cases, a suggested course of action is worked out by the defense attorney, prosecuting attorney, and probation officer before the case is actually heard.

In court, the clerk reads the charges, and the judge asks how the defendant pleads. Lawyers regularly advise the minor to plead "not delinquent," because a guilty plea closes off chances to appeal. Even if the lawyer is sure the defendant is guilty, he or she can plead something like this: "Not delinquent, though I admit to the facts sufficient to delinquency in this case." This still reserves the right to appeal should the court be too harsh.

The defendant may be told he or she has the right to a jury trial, but most juvenile court proceedings are "jury waived." One assumption is that the judge is experienced and well versed in matters of juvenile crime and restitution. In point of fact, a child will never find a "jury of his or her peers." Another reason is that if the lawyer later decides to appeal to a jury, he or she will already have heard the prosecution's case, and can conduct a better defense.

During the hearing, the judge will hear the case presented by the prosecuting attorney, the defense attorney, and the recommendations from the probation officer. If it seems in the best interest of both the community and the defendant, the judge is likely to rule: "This case is continued over without a finding." The defendant is put on probation for a specific period of time, usually six months to a year. If the teenager stays out of trouble for the designated time, the case is then dismissed and the record is sealed as if it had never happened. In many states, juvenile records can be sealed regardless of a conviction. In both cases, defendants can answer no to questions about arrest and conviction on applications for work, government jobs, or the military.

The judge may also fine the defendant. This fine may be suspended, pending the defendant's good behavior, or the defendant may have to pay by the time probation is up. The amount varies but is usually a sum the court feels the defendant can earn in the specified time. It goes without saying that the way to make a fine effective is to insist that the person who received it, pay it. If this means that a teenager has to forego some pleasures or sweat a bit to earn it, the lesson is likely to sink in.

Continuing a case over does not mean that it has been treated lightly. Some first offenses, such as drunk driving or willful destruction of property, are taken very seriously. Increasingly, courts are also using restitution and community service as sentencing options. The judge may require the defendant to pay for damages or to perform public service, such as doing janitorial duty in a courthouse or state hospital. Restitution and alternative sentencing can be highly effective ways to teach minors the consequences of juvenile crime.

During probation, the defendant will be asked to be law-abiding, to attend school, obey his or her parents, and sometimes even told not to associate with certain kids or hang around certain areas, such as deserted houses or parking lots. The defendant may also be told to get a job or attend an alcohol or drug abuse program. He or she will have to report to the probation officer at certain specified intervals. Probation officers are trained professionals who are truly interested in the welfare of minors, will insist that they do report, and will try to teach them to behave more responsibly.

If the conditions of probation are violated, the case could be reopened and a finding of delinquency imposed.

A teenager who becomes a repeated offender has a serious underlying problem, and therapy may be required. The earlier one intervenes in this kind of antisocial behavior, the better the chances of untangling the reasons for it. It is not the type of problem that parents can easily solve alone. It takes a third person to make this possible.

I do not mean to leave the impression that teenage years are fraught with danger, disobedience, and crime. Most adolescents are not in constant turmoil nor are they trying to destroy themselves and their surroundings. Most of their experiments are healthy attempts to stretch their abilities and knowledge and to test their inner control and self-mastery.

Far from being antisocial, kids this age are apt to be idealists. They long for a sense of belonging. They like the idea of future plans that promise growth, fulfillment, and acceptance. Sure, they get off the track occasionally, but if their parents' reaction is to steer them toward genuinely productive and responsible tasks, teenagers can reward their parents and their communities with prodigious efforts in useful directions.

10. Drugs

Our lives today are filled with many drugs. To help children learn to live wisely and safely among all these substances, parents need to examine their own habits regarding drugs, so they don't unwittingly set a poor example. Few parents smoke dope or take heroin for recreation, but many parents start their day with an instant fix of coffee or reach for the Valium to get through a difficult period. You can't stop taking all medicines, but for your own sake as well as your child's, you do want to avoid unneeded dependency on any drug. Use caution. Look for other methods of relief whenever possible. Solve your problems, rather than trying to drink or drug them away.

Parents can't do much to prevent their children from coming in contact with many of the substances that are available to them today. Vigorous citizen campaigns to get drugs out of schools, to eliminate dealers, and to take political aim at better control of hard drugs and alcohol will help in the long run, but these efforts can't bring about changes fast enough to help your kids right now. You will have to try to protect them with knowledge of what drugs are all about as well as an objective and intelligent attitude.

Parents who discuss drug use in a rational way, before it becomes part of their children's environment, lay the groundwork for rational responses on the part of teenagers. Parents who say nothing, and then explode when their teenager has some contact with a drug, make it very difficult for the adolescent to make sensible choices. By the time they reach junior high and high school, teenagers are people with independent ideas, growing ability, and self-control; if you treat them as such, they are less likely to get into serious trouble. Adolescents need room in which to explore and experiment, even to rebel. If you clamp down, and do nothing but forbid, criticize, and judge, they won't develop good judgment; their self-esteem will diminish and open, productive discussion will not be easy to initiate. In other words, they will tune you out.

Good communication is never more important than it is over the issue of drugs. If you give kids the chance to talk and explain their views, you may develop a dialogue that will help both sides. You can then start setting up some early-warning systems to help your teenagers fend off the peer pressures they are bound to get. You won't stop them from reacting to these pressures, but young people who have some preparation can better handle peer group expectations. Knowing ahead that they will be asked to try different things gives them a chance to think about what they want to do and to make more studied decisions.

Virtually all kids try some kind of drug at some time in their adolescence. Teenagers are experimenting with life and want to try everything, and sampling something a couple of times doesn't cause ruin. When a youngster finds that a drug offers escape from worry is the time trouble starts, so parents' listening skills should be directed toward these problems. Encourage kids to talk freely about their anxiety concerning school, social life, personal development, and perhaps even family tensions as well.

Usually the first reason a youth will give you for taking a drug is "I like it." This is not always a cop-out explanation. Once someone becomes a drug abuser, however, there are other underlying psychological issues to deal with. But to deny that drugs lead to feeling good is to deny a fact. Parents must be willing to admit this fact to their children and focus the discussion on other, more individual and personal, issues.

Marijuana

Marijuana is second only to alcohol among substances teenagers abuse today. It is easy to get. Head shops sell marijuana smoking paraphernalia right next door to many city schools. According to a 1979 Gallup Poll, one out of every five Americans has tried it. Two thirds of all college students have smoked it, and 40 percent use it regularly, though not heavily. Sixty percent of all high school students have tried it.

Daily use of marijuana by high school seniors began dropping recently, in sharp contrast to its rapid rise up to 1978. There has also been a shift to less frequent and less intense use of the drug. The best news so far is that marijuana use is leveling off in junior high schools. It is no longer true that kids try it at younger and younger ages, according to the National Institute of Drug Abuse.

Many kids use marijuana in a social way, sharing a joint with one or two friends at a party or a concert, once or twice a week or a month. They may even smoke it alone from time to time. Someone who frequently smokes marijuana alone, however, may have other problems that need attention.

Pressure on kids to try marijuana is reflected in the letters I receive every day. "All the kids in our crowd are starting to smoke pot. I'm too scared, but I'm more scared they won't like me if I don't. Should I try it, even if I don't want to? — Help Quick." Young teenagers are afraid to displease their friends by not following the crowd. They have the impression that "everyone is smoking dope all the time," but that isn't true. A few kids are real "pot heads," who light up even before they get on the school bus in the morning, but generally, schools are not filled with students nodding over their English papers. Heavy drug use by children in school is low, much lower than heavy use of alcohol. Marijuana's illegality simply adds to the lure for kids who are looking for dangerous ways to test their courage. Marijuana has become a popular bone in parent/teen contention over control.

Most people describe a marijuana high as a sense of well-being, gaiety, giggliness, and talkativeness. It makes them mellow, reduces their inhibitions, and enhances sensations so that sight, sound, and touch are perceived more strongly — one reason people often use it before a concert. It is not an aphrodisiac, but because it smothers inhibitions and heightens sensations, it can intensify sexual feelings. Marijuana distorts the user's sense of time, so that good feelings seem to go on and on. Unlike liquor, pot makes users introspective, not aggressive or belligerent. A marijuana high, using common, unadulterated "street" marijuana, produces a gentle and mild euphoria that lacks the potent consciousness-altering qualities of the true hallucinogens.

The effects of marijuana are variable and quite unpredictable, however; they depend on the strength of the drug, and to a great extent, on the previous experience of the user, the circumstances in which it is used (the setting), and the mood of the smoker (the set). One's frame of mind before smoking is augmented by the drug. A person feeling good and optimistic about the high will normally have a pleasant time. A person who is apprehensive about smoking marijuana, worried about being arrested, or anxious for any reason will find that these fears become exaggerated — the high may not be a happy feeling at all. High doses may make the user drowsy, forgetful, or disoriented.

Teenagers write "I like to smoke marijuana because it makes me feel good." "I smoke pot because it helps me relax and forget my worries. What's wrong with that?" "We smoke a joint because it makes us enjoy the music more." "My boyfriend tries to make me smoke grass because he thinks then I'll make love to him." "Why do we smoke pot? Because all our friends do, that's why." This last statement is probably the underlying reason, at least for younger kids. High school seniors are becoming more cautious. In 1980, 50 percent said they believe marijuana presents "great risks"; in 1978, only 35 percent said so.

The intoxicating ingredient in marijuana (or cannabis, its Latin name) is tetrahydrocannabinol, or THC. The immediate physical effects of THC are to increase the pulse rate and cause the eyes to become bloodshot. Other effects such as dizziness, dryness of the throat, resulting in thirst, and hunger are harder to detect.

First-time smokers often experience no unusual sensation at all. With repeated use, there is a release of inhibitions, which produces feelings of freedom and bliss and seldom any hangover. Unlike occasional users, heavy users may build up tolerance and look for stronger pot. Still, there are no withdrawal symptoms when they stop smoking.

THC affects the way the brain perceives time and sensation. This results in a reduction of motor coordination and impairment of short-term memory. The statistical connection between marijuana and auto accidents is still somewhat controversial, but common sense tells us that to drive under the influence of a drug that affects our motor responses and our sense of timing is sheer folly.

Alcohol certainly produces a much more disabling kind of intoxication. It can have a more severe effect on the central nervous system and, so far as is known, long-term use is far more harmful. Although a strong marijuana habit may be hard to break, it is not caused by physical addiction, whereas alcohol is dangerously addicting and causes severe behavioral changes. Alcohol abuse is also associated with physiological damage such as deterioration of the brain and the liver. However, marijuana is not harmless.

What are the physical dangers of smoking marijuana? It would be helpful if parents could point to incontrovertible evidence, similar to the cancer risk for cigarette smoking, but wide-scale marijuana use is relatively new in this country, and research has had a slow start. Some reports of ill-effects that appeared in the media and in scientific and medical journals were later refuted, leaving the public confused. One frustrated researcher described marijuana as "a substance which, if injected into a rat, produces a scientific paper."

The most thorough examination of the marijuana question is Dr. Lester Grinspoon's book *Marijuana Reconsidered.* Dr. Grinspoon examined all the reports of physiological effects from long-term marijuana use — such as brain damage, memory damage, lowering of testosterone level, impairment of the immune response, chromosomal and fetus defects, and damage to pulmonary function — and concluded that none of these has yet been conclusively proven by large-scale, thorough scientific research. Furthermore, in carefully controlled investigations, with hundreds of heavy marijuana smokers in Jamaica, Costa Rica, and Greece, no conclusive evidence of physical harm was found. There has never been an authenticated death attributed to marijuana. This does *not* mean that marijuana is harmless. I hear increasing complaints of memory impairment from erstwhile marijuana smokers. Dr. Grinspoon feels, as do I, that this drug has no place in the lives of adolescent children. What it does mean is that the verdict is not yet in on physical hazards.

The psychological effects of marijuana are of concern. A user, especially a novice, may suffer an acute anxiety reaction to being high, with paranoidlike fears about losing control or being arrested. These reactions seldom reach panic proportions; reassurance will usually calm the user down. True psychotic reactions are not substantiated by research. Although psychoses have been claimed in some reports, preexisting emotional disturbances or the use of other drugs seem to have been involved. Nevertheless, there is grave concern over other aspects of adolescents' reaction to heavy marijuana smoking. One is the fear that marijuana reduces a user's ambition and drive, the so-called antimotivational syndrome. This letter from a mother describes a typical worry about motivation: "My son was always a pretty good student, until he got in with the pot smoking crowd in the ninth grade. He promised me he wasn't using it himself, but I got suspicious because his marks have dropped so much, and he doesn't do sports anymore. He just sits around his room and listens to music. I finally searched his room and found evidence he can't deny. Don't tell me marijuana doesn't take away the will to work. My once-active boy has become nothing but a burn-out. — Beside Myself."

Heavy use of drugs is certainly associated with low motivation. Whether marijuana actually causes the change in behavior or is a result of some developmental emotional storm is not definitely established. Lethargy and disinterest in activities are symptomatic of adolescent struggles to grow up. Studies show that there is no difference in grade-point averages between marijuana users and nonusers. Other reports find that marijuana has no significant effect on learning performance or motivation. But some parents can see a lack of will and energy with marijuana smoking going on at the same time; to them, which came first scarcely matters. What is obvious is that the drug is adding to their adolescent's problems.

"Isn't it true," asks a father, "that using marijuana leads kids to try harder drugs like heroin?" This is not true in the chemical sense; that is, there is no chemical property of marijuana that causes a user to crave harder drugs. In fact, most casual users find they need less, not more, marijuana in order to get high. While it is true that many heroin addicts first tried marijuana, they also tried alcohol and nicotine. The National Commission on Marijuana and Drug Abuse concluded that "the overwhelming majority of marijuana users do not progress to other drugs. They either remain with marijuana or forsake its use in favor of alcohol." It is a fact, however, that people who drink alcohol and smoke cigarettes are more likely to try marijuana. Smoking cigarettes by age eleven or twelve is one of the most consistent indicators that a child will smoke marijuana.

It stands to reason that a person who is associating with a certain group just for the purpose of using a drug will get into a pattern of drug use. He or she will be in contact with kids who deal and who get pinched. Furthermore, if the teenager's friends are kids who have little interest in life except getting high and looking cool, then this kid's schoolwork and, far more important, his or her testing and exploration for personal growth and development are bound to suffer. This is the time when the issues that arise will affect the adolescent's whole future and the consequences of avoiding decisions will be profound. No one can learn to make decisions by copping out. Teenagers who depend on marijuana to get away from the necessary tensions of growing up are prevented from learning how to solve problems and from developing social skills.

In trying to influence your children not to use marijuana, be calm and loving. If you act as if your kids have started down the road to destruction, you will quickly slam the door to further communication. Keep them listening to you, help them believe you accept them even if their views on some things differ from yours.

Teenagers are not affected by a litany of dangers they don't believe are true. They are interested in provable facts about their health. They may not be scared by the threat of arrest, but they will be impressed if you know the severity of possible sentences in your area, and the consequences "a record" can have on their future, if you live in a state where marijuana use has not been decriminalized.

Talk openly about heavy marijuana use, about the change in lifestyle of a "pot head," and point to a real example. Talk about the type of friends drug abusers have and what kinds of goals they exhibit.

Your discussion will be much more effective if you show that you also understand the temptations and pleasures that come from the relaxation of tensions, the sharpening of sensations, and the feeling of euphoria. Whether you have tried marijuana yourself or not doesn't matter. You can imagine what it is like. However, if you have tried marijuana or any other drug, you should remember that everyone's experiences are not necessarily the same as yours. Don't overgeneralize and be open to what your children say about what these drugs do to them.

If you believe that your child is using a great deal of marijuana, or using it so often that it is becoming a big issue in his or her life, step in firmly. Clues that might indicate marijuana abuse are: changes in normal behavior; daydreaming; vagueness and inattention; loss of interest in previous activities; avoidance of parents; dropping old friends and taking up with new ones; secretive phone calls; sporadic flows of unfamiliar visitors; redness of eyes; tremors; strange odors or unusual attempts to freshen the air; and headaches and nausea. As these changes are not uncommon in adolescence anyway, determining whether they are caused by marijuana is hard. To make a false accusation will throw all mutual trust out the window, so if you have suspicions but are unsure, don't ignore the problem. Spend more time with your child; be cool, unemotional, and open to his or her opinions to gain better insight into what is going on.

If you are convinced your child is abusing marijuana, find out why the drug is being used. A sudden increase in the use of any drug frequently reflects some major change in the adolescent's life, such as loss of confidence, anxiety over academic work, loss of a girl- or boyfriend, some serious family conflict, or even a deep concern about the safety of the future — indeed, that of the whole world. Feelings of boredom, lack of challenge, of being overly restricted or alienated and depressed are common as teenagers struggle toward their uncertain future. Adults often fail to realize how scared kids are about the threat of nuclear war and annihilation. A drug like marijuana that provides both relief from anxiety and a way to show defiance against a world that seems to be against them is doubly attractive to adolescents.

Calling marijuana use criminal or deviant behavior will not discourage most kids from smoking it. Scolding, nagging, getting angry, and blaming friends will not undo the events that led up to the teenager's need for a drug. Speak with honesty and with love and support: Punitive threats or harsh judging will not help you to get to the bottom of whatever it is that made marijuana an attractive outlet for your teenager.

Some parents can persuade their teenagers to stop using marijuana for a definite period of time — several weeks or months — to find out if they can cope with problems in a more satisfactory way. Some parents form groups to take a communal stand against marijuana use in their community and school. This is a good plan if there is cooperation from the school, police, and a sufficient number of parents to establish some rules with real teeth in them and to provide some alternate activities for teenagers.

Perhaps the teenager can work with adult support and funds to create a community youth center or project to generate acceptable recreational activities, such as athletics, music, art, or career exploration. Otherwise, parents need to help their adolescents develop individual interests and talents on their own.

If you can't talk with your teenager, or feel he or she isn't leveling with you (a common thing and, in fact, part of the problem with serious users of marijuana or any drug), find some other adult your young person can talk to.

Your child may feel more open with a teacher, doctor, religious leader, relative, or older friend. If you can't find such a person or the problem seems too severe, reach for professional help. You can find drug therapists or counselors through your doctor, mental health clinic, or hospital. If your child refuses to go, go yourself, and he or she may follow.

If your child is getting this kind of help, keep in touch with the situation. Keep pressing for new solutions, and show by your love and concern that you really care about your kid's welfare. This is the most important thing you can do. Many adolescents' anxieties are caused by their perception that their parents don't know what is going on. This is important. When teenagers feel neglected, they interpret it as meaning their parents don't love them. And feeling unloved is a powerful force for harmful use of drugs. Finding other ways to gratify the needs of adolescents will bring the best long-term results.

Other Illegal or Illicit Drugs

Many drugs other than marijuana are also readily available to teenagers today, both prescription and street drugs. Children do not expect their parents to know all about these drugs and how they affect people, but a nodding acquaintance with the basics is very helpful. Most important, find out where to get information, as new drugs keep appearing on the scene. The best sources are hotlines and crisis centers, or you can look up facts in the *Physicians' Desk Reference* (PDR), or even better, the *Nurses' Guide to Drugs.*

Most schools and libraries have books for kids on drug use, though the teenagers may not see these as impartial. The Council on Drug Abuse puts out pamphlets that are up-to-date and fair. You can write for these at: National Institute of Drug Abuse, 5600 Fishers Lane, Rockville, MD 20857.

Also talk to your kids about drug use in general to help them understand the cause and effect of chemicals on the body. Even when they know the hazards of various substances, they need to be aware that many street drugs, including marijuana, are not pure. Because the manufacture and sale of these drugs are illegal, there are no controls over the dosage, toxicity, and additives. There can be, and often is, downright fraud. Drug peddlars, even teenaged ones, are out for money. They don't care what happens to their clients, especially if they are themselves junkies. It's a hard lesson for kids to learn that "one of their own" may do them in on purpose, or trusted friends may purchase impure stuff unwittingly.

Young people should be warned against the practice of mixing drugs. One of the worst mixtures is alcohol and tranquilizers. Teenagers may believe it's harmless but the mixture magnifies the action of each. This is a 2 plus 2 equals 6 situation. The combined reaction is worse than the sum of the individual reactions and a deadly overdose is possible. Some unsuspecting kids will buy a substance because it's cheap. "It's great! Dynamite! Won't burn you," the pusher promises, and a nightmare trip ensues. Another terrible trick is to grab a handful of mixed pills and swallow them on a dare; children should realize the physical and mental damage that such a drug "salad" can produce.

Today's generation of adolescents is more sophisticated and street wise about drugs than were the kids of the sixties. There are fewer bad trips and overdosing, or OD's, because more is known about drugs and how to use them. A small, experimental dose of most drugs is relatively harmless, but it is still hard to be sure exactly what dose or even what drug you are getting on the street. And bad trips still do occur.

The following is a brief description of the commonly used drugs and their special properties; it will help you in overall discussion of drugs with teenagers. But if any serious drug situation arises, you will need to turn to professional help.

Hallucinogens

PCP (phencyclidine, angel dust, super weed)

This is not a true hallucinogen, but is used as such, and has recently been a most troublesome drug. PCP is a tranquilizer for horses; it is very strong and has the potential for serious bad trips. Large numbers of kids first meet PCP by chance. Sprinkled on marijuana, it is undetectable, but the effect is far more potent and potentially very dangerous. Its strength varies greatly depending on who made it. In Boston, for instance, the strongest type of PCP is called crazy eddie or moon bars.

More bad trips are caused by PCP than any other street drug. In extreme cases, it causes a drop in blood pressure, paralysis, coma, and death. More commonly, it has a dangerous psychotic reaction, possibly with suicidal or homicidal tendencies. This psychosis may last up to several weeks. The user may have amnesia, and remembering nothing about the bad trip, take PCP again.

"My friend got some stuff he said was THC. We were going to try it, but luckily I got sick. He tried it, and wound up in the hospital like he was mental or something. Is that what THC does to a person? — Lucked Out." No, it is what PCP can do. The friend was sold PCP, disguised as THC. PCP is the most misrepresented drug on the market. It is often peddled as mescaline, LSD, or psilocybin, as well as THC or just plain T, but none of these are readily available on the street. This is why it is necessary for kids to *know* what they are being offered.

"Kids at school are using 'super joints.' They say you get a terrific high, but I'm sort of scared. Should I be? — A Little Square." Darned right this writer should be scared. Super joints are marijuana with a little added PCP. This is like sprinkling a little gasoline on your fire — it may explode right back in your face. During a high, people do things they wouldn't ordinarily do. It is easy to overdose on PCP, particularly when mixed with other drugs, like alcohol, barbiturates, or other tranquilizers. Warn kids of this, too. A visit to the psychiatric ward of a hospital would probably convince them that PCP is nothing to fool around with. PCP abusers are likely to abuse other drugs as well. What makes this a difficult problem is that the effects of PCP may resemble the effects of other drugs — narcotics, stimulants, depressants, and cannabis. Some common signs of PCP abuse include numbness of limbs, paranoia, muscle rigidity, inability to speak, blank stares, and violent behavior.

Arguments with a PCP abuser can trigger violent behavior. PCP abusers' sense of reality is severely distorted and their behavior is therefore unpredictable. The best thing to try in dealing with a bad PCP trip is to steer the abuser to a quieter and more relaxed environment.

PCP abusers become particularly disoriented in water. Of nineteen deaths associated with PCP in California, eleven were caused by drowning — one while in the shower.

LSD (lysergic acid diethylamide, or acid)

This is the only real hallucinogen that can be bought on the street. Right now it is fairly rare and what is sold as LSD is most commonly PCP, which is cheaper and easier to make. While one can't really overdose on LSD, very bad trips can result from too strong a dose. Bad trips can also occur when an unstable person takes the drug in a hostile environment or when a person is unaware that he has taken LSD.

LSD is often used to try to gain new insights. It was popular in the late sixties when kids were questioning the lifestyles and values of their parents' generation, hoping to find answers through this drug. Whatever convictions they may have come to while high didn't result in permanent answers once they came down.

The setting of the user is particularly influential in getting a good or bad trip from LSD. A person who is on a bad LSD trip can usually be talked down. One reputation of LSD is that it may cause "replays" or flashbacks to an unpleasant high, which occur for no apparent reason. Fortunately, LSD use is down, possibly due to fears of bad trips and of chromosomal damage, although the latter has not yet been scientifically proved. Most kids who want hallucinogens now will probably buy PCP being sold as mescaline.

Inhalants

Certain glues, aerosols, paint, inner tube buffing compounds, and other vapors are sometimes sniffed to produce a high. Sniffing these petroleum products is dangerous, for there is such a fine line between getting the right amount of the drug and getting too much. Many sniffers have passed out from lack of oxygen, which could permanently damage the brain. Sniffing sprays is also very hazardous since it's difficult to separate the chemical from the gas used to power it. Freon, for instance, can freeze the larynx and/or lungs, causing suffocation. Warn kids that any petroleum product is basically toxic.

Opiates

These are the narcotics, the hardest of the "hard" drugs, which are derivatives of the Oriental poppy. Opium is seldom used in the USA, morphine is not a street drug; heroin (junk or smack) is the most common narcotic in this country.

Opiates slow the body down. Temperature falls, blood pressure falls, all the other body functions slow down. Users often feel nauseated at first, as their body tries to reject this poison. Tolerance increases, meaning a user has to have bigger and bigger doses to get the same high. Withdrawal is very unpleasant: Flu-like symptoms occur, and then cramps, tremors, and sharp spasms, which is why it's called "kicking" the habit.

Heroin is used by kids in city ghettos, and by middle-class kids in suburban high schools. Heroin is highly addicting physically and is easy to overdose on.

"My cousin wants to turn me on to heroin. He says it isn't all that bad. He just 'chips,' he says, and it doesn't get the better of him. Can people control their habit like that, or is he just putting me on? — Wants to Fly." "Chipping" means using heroin on an occasional basis, and new evidence shows that more people are able to do this than was once supposed. It is also a fact that some adolescents who abuse heroin later give up the habit spontaneously, possibly when they have matured enough to feel capable of handling their adult responsibilities. Basically, however, heroin remains a drug no one should fool with. Tell your children the truth: that it is dangerously habit-forming and hard to give up, that only a very few can get away with such experiments.

The other grave danger from heroin comes when it is injected directly into the veins, called mainlining. Infection and hepatitis from dirty needles is almost inevitable. Mainlining also creates telltale scars, called tracks, which no healthy teenager wants to bear.

Heroin was actually invented as a nonaddictive pain killer to substitute for morphine. It turned out to be highly addictive but its pain-killing properties are what users are looking for, and they get people into deep trouble. Kids who grow to depend on it are those who feel such pressure at home or school that they believe they can't control their own lives and have no where to turn but to "junk." Their frustrations turn to self-hatred, and heroin is used as a kind of psychic suicide. These kids are not looking for a little fun, a kinky high — they are seeking oblivion from pain. By numbing awareness of problems, heroin reduces an abuser's ability to cope, setting up the addictive cycle that's so hard to break. The more successfully a drug eliminates pain, the more easily it is abused.

It is not wise to pull away the support of the drug abruptly from a dependent person. Careful and experienced help is needed to shore up the confidence to handle one's own life as well as to get off the drug. Most heavy heroin users probably live at home, but this isn't the best place to be. Even young addicts become deceitful, real con artists who won't usually stop taking the drug for the sake of their parents.

Difficult as it is to admit that one's own child is addicted, the best place to turn is to a treatment center that specializes in young heroin users.

Tranquilizers

Tranquilizers are the most widely used of the legal drugs. Until very recently, many doctors prescribed them liberally, especially Valium and Librium, believing that these were harmless and beneficial for relief from anxiety. The most commonly used adult tranquilizers logically enough are the ones most commonly used by teenagers: Valium, Librium, Thorazine, Miltown, and Equanil. These drugs are depressants that act on the nervous system, relaxing the muscles and affecting parts of the brain. Unlike barbiturates, tranquilizers have special anxiety-reducing properties. When taken over a long period of time even these "mild" drugs can be addicting. Of course, there are other problems with tranquilizers, too.

"We were partying last weekend, and my boyfriend was pretty high (as usual) on beer. Someone had some Valium, and when he took it, he just passed right out. We couldn't wake him up at all, and it was panic city. One of the older guys took him to the hospital. He was okay after a while. What was wrong with him? — Sally." This boy was the victim of double depressants, as both alcohol and tranquilizers depress the central nervous system and can cause blackout, and sometimes coma and even death. So disabuse your children of the idea that a tranquilizer is nothing more than a stronger aspirin. It has lethal potential.

Barbiturates

Even more powerful depressants than tranquilizers are the barbiturates ("downers"), or sedatives, which are prescribed by doctors for sleeplessness and high blood pressure. Some of the common "barbs" used by students are "reds" (Seconal), "yellows" or "yellow jackets" (Nembutal), "blues" (Amytal), and "sopors" or "ludes" (Quaaludes). The overdose possibility of these downers is extremely high when they are taken in large amounts or mixed with alcohol or other drugs. Sleeping pills are among the most dangerous drugs, and are more addicting than tranquilizers. Thousands of avoidable accidents and hundreds of deaths occur each year from their misuse. It's hard to stop using them without being under a doctor's care.

Doriden, sometimes prescribed for sleep, is called "jugs and beans" by kids. Doctors call it "queen of the killers," since it has worse side effects and is more addicting than other depressants. It is similar to Quaaludes, but is retained longer by the body and stopping the drug may cause convulsions similar to grand mal seizures for up to eight days after use.

Teenagers usually are so full of energy and activity, one wonders what they find appealing about drugs that make them sleepy, confused, lethargic. The answer is that adolescents who suffer many anxieties and insecurities use downers to help them forget their troubles. For instance, a student who does poorly in a subject, who doesn't understand it and never gets caught up, may face a test with a sense of sure defeat. A downer keeps him or her from thinking about it. The drug also prevents the user from preparing for the test; but the risk of failure is no deterrent, because the student is convinced that she or he will fail anyway.

Tolerance of barbiturates builds quickly, and that is why they are so addicting. At first it takes only one pill to go to sleep, then two, then three. When a person can't sleep without pills, it is time to see the doctor.

Barbiturates kill more users — adults and children — than any other drug, legal or illegal. Fifty percent of all drug deaths are caused by barbiturates, alone or in combination with other drugs. Countless traffic accidents are undoubtedly attributable to barbiturates as well. An overdose of barbiturates is not something that can be handled at home. It is important to call a clinic or hospital immediately.

Stimulants

The most familiar stimulants are coffee and nicotine, but when we speak of stimulant drugs, we usually mean cocaine or amphetamines, the synthetic stimulants that resemble adrenalin. These include plain amphetamine, or Benzedrine, Dexedrine, and Methedrine (called "speed," "bennies" or "beans," "whites," "uppers") and make up 5 percent of all drugs prescribed in this country.

Eight billion such tablets were produced in 1968. Most abusers of such tablets are middle-class, young, economically secure and often well educated. The drugs are also used widely in colleges, where students are drawn to stimulants that make them feel brighter, more energetic and competent, and able to put in long hours at the books. Speed does not help in complicated intellectual work, but the user feels it does.

Amphetamines mask fatigue and give the user an increased sense of confidence and interest. They prevent the brain from receiving the body's signals that it is tired and hungry, which is why they are effective diet pills, but a person can burn out by overdoing and getting excessively fatigued. People high on speed are often hyperactive, suspicious, and unpredictable. They may be pleasant one moment, then suddenly become violent and aggressive, for no apparent reason. "Wired" is the term students use for how speed makes them feel.

Stimulants may be relatively safe in small doses, but dependency is a high risk. "I started using some of my Mom's diet pills. They worked like a charm. I wasn't eating at all hardly, but I felt great and was doing terrific in school. Then we went away on vacation and Mom didn't bring her pills. I felt hot and cold and jiggy and depressed. Just awful. Why do doctors give out these pills if that's what they do to people? — Skinny." Users often feel badly when they get off stimulants, as the body is struggling to regain its equilibrium. They feel nervous, jumpy, and depressed, and want some more of the pills. That's why even short-term use risks dependency. People often use Valium or some similar drug to fight off the depression so often associated with "crashing," or coming down from speed. Some doctors seem unaware of these dangers with this drug, but of course in Skinny's case the diet pills were prescribed for the mother, not the child.

Psychological damage from stimulants may include short-term or possibly long-term psychoses. There is strong suspicion that prolonged use leads to deterioration of mental functioning, possibly cardiovascular and brain damage and fetal harm as well. Many teenagers believe that pep pills and diet pills are harmless. A person who is tired needs to rest; a person who is too fat needs to learn to eat more sensibly. There are no short cuts without risks. Speed, by its very nature, is the essence of excess, so it's hard to use it in moderation. Kids themselves say, "Speed kills."

Cocaine

Cocaine (coke) is a mild stimulant that is usually sniffed (inhaled) but can be swallowed or injected. Cocaine affects the communication of nerve cells, or neurotransmitters, producing a pleasant stimulation. It deadens the appetite by acting on the hypothalamus, and like other stimulants, heightens short-term sexual interest.

The special property of a cocaine high is an enhanced awareness of self. One user described it as "the greatest ego-inflating drug there is." The "coke feeling" is a sense of self-confidence and mastery, of superiority and exhilaration. Cocaine helps one perform simple, routine tasks. Indians in South America chew coca leaves for the cocaine they contain, which masks hunger and fatigue and makes dull, hard work seem easier.

Some students use cocaine in place of coffee at exam time. It gives the user the illusion of being more capable, as do amphetamines, caffein, and other drugs that affect the central nervous system. No drug can give a person more intellectual capacity than he or she naturally has. Coke can only deaden nervousness — such as stage fright, which makes it a popular drug with performing artists.

Occasional use of cocaine does not seem to be harmful and there is no "hangover." No true physical craving results, but people can develop strong habits because its use is so pleasant. There are unpleasant effects from cocaine abuse, including restlessness and exhaustion, suspiciousness and confusion due to insomnia. Sniffing creates coldlike symptoms, nasal drip and irritation of the nasal cartilage, and occasionally actual perforation. Toxic overdose is possible, though rare.

Large doses produce an effect like excitement, with rising rates of metabolism and blood sugar. Very high doses produce a weak and erratic pulse, tremors, nausea, vertigo, convulsions, unconsciousness, and death. Such overdoses are rarely seen, however.

Regular use by high school seniors was increasing rapidly in the late seventies, but rose only .3 percent in 1980. About .2 percent, or roughly 6000, U.S. students use coke; 15 percent have tried it at some time in their life. Despite the fact that its very high cost and lack of availability limit its use, cocaine has become the in drug among the upper-middle-class, young professionals and college students.

One reason for its popularity is undoubtedly its association with entertainers, writers, and intellectuals. Sarah Bernhardt, Robert Louis Stevenson, and Sigmund Freud were said to have used it. Sherlock Holmes is one of the best-known, though fictional, afficionados. Cocaine has been celebrated more recently by such groups as the Grateful Dead and the Rolling Stones. With models as illustrious as these, it is small wonder that young people wish to try this drug.

Abusing Drugs

No one has been able to say exactly who can use drugs safely and who cannot. Not even experts can explain why some users become abusers. Probably it is a combination of genetic and psychological factors as well as experience. One ten-year study of students in the suburbs came up with a profile of the student drug user: insecure; out of things; not doing well in school; not considered responsible by others; in other words, a kid who is in trouble in general.

The line between addiction (or true chemical dependence) and habituation (psychological dependence) is often impossible to draw. It matters most in terms of how the user is treated medically for withdrawal. The main thing teenagers need to know is how dependence on most any drug can creep up insidiously on a steady user. "I take some drugs now and then, and use Valium when I can get it. But I'm not really 'on' anything. I can quit anytime I want to." This is the time-honored boast of the deluded abuser. Three of the most addictive substances (not counting nicotine) are alcohol, barbiturates, and narcotics, all of which serve as analgesics; they make users less aware of both physical and mental pain. Therefore adolescents who have many fears and apprehensions have a high risk of dependence.

Many parents believe their child would never take any drugs. When they find out he or she has, they get scared and condemn the child angrily. This doesn't solve anything. There really isn't a "drug problem"; there is a child problem. It is more effective to use the event to kick off a good discussion about where a lot of drug use can lead. Through books and real-life examples, you can show where it has led others. If your child says "Well, Johnny is doing it," ask

"Why? Is Johnny happy? Does he really have respect for himself and his body?" Ask if it's worth the risk of putting poison into one's body.

It is very scary if your child's first drug experience involves a bad trip, but it is important not to panic. When someone is "freaking out" you can sometimes talk him or her down with soothing reassurances that everything is going to be all right. This doesn't work with angel dust (PCP). In fact, the attempt may add to the user's delirium. If you don't know what drug was taken, recruit the help of your child's good friend. Many bad trips can be treated like a bad dream or feverish delirium. Your calmness will help bring the user down. Call for professional help if behavior becomes destructive.

If you do have to get outside help, try all private means first. Ambulance attendants are well trained in how to respond to drug overdoses. Try not to bring in the police or juvenile authorities as the incident will go on the child's record. The authorities might even act in ways contrary to your wishes. Furthermore, it will seem like betrayal to the child.

Ongoing use of any drug cannot be ignored. Clues to heavy use of so-called hard drugs are similar in some ways to those of marijuana abuse: changes in lifestyle, friendships, and living patterns. With these drugs, money becomes an enormous problem. Addicts become ruthless and devious about taking money. Finding cash gone from your pocketbook, or small appliances "lost," are strong warning signals. Disappearances of pills from the medicine closet, strange pills showing up in pockets or drawers, sunglasses worn at odd times, should make you suspicious. So should overfriendliness or listlessness or drowsiness. These things are not as easy to spot as they sound, for it all comes on gradually. Parents are usually subconsciously aware that something is wrong before they can articulate it. Don't talk yourself into believing everything is all right if it isn't, or let your child talk you into believing it, because early interference with drug abuse is critical. You have to find out what is going on by seeing your teenager clearly, not as you wish or hope he or she might be.

If your teenager is on a self-destructive course with any drug, more help is needed than a parent can give. Try to find the best possible drug therapist or group therapy. Therapy is really just a special kind of teaching, to help a teenager learn to respond to problems in the adult world in a more mature way. It is important that your child can build a relationship of mutual trust with the therapist. You may have to search hard to find just the right person to help the teenager see that drugs don't really deliver what he or she wants out of life.

You may reach a point where it is beyond your ability to deal with a child's drug abuse problem. It is important to accept this. Parents should then give up, not in guilt, but in recognition that the situation is simply beyond their control, and it is up to the child and to experts in drug abuse to cope from now on.

The National Institute of Drug Abuse report *(Student Drug Use in America, 1975–1980)* reveals a heartening decrease in the use of most illicit drugs, such as barbiturates and PCP, in the last year. Cocaine and heroin use, which had been rising in previous years, remains constant. Increased use of stimulants is troubling, however, as this is the most commonly used illegal drug after marijuana. Though the use of stimulants has risen, especially by females, fewer students say they use speed to get high. Therefore, it can be assumed that these drugs are being used primarily to help lose weight. That doesn't mean it's a harmless practice, however.

There is some evidence that kids with strong religious values, kids whose families help them with their problems, and kids who participate more in extracurricular activities, hobbies, clubs, and so on, are less likely to be drug users. Certainly not all drug users are poor, disadvantaged kids from the ghetto. Whatever their family background, teenagers who feel they are failures, who have a low sense of self-esteem, and who believe they are unable to cope with their problems are more apt to get seriously involved with drugs. These are the conditions that parents must work to prevent.

Conclusion

Drugs are what parents generally dread most about the teenage period. However, drug use will surely continue so long as it is our cultural belief that you can find happiness or be able to cope with life's problems just by swallowing something. Kids may spell relief M*A*R*I*J*U*A*N*A, but they are only aping their elders.

To lessen the drug problem, we have to change our ways. Recent knowledge about the dangers of tobacco has really changed our national smoking habits. Daily use by adults has been dropping, and by 1980, teenage smoking too went down significantly. The shift proves that adults can help educate the next generation of teenagers to a more moderate and rational drug use by setting a moderate and sensible example themselves. Don't allow illegal drug-taking in your home. Clean your medicine closet of dangerous legal drugs. Give up some useless dependence of your own, and show your kids it can be done.

In addition to being a pill-popping society, we have a strong winning syndrome. To lose is to be a nothing. Kids who get heavily into drugs are kids who feel they are losers. They believe nobody loves them because they aren't number one. They give up, and turn to drugs. When parents make kids know they are number one with them, that they love them no matter what, and that they accept them as individuals, even if they fall down now and then, their kids will not be downed easily by drugs, or anything else in their lives.

11. Smoking and Drinking, the Legal Drugs

We don't often think of either cigarettes or alcohol as drugs, but they are. Any substance we take that causes changes in our body or behavior is a drug. Science now has discovered that almost every drug we take, from aspirin to caffein, has more serious consequences to our health than we used to suppose. Nicotine has some of the worst effects; drinking alcohol in moderation is not necessarily harmful, but the potential for grave problems is always there. So parents should be concerned about the example they set for their children with both of these legal drugs.

If Dad comes home from the office saying "Boy, what a day I had. Get me a martini, quick!" it gives his kids a potent message about using alcohol to feel better. If Mom reaches for a cigarette every time she goes to the phone or picks up the newspaper after breakfast, her children get the idea that nicotine does something positive for you. Sooner or later children will try these things themselves; a healthy kid is a curious kid. Even in the good old days, children smoked corn silk out behind the barn, or got a bit tiddly on stolen swigs of rhubarb wine. But they seldom got drunk or stoned. Now the use of all kinds of drugs is far greater than ever before.

Teenagers drink and smoke now more than in the past. The main reason is that the stuff is more available, and advertisements about nicotine and alcohol are constantly before kids' eyes. So are adult drinkers and smokers. Another reason kids use drugs is that there are more pressures and tensions in adolescence than there used to be. Home life is not as secure and stable for children as it once was, and their vision of the future is not always a bright and optimistic one.

Parents have insidious influences to combat. Liquor companies present the woman who drinks their brand as sexy, sleek, and desirable. Cigarette companies show the man who smokes their brand as a handsome, brawny, and virile outdoorsman. Parents have to convince their children that those attractive people in the ads and commercials aren't attractive *because* of what they drink or smoke. They are just models. You have to arm the young to fight commercial distortion and persuasion. We can't defend them against all the messages in the "soaps," the serials, the TV dramas, magazines, and newspapers, but healthy skepticism, plus early and continuing family discussion of the true effects of nicotine, whiskey, pep pills, and the like, can help a lot.

Young children who are raised in strict families often become boringly moral and evangelistic, with deeply-rooted aversions to drinking and smoking. Then puberty strikes and these attitudes seem to fly out the window — at least for a while. Adolescents are compelled to try new things they previously shunned as dangerous or evil and their experiments are usually not harmful. Eventually they regain their good sense, other things being equal. What makes the difference is their basic respect for themselves and a free, two-way communication with parents.

As discussed in earlier chapters, communication is essential. Present kids with clear, understandable, well-documented facts about the dangers of drugs and allow them to speak to you about parts of their lives you may not approve, without fear of being scolded, ridiculed, condemned, or disliked. Parents who are suspicious and fearful that their kids are doing unhealthy things should stop and listen to them in a way that will encourage honesty and foster understanding.

Smoking

Cigarettes are likely to be the first venture into drug-taking for teenagers. Nicotine does not seem much like a drug, because it does not noticeably alter one's thinking or behavior, but it definitely is one. Smoking is still pervasive in our environment and to kids it looks cool and grown-up. Tobacco ads present the smoker as young, healthy, appealing, popular, and having a swell time. That example, plus peer pressure and kids' natural curiosity about all adult things, compels most average young teens to at least try smoking.

"I like to smoke when I go out. I think it looks good, and it makes me feel better when I'm nervous. I read what they say about cigarettes being hazardous to your health, but this doesn't apply to younger people, does it? — Kool Kat." Smoking does give people who are ill at ease something to do with their hands, something that has the aura of sophistication and chic. This aura lingers, despite the incontrovertible evidence that nicotine is a serious danger to health. Kids find it hard to believe that the danger applies to them. In general, teenage is a very healthy time — none of your children's friends has lung cancer or heart trouble. It's hard for them to see that what they do now may have a lethal payoff years down the road.

For a while, the more bad publicity given to smoking, the more exciting the habit seemed to appear to some adolescents. Those who were seeking ways to taunt their parents found cigarettes to be effective. Those who didn't smoke were called chicken, a harsh label for a youngster to bear.

Adult smoking went down from 42 percent to 33 percent between 1965 and 1975. Teenage smoking went up 43 percent in that period, mostly among girls. Fortunately, the tide has now turned for adolescents, too, and since 1979, there has been a drop in tobacco smoking for both boys and girls in high school — down nearly 3 percent for girls, almost 5 percent for boys.

This boy's thinking shows why teenagers were slower to believe the facts. "Adults just want to have all the fun," wrote a boy named Josh, after his parents lectured him about smoking. "They smoke themselves, and drink too, and then say we shouldn't do these things. It isn't fair!" Josh's conclusion is offbase, but his parents are not setting a wise example. They are right, however, to talk up the dangers of nicotine.

Nicotine has no good use for human beings at all. It is both a stimulant and a depressant, and it is toxic. It causes habituation — that is, the psychological need for the drug — as well as dependence — the physical need for it. This double whammy is what makes it so hard to quit smoking.

Most harm is done to those who start smoking early. A study done by the World Health Organization in the midseventies revealed that most smokers in Western European countries start the habit by age nineteen or twenty. Many start much earlier. Only one out of every three smokers can stop. Most adolescents in this country resemble this girl: "I smoke some, only a few cigarettes a day. I know it is going to be bad for me later on, but I can stop when I want to. I think I will want to stop next year. — Not Hooked." This is wishful thinking. She doesn't have any idea how hard it will be. "Not me!" she thinks, but she's wrong.

Parents' first obligation to their children is to quit smoking themselves. The best prevention against smoking is to grow up in a nonsmoking family. If someone in the home smokes, one out of four kids will smoke, too. If no one smokes, only one in twenty will get the habit. If you have been a smoker and give it up, you will set a valuable example. If you just cannot quit, admit it and make it clear what a grim battle it is. This may serve as a powerful warning against the habit.

Discourage your children, if possible, from starting to smoke at all. If they don't take your advice, there are many antismoking arguments to make. Be sure they understand the true dangers of smoking. If they don't seem convinced by your arguments, get more facts from the American Cancer Society. Be sure they hear this quote: "Statisticians estimate that life is shortened by fourteen minutes for every cigarette smoked and inhaled. Cancer of the lung favors smokers eleven to one, and under the age of sixty-five, smokers are two to three times as likely to die of heart disease as nonsmokers."*

**The Family Handbook of Adolescence*, by John F. Schowalter, M.D., and Walter R. Anyan, M.D. New York: Knopf, 1979.

One approach that has meaning for most young people concerns staying in top physical shape. Smoking cuts down on wind and affects circulation. No serious athlete smokes.

The effects of smoking on physical appearance may have an even more profound influence on teenagers. Bad breath, yellow-stained teeth and fingers, and a phlegmy cough are not attractive at all, especially at an age when appearing fresh and healthy is important. The antismoking campaign ad that shows a handsome boy starting to kiss a pretty girl, and then backing away with a graphic "Yuck!" expression should reach kids.

Appeal to your children's deep desire to take control of their own lives. Getting hooked on anything means that it has control over you. It is unwise to bribe kids not to smoke or punish them severely if they do. The decision to become nonsmokers has to be clearly their own.

Appeal to your daughters as future mothers. Pregnant women who smoke have a far higher rate of miscarriages than nonsmokers and their babies have lower birth weight, leading to birth defects and retardation.

Finally, appeal to your children's sense of altruism. Smokers blow their toxic gasses at everyone who comes near. This increases both smokers' and nonsmokers' chances of getting bronchitis, among other things. Teenagers have broad streaks of altruism and generosity that may lead them to be moved by this argument.

Children who are trying to quit smoking need help but not nagging. If they are unable to stop on their own, there are groups organized for breaking the habit that can help. Call the American Cancer Society in your area for resources.

Alcohol

Alcohol is the number-one drug of abuse in this country. Hardly anyone gives a party without serving cocktails or wine. "Have a drink?" seldom means tea or lemonade. As a result, parents don't consider drinking to be in the same category as other drug problems among teenagers. Most adults are used to alcohol. People are now waking up to the fact that teenagers are drinking more. Two thirds of all eighteen-year-olds drink, the same proportion as the adult population. There are alcoholics among adolescents, too, some as young as eleven.

Statistics on teenage drinking are hard to come by, but the Research Triangle Institute reports from studies in 1974 and 1978 that the percent of youth who report having been drunk is on the rise. They estimate that roughly 30 percent of young drinkers are alcohol misusers.

Kids often drink because their parents do. Forty percent of American teenagers who abstain from alcohol come from homes where liquor is not served. Also, kids drink because alcohol is relatively cheap, it seems safe, and it makes people feel good. And finally, it is easy for the young to get. Kids who are below the legal age can sneak it out of their parents' liquor closet, or get an older person to buy it for them. They may even be able to call the liquor store and have it delivered.

Kids drink because their friends do. Alcohol is almost as much a part of the teen scene as it is the adult scene. "I went to a party with some older kids, and I couldn't hack it. I felt really shy. Then my girlfriend gave me a couple of beers. Pretty soon everyone was talking to me and I was talking back like we were all old friends. I had a good time." "I'm new in this school, and kids have been teasing me about my accent. Last week a big guy punched me out, and I couldn't fight back. I cried, and they all looked at me like I'm a coward. When I got home, I took some of my Dad's whiskey, and it made me feel much better about everything." "Every time there's a party, the kids get so loaded, it really isn't any fun. I don't drink much, but you've gotta pretend, or they'll start hating you."

Alcohol is the same social lubricant for the young that it is for adults. Like their parents, many teenagers believe a party is no fun without alcohol. "Let's have a picnic. Who'll bring the beer?" Drinking right in school is not unknown; ask the janitor who empties the wastebaskets! Kids drink together and alone, on the beach and in the park, and they drink in cars, which is a horror in itself. Those empty six-packs on the side of the road are largely jettisoned by teenagers, who can't trash the cans at home for fear of getting caught.

Kids think of drinking as risky, courageous, rebellious, and a machismo thing to do, which makes it attractive to young people trying to show the world they are grown up and independent.

Parents have to assume that alcohol will be in their children's future, so children need to understand as much as possible about it before they hit teenage. You can help by acknowledging your own attitude toward drinking. If you do drink, don't deny it. Explain why you drink and how you keep from drinking too much. If you have friends who overdo it, use them as object lessons in alcohol abuse. If one parent is a problem drinker, acknowledgment is hard but it can't be denied. The biggest problem teenagers have with alcohol is their parents' abuse of the drug. It causes untold grief in the young. An excellent program for the teenaged children of alcoholic parents is Alateen, sponsored by the Al-Anon Family Groups. Teenagers meet together and talk out their feelings, and come to understand the disease of alcoholism. If you have this problem in your family, try to get your teenager into an Alateen program.

All kids want and need as much information about alcohol as they can get. "What does alcohol actually do to the body?" Alcohol is a depressant, similar to ether, that works by putting the brain to sleep. This doesn't come about slowly either. Alcohol goes directly into the blood stream and spreads through all the body's fluids. It especially affects the brain, where there are lots of blood cells.

"How long after you have a drink do you get over the effects?" The body starts working to get rid of the alcohol immediately, as it does any other substance that pollutes it. The liver does most of the work, breaking down the alcohol chemically, in a process called oxidization. It takes about two hours for the liver to oxidize one standard drink.

"How much can you drink before you get drunk?" This is a tricky question, because intoxication depends on so many things, size and body weight, the amount of food in the stomach, how quickly you drink, and your frame of mind. A heavy person who has recently eaten some food and who sips slowly and is in a pleasant mood can drink a great deal more without feeling the effects than a small individual who hasn't eaten, gulps down the drink, and feels anxious, tense, or nervous. In the latter case, the drink will literally "go right to his or her head."

Different people are affected at different rates and the rate also varies from time to time with the same person. "I was out with the gang Friday night, and had a few beers, no more than usual, but I got so loaded it was unbelievable. That never happened to me before. I had to sleep over at my friend's house. What got me so drunk all of a sudden? — Surprised." Being tired or nervous can intensify the way alcohol affects a person. Furthermore, at this point people often lose track of how many drinks they have had, and drink them too fast. Kids have this myth that "just a few beers" isn't really drinking. One standard beer is the equivalent of a shot of whiskey or a glass of wine. The alcoholic content is exactly the same, and that's what counts.

A girl wrote, "All we ever had to drink at home was a little wine on holidays or special occasions. Now I'm old enough to go to parties, and I'm worried I won't know how to handle drinking. I'm afraid to say no. — Helen." Helen's parents might tell her that she can refuse a drink anytime, just by smiling and saying "No, thanks, some other time. Would you give me a coke or some club soda?" There are many polite ways to say no without resorting to the put-down response "Oh, I never drink that stuff!" Timid refusals stir up more hassles than pleasant and confident ones. A person doesn't need to apologize for refusing alcohol.

Your kids are probably going to accept a drink at some time. You can give them rules for safe drinking:

1. Always eat before you have an alcoholic drink. Milk is a very good base. And keep snacking as long as you're drinking.

2. Nurse your drinks. Spread the effects over a long enough period of time. Learn not to take a second drink until the effects of the first have worn off. Remember, alcohol has a "down" side as well as an "up" side. Most people reach for another drink when their alcohol blood level is still up, but they don't feel high. The trouble is that the high is still going on.

3. Don't drink straight shots; do go heavy on the ice cubes. Be careful of the mixers you use, however. Sweet mixes screen the alcoholic content, and carbonated drinks make the alcohol work faster. The best mixer is water.

4. Never drink if you are very angry or upset about something. The effects are fast and unpredictable.
5. Let someone else drive if you feel at all tipsy.
6. Repeat: drink *slowly.*

"I made a fool of myself at the last party I went to. I tripped over a chair, broke a couple of glasses, and finally threw up on my girlfriend. What a jerk! How can I tell *before* that I am getting loaded like that? — In Dutch." This is the crucial knowledge for anyone who wants to drink sensibly. The sensations are experienced differently by different people, and that's why each drinker has to learn by trial and error. Most people find they have a warning light that tells them to slow down. It may be giddiness, slurring of speech, or numbness in some part of the body. It's important to learn one's own alert sign before it's too late.

Is it wise to have one's children learn to drink at home? Serving wine on special occasions can give children a wholesome attitude toward the use of alcohol. In societies where it is used only in rituals, sipped slowly among family or friends and usually during meals, alcohol is seldom abused. Most parents prefer that their kids learn about drinking in the safety and privacy of the home, rather than out in public. I am not suggesting that you get your kids drunk regularly so they know what it's like; I do feel that when parents allow a little experimenting at home, the children will find that some of the glamour surrounding alcohol is dispersed. They will still want to drink with their friends, in all probability, but it won't be such a big deal if they have already associated alcohol with family scenes.

Serving your kids' close friends who are minors is a problem for many parents. If you know that their parents allow them a beer occasionally, as you do, you will probably serve them, ignoring the legal implications. You certainly don't want to press alcohol on a teenager whose family doesn't approve. And you have to be scrupulous about not serving kids who have to drive afterward.

There are many theories about how to sober up, and all of them are myths. The cold shower, the walk around the block, or the strong black coffee make friends feel helpful, but do not hasten the breakdown of alcohol in the body. There are no cures for hangovers either. Drugs that stimulate the central nervous system, such as caffein or diet pills, don't help. The headache, nausea, dizziness, shakiness, and irritability are caused by the toxic effects of the alcohol and by fatigue. An anesthetized brain fails to inform you that you are tired, so you stay up late and overdo it. You don't sleep well while drunk, anyway. The best solution is to learn to drink more sensibly.

Alcohol becomes more dangerous, even fatal sometimes, when combined with certain other drugs. If taken with antihistamines for instance, the depression of the central nervous system is increased, producing drowsiness, even coma. With narcotics, such as codeine or heroin, alcohol creates an even more dramatic depression, and may cause cardiac arrest. It is even dangerous to mix aspirin or Tylenol with alcohol, as stomach or intestinal irritation or even bleeding can result.

The biggest drinking problems for teenagers concern driving and sexual behavior, often both together. "Every time we go out, my boyfriend insists I drink along with him. Then we go parking and end up going further than I meant to and I feel real bad the next day. I really like him a lot, otherwise. What should I do?" Alcohol relaxes inhibitions, making it easy for a person to ignore their conscience, and "go too far." Even a small drink may encourage the uninitiated drinker to throw caution to the winds. This, of course, is another reason why the drug is popular with teenagers. Some kids may ply reluctant partners with booze to get them to agree to sexual relations. They may also rely on alcohol to overcome their own anxieties in the same situation.

Teenagers who are just starting to go out need useful advice about how to handle friends who have drunk too much. Girls need to recognize signs of trouble early, and be reassured that they will not lose popularity by refusing to go out with boys who get sloppy drunk and/or try to seduce them. Girls *can* stick up for their rights without being killjoys. Boys need to be warned about extra pressures on them to show virility by drinking a lot. Of course some people will label others "straight" or "old-fashioned" and ostracize them if they won't get loaded every Saturday night. Kids who are good company will be accepted and liked, even though they don't get drunk.

The combination of drinking and driving is the most serious

problem connected with alcohol. Kids must be taught the physiological reasons that make alcohol dangerous for drivers. Alcohol, a depressant, impairs reaction time. It can make a driver fatally slow in perceiving trouble and stepping on the brake. It interferes with the ability to judge speed and distance. Also, one's judgment is altered and behavior becomes erratic. The veiling of inhibitions may cause a drinking driver to ignore the traffic rules, and his aggressiveness may lead him to race anything in sight or take chances. Drinking increases boldness and the desire to show off, while impairing muscle coordination, attention span, vision, and hearing. It doesn't take much imagination to see how all this affects one's speed, competitiveness, and ability to maneuver. Too often, the result is a car wrapped around a utility pole, injury, or death.

The seriousness of this danger must be discussed with boys and girls long before they get their licenses. Ask them to read aloud newspaper stories about alcohol-related accidents. Show them statistics. Talk about the laxity of drunken driving penalties in this country compared to those in foreign countries, and the terrible toll drunk drivers take in lives and crippling handicaps every year, especially during holidays. Make very, very strong rules for the whole family about drinking and driving, and seek your kids' cooperation in obeying them for everyone's sake. Make a contract with them: if they or their companions are ever too intoxicated to drive safely, they can call you. You'll pick them up, and there will be *no lecture.* One mistake is better than two. Students Against Drunk Driving (S.A.D.D.) is a program that promotes such a contract. Finally, make sure your own example is one you want your kids to follow.

Drinking and driving is a serious problem and it makes sense to mandate alcohol education along with driver education. Some schools do this, but the quality and effectiveness of the courses vary widely. Good alcohol education in schools is important to supplement parents' teaching. Professionals know more than most parents do, and when kids learn together, they will be more open with each other about the effects of alcohol when they're out partying. The most effective education deals with how drinking comes up in kids' own lives: What alcohol does to a young person physically, mentally and socially. The prospect of losing control or making themselves obnoxious to others impresses teenagers.

Alcohol can be a wonderful relaxer at the end of a hard day; don't be afraid to comment on its good qualities. Kids should think of alcohol as a pleasant adjunct to life and not a necessary or all-important thing in itself.

Problem Drinking

If your child gets drunk a couple of times, don't overreact. Overimbibing once or twice is not a sign that grave trouble is on the way. People who drink moderately and drink for pleasure are not likely to abuse alcohol, but people who drink to solve personal problems, to ease pain, or to forget worries are in grave danger. This is something kids should understand. There are many pamphlets listing the danger signs of alcohol abuse, and you'd be wise to have your children look them over. They can be obtained from alcohol abuse programs.

Drug abuse agencies list questions for drinkers to ask themselves if they think they have a drinking problem: Do your friends drink more than you do? Do you drink to lose shyness and build your self-confidence? Do you drink to escape from study problems or home worries? Does it bother you if someone says you drink too much? Have you ever had a blackout? Most teenagers believe they are too young to become alcoholics, that if they drink only beer and wine they are not in danger, and that they can stop drinking any time they want. Even the "just on weekends" drinker can be an alcoholic. Anyone who worries about keeping his or her drinking under control *should* be worried.

There is no known "alcoholic personality." Young people who are especially unsure of themselves, who feel inadequate and hopeless, and who are on the fringes academically and socially need to be especially careful about drinking.

Parents may be relieved that their kids are "only drinking" and not messing with other drugs, but alcohol is just as insidious in its effects, and it is more addictive than many other substances. If your child seems to be drinking too much or too frequently, start talking *and* listening.

Talk about your admiration for people who control their drinking and how pathetic drunkenness is. But don't issue dire warnings about "becoming one of those winos in the gutter." Talk instead about their reputation in school and possible embarrassment with other kids. Don't tell your children they are bad and weak. Talk about how seriously alcohol can limit kids' successes in sports, hobbies, studies, and with friends too.

If your teenager feels he or she needs to drink, and goes on drinking beyond reasonable limits, or if drinking is a problem to him or her and to others, that kid has an alcohol problem that calls for immediate professional help.

Alcoholism is hard to treat at any age. With students, drinking is often related to problems of failure, inadequacy, or alienation. It might be disastrous to take away the alcohol without addressing the underlying causes for the need to drink. Parents will give more help assuring firm love and support than denigrating or shaming their teenager. An effort to strengthen their child's character and confidence and hope for future success will do the most good.

It is not easy to get an adolescent to see that he or she needs help, however. If you meet resistance, find an agency that will work with your child and ask advice for getting started. Groups like Alcoholics Anonymous, which have special programs for adolescents, seem to be the most successful. There are AA groups listed in most phone books, or you can write to the national headquarters: Alcoholics Anonymous, General Service Office, Box 459, Grand Central Station, New York, NY 10017. Many hospitals and mental health agencies also have excellent programs for young people. If you can't find a local agency, write for information to the National Council on Alcoholism, 773 Third Avenue, New York, NY 10016.

12. Moods, Depression, and Suicide

Torn by demands from parents, peers, and themselves, teenagers can be high one minute and low the next. They exult in new freedoms and choices some of the time, and at other times are confused and scared by the awesomeness of adult roles. Human growth, whether physical, emotional, or intellectual, is often erratic, contributing to the unevenness of adolescents' moods and behavior.

One mother says she never knows which daughter is coming home from school, "the happy, confident, and gossipy Mary or the closed-up, worried-looking, and solemn one. The first Mary talks up a storm and does her share of jobs with good grace; the second one stays in her room, plays the radio, and contributes nothing to the family." Parental patience and calm will help the most.

While they are giving up the comfortable ways of childhood and not sure yet what they will be like in the future, many teenagers feel very low in self-esteem. "I'm thirteen and I think my life is falling apart right in front of me. I don't know what to do. I can't just watch it leave. I don't know myself; I actually don't know who I am. What kind of personality do I have? That's a dumb question . . . I don't have any. Well, maybe some. Like boring, serious, hard-to-talk-to, and a few other good ones. — Loser for Life." Most kids are not this hard on themselves — by far the majority just feel insecure and changeable.

Do adolescents ever tell their parents what they are truly concerned about? They do if they know it is okay to mention serious personal things without fear of ridicule, mockery, or contempt — in other words, when parents show genuine interest in hearing what kids really want to reveal. It's best not to pry, not to interrogate. Just listen. This is what makes them feel "My parents understand!"

Allow children to be angry and sullen at times, and be sympathetic to their feelings. This doesn't mean letting yourself be used as an emotional punching bag, and sworn at or put down. It means making clear to them the mechanism of relieving feelings by acknowledging their existence, identifying them, and talking them out. If you have proved that you are available to them, through nonjudgmental, active, and responsive listening on your part, they will turn to you often, though maybe not always. Sometimes kids need to be alone with their problems, but then comes a time when they want to talk.

The prospect of separating oneself from one's parents is scary. The resurgence of biological and social drives in puberty sets up conflicts both within the adolescents and between them and their parents. In trying to "get it all together," there are inevitable ups and downs. These mood swings don't mean your teenager has an abnormal, unhappy, or depressed personality, however. Parents just have to accept this disequilibrium as necessary and important in this phase of growing up.

Anxiety

Fear is the normal human response to threat. In a stressful situation, the heart and lungs pump harder as adrenalin pours into the system to get the body ready to fight or flee. The anxious response to nonphysical stress, such as a tough exam or speaking up in public, involves these same physical reactions. There are many things in an adolescent's life that loom as threats and create temporary anxiety, such as fear of disapproval or failure or abandonment. Anxiety can also come from a more diffuse, undefined sense of threat. The person may have no conscious awareness of conflict or of anything emotionally wrong, but still feels a sense of real apprehension. A mother writes, "My sixteen-year-old-daughter, Marj, has been acting very upset lately. She looks tired all the time, and isn't sleeping well at all. She seems nervous about everything, but when I ask her what's wrong, she says she's just tired. Marj was doing honor work at school, but her performance has dropped off. Do you think she's mentally sick?" Being on edge all the time, tense and easily startled, not sleeping well and feeling tired are all symptoms of anxiety. Marj can't identify any special thing she is worried about, but there are plenty of possibilities at her age: Fear of breaking free from parents, worry about college and career choices, concern about developing intimacies, moral values — all might trigger underlying fear of failure, disapproval, or loss of parents' love, making a teenager anxious.

Even a great success, like Marj's performance in school, can create anxiety, especially if parents are so loud in their praise that the student gets worried about having to keep up such a high standard. A student may also worry that doing well leads to growing up, becoming independent of parents, and thus being alone, unprotected, and abandoned, an illogical, unconscious, but real fear just the same.

"I have been having these terrible pains in my stomach, so I can hardly stand up sometimes. I can't eat in the morning, or I throw it all up. My head aches and I sweat and feel shaky. I went to the doctor twice, but he says there's nothing 'organically wrong.' Mother accuses me of faking because I don't want to go to school. I'm not! I'm sure I must have cancer or something they can't find. It really hurts and is getting worse. — Probably Dying." Just because no germs or anything organic can be found does not mean physical pain is not real. Psychosomatic symptoms are a way the body responds to too much stress. It isn't faking. The symptoms are very real to the sufferer. All diseases have emotional as well as physical factors, and doctors are just beginning to understand how great an effect the emotions have on the body. Probably Dying needs support, not accusations. First, her mother needs to talk to the teacher, not the doctor, to see if there is something disturbing her so much at school that it is literally making her sick. The problem may be a conflict at home that the student is projecting on to the school. Projection, or ascribing one's own thoughts, feelings, or conflicts to someone else or even to one's own family, is common in adolescence.

Extreme anxiety may be expressed in fatigue or frustration, in hyperactivity, or even in reckless, destructive behavior. If this kind of behavior occurs frequently, or if it disrupts a teenager's normal life at home or school, try to go over your child's life with him or her and see if you can identify what's causing the distress. If normal parental reassurance does not help, or if you can't find any rational reason for the tenseness, then talk the situation over with a professional. Counseling may be needed to get at the root of the anxiety.

Depression

Adolescent mood swings may be so severe that parents fear their child is in a serious depression. Usually this isn't so. A teenager who seems blue or withdrawn is in most cases going through a period of intense problem solving. It is important to give kids time and space in which to do this. They need to be alone sometimes. In fact, those kids who seem to spend no time alone may actually be the most distressed and unable to stand their own company.

Most kids are reasonably happy a lot of the time. However, teenagers do feel lonely at times, too. Research shows that high school students say they are lonely far more often than the elderly do, perhaps because it's assumed that students are sociable — always in the midst of happy throngs. This is a romantic time of life, and everyone is supposed to have a boy- or girlfriend. The kid who is alone on Friday or Saturday night can feel desperately lonely and depressed, but this is not true depression and is only temporary. Let that phone ring, and the girl or boy is up and off like a shot, the lonely feelings left behind like an old shirt.

There can be a positive side to depressive feelings, too. Sometimes certain adolescents, more likely girls, may even revel in their low periods, finding a richness, a sense of deep reality that life can be hard and people don't always "live happily ever after." It is a character-building experience for kids to learn how to bear anxious and depressed feelings and stress, and then be able to get up and keep going. Girls can even enter a sort of morbid competition — "I'm more depressed than thou" — but they bounce out of this mood as soon as there's a call for action. A truly depressed person cannot throw off such feelings.

There are other things in teenagers' lives that create a justified feeling of depression. They worry about living their lives as adults, partly because it looks like a pretty grim world out there: They know about war, nuclear threats, pollution, and so on. Feeling down in the face of these realities is normal, but temporary. Outside influences, stern as they may be, do not cause true "clinical" depression.

True Depression

What distinguishes a full-blown depression from a fit of the blues is that it goes on and on and doesn't get better. The black mood grips all aspects of the person's life and behavior.

"What is wrong with me? I've completely lost my will to work. I can't study. I feel so hopeless! I don't want to be like this. I make myself sit in front of my desk — I tell myself that I won't eat or drink or move or talk to anyone until I get my homework done — but even that doesn't work. Not that anyone calls anyway. They all hate me. I even hate myself! How can I get out of this lousy hole? — Messed Up."

Feelings of guilt, dejection, helplessness, hopelessness, and worthlessness underlie true depression. The sufferers, like Messed Up, blame and punish themselves for their inability to concentrate, and for their poor work and their unsociability, when the fact is all their energy is going into fighting the depression. Crying, withdrawing, sleeping and eating problems, and changes in thought and in schoolwork are ways depression shows itself.

One common characteristic of depression is rock-bottom self-esteem. Depressed people have lost their sense of self-worth to such a degree that they feel helpless to carry on. Unexpressed rage is another important part of adolescent depression, the anger being directed either at themselves or at their parents. This rage may not be due to any action on the parents' part. Teenagers sometimes feel angry at the best of parents. If, in childhood, teenagers have idealized their parents and then discover in adolescence that they are only normal human beings after all, teenagers sometimes feel so disillusioned it triggers a depression. Some teenagers find traits in themselves that they despise in their parents, which drives them to fury, self-hatred, and despair.

Sometimes parental actions are the factor. When parents use heavy shame and punishment instead of positive reinforcement to raise their children, it may lead these children to feel so worthless and inadequate to face adult issues that they develop depression in adolescence. Or parents may unwittingly set a child up for depression by being overprotective and overdirecting, expecting absolute compliance, or by trying to use their children to fulfill their own unachieved goals. "I am about to flunk music, and my parents are going to kill me. I don't know what's the matter, but I have started hating the piano. I can't seem to do anything right anymore. All the other kids are really good, and they look at me like I'm some kind of nerd. I never had any social life in school anyway, because I always have to come home and practice. I don't have any friends. I sit in my room and cry. I feel like I'm falling apart, but I don't dare tell them. — B minor."

Protecting children from too many things, not letting them explore for fear they may make a mistake, directing everything they should or should not do or be, does not come across to children as love. It comes across as lack of faith in their ability to do anything for themselves. Becoming a responsible person is more important than getting A's on tests or learning to play like Paderewski. If kids are not encouraged and seen as able to manage for themselves a good part of the time, they may simply fall apart when life becomes hard. Some turn to drugs or antisocial behavior; others become depressed.

Certain diseases, like infectious mononucleosis or hepatitis, make people feel very depressed, so a medical checkup is an important first step in dealing with depression. This kind of depression clears up along with the disease. A child with a known handicap, such as a loss of a limb, paralysis, or chronic illness, may reach a crisis of despair in adolescence, when he or she fully realizes how much his or her life is going to be curtailed. Therapy can be very helpful.

Whatever the reason for depression, there is much parents can do to help. First it is necessary to recognize true depression. A depressed adolescent may be flat, tired, bored and listless, and slowed down in every way; or, occasionally, a child may be abnormally restless and hyperactive, making the depression less obvious. Slovenliness and unaccustomed lack of concern about looks and clothes may be a sign of true depression. When a teenager feels no joy in life, no love, and above all, no hope, and these feelings don't go away, then it is time for a parent to step in and get professional help.

A family physician, pediatrician, or mental health center can provide a referral to a therapist who specializes in adolescent problems. The therapist must be someone the teenager will like and trust. Don't be afraid to shop around until you find this person. A therapist may be a psychologist, a psychiatrist, or psychiatric social worker. Treatment may be individual or family or group therapy, the last being excellent in many adolescent cases. What works best depends on the particular individual and the particular problem.

Most depressed teenagers really want help. Ask "How do you feel about consulting someone who can help us understand how you feel?" It is wise to tell them that it is not a sign of weakness or craziness to ask for help. Most people who seek psychiatric help are not crazy, but simply have problems that keep them from functioning in the usual way, and don't know the reasons why.

Explain that therapy and counseling are special kinds of teaching that help people "unlearn" some ineffective way they have been responding to something in their life, their school, or their family relations. Perhaps they haven't outgrown some childhood responses. Perhaps they have ideas or emotions that don't fit their lives anymore, now that they are mature.

A therapist who empathizes with young people will listen to them in a nonjudgmental and accepting way, helping them recall incidents that they have pushed back into their subconscious memory but that have gone on influencing them. The therapist then helps them see how these old influences make them think and feel and act in inappropriate ways, causing their fear and depression.

The book (and movie) *Ordinary People* showed how one therapist worked to help his patient recall his past and how a parent can help. The father in this story responded to his son's depression by always trying to be there for the boy. Even when he wasn't sure exactly what to do or say, he made every effort to reach his son whenever he sensed the boy was down. He shored him up and supported him, and also tried, without nagging too much, to encourage him to work with his therapist. It took an astute and caring psychiatrist to uncork the bottled-up emotions that were driving the boy to despair, and the father's love and respect provided a foundation on which a fresh and stronger personality could grow.

Sometimes a person with a severe depression may have to be hospitalized because helplessness, disorganization, and possibly self-destructiveness means he or she needs the protection of a safe environment. Early medical help can save a depressed person untold suffering, and the ravaging effects of the illness.

Psychoses

Psychosis is a general term for emotional disturbances that involve loss of contact with reality. One is manic depression, which is characterized by extreme highs, or manias, followed by deep depressions, though a person may have only the manic or the depressed phase. Many manic depressives are helped by lithium medication. Another psychosis is schizophrenia, which involves loss of touch with the environment and disintegration of personality. This illness frequently makes its appearance during adolescence and, unfortunately, is difficult to cure. It is often hard to distinguish one mental disease from another because symptoms such as paranoia, delusions, hearing voices, and so on, overlap to some extent. Doctors may therefore be reluctant to label a young person with a particular malady. What is important for parents is to recognize when any emotional upset is serious enough to call for help.

People who are psychotic are often unable to distinguish between what is happening and what is imagined, and so they respond to imagined perceptions or delusions. Or they may be aware that their thoughts and voices are unreal, may even say "I'm going crazy!" Parents should not try to smooth over such acts or mask their own alarm by reassuring their adolescent that "Everyone feels that way at times." Such thoughts are not normal and require the best possible treatment. Call your local psychiatric or psychological association to help you find the best therapist.

Fear of Death

"I hate the idea of dying. I can't go to sleep sometimes because I get crying about it and can't stop. My aunt had an operation for cancer, and it made me afraid that my parents are going to die. It makes me so sad. What would I ever do? — Orphan??" The first realization that we are all mortal is a painful one for young teenagers. It often takes the form of worrying, like Orphan, about what will happen if one's parents die. This may be your children's first recognition that parents can't always "fix it all up" for them, but you can reassure your kids that most children will be grown up and parents themselves, or even grandparents, before Mom and Dad die. If anything unexpected should happen, someone will look after them, *no matter what.* There is always someone, another relative, friend, or a concerned person from an agency who will take care of children.

Sometimes kids go through a period of being afraid to go to sleep lest they never wake up. Parents can explain how unlikely this is, but also should help them see that death is a part of life for everything that ever lives. Religion may help, if this is a part of your life, but whether one believes in heaven or not, we all have to learn to accept the knowledge of death and feel good about living. Children suffer when there is no one able to talk with them about death, so this should be discussed. Something that is natural and inevitable should never be a taboo subject. Parents can stress the idea that every person passes something along to others that death cannot destroy. Vital memories stay alive in those who loved, and were loved by, the one who died. In this way people continue to have a real and effective influence after death. Furthermore, people who have children pass their genetic material along and their existence continues to have an effect on all future generations.

Suicide

Young children quite often threaten to kill themselves. "You'll be sorry after I'm gone!" they may say. This is an obvious attempt to get parental sympathy and parents tend to brush aside the idea that suicide threats should ever be taken seriously. However, even very young children sometimes do take their lives, and the possibility must be reevaluated in each instance.

"My head is all messed up inside. I'm seventeen and the last few years have been tough. For one thing, my body is not very big and masculine. This is always on my mind. I am afraid it will ruin my chances of being happily married. Also things are very heavy at school. Senior year is so important, but I never can seem to keep up with my work and all the other things I'm supposed to be doing. I get so mad I feel like hurting myself. One person in our school already killed himself, and one of my friends almost did too. Thinking about them makes me hang on to myself, but I don't know how long I can last. — Sickie." When young people feel inept or useless, unloved or unworthy of love, they may turn on themselves. The problems of Sickie, who wants to hurt himself and thinks of taking his life, have to be taken seriously. He will probably work his way out of it, but he certainly can use help.

Parents fear that if they talk about suicide when their children are very upset, it may put that thought into the kids' minds. The thought is already there. Virtually every child has considered the idea, most not seriously, but others only too seriously. Suicide is now the fastest growing cause of death among adolescents, second only to accidents. In addition, a number of accidents, such as auto crashes and drug overdoses, are sometimes unrecognized suicides.

Most of these deaths could have been prevented if adults close to the victims understood more about suicide. One myth is that suicide only happens to certain kinds of people. "Oh, but he wasn't the type to take his life," people often say in surprise. There is no "type." Suicide happens to all kinds of kids at all levels of society, and at younger ages than ever before.

Another myth is that people who talk about suicide ahead of time will never actually do it. This is not true. "I am a fifteen-year-old girl and feel like I'm falling apart. I've got this big empty feeling inside me all the time. I can't do any work or carry on a decent conversation. It seems like the teachers and kids are just pulling me apart and letting me die. I feel like I'm on the brink of existence — a mechanical wind-up toy. I told my mother about it, but she doesn't care. Please help me! — Nora." Almost all suicides announce their intentions clearly, and many times, before they finally act. Nora's family should be most concerned.

People who are thinking of suicide don't like themselves very much, and may behave in a way that makes others dislike them, too. It is hard even for parents to be sympathetic to a child who is gloomy and complains a lot. They are tempted to say "Why don't you pull yourself together?" On rare occasions a person has been snapped out of it, but this usually happens only in the movies. Parents shouldn't brush it aside when a child becomes unusually discouraged and uncommunicative, sits around listlessly and sighs a lot, has apparently hypochondrial complaints, wants to be alone more than usual and breaks off friendships, does poorly in school, and seems sad and frustrated. The family should be alert to warning statements, such as "I'm no good at anything"; "What is there to live for?"; or "I wish I were dead." Many teens will write about their emotions more easily than they talk about them. Teenage girls, especially, are likely to turn to a diary to express the daydreams, conflicts, and secret thoughts that they don't want or don't dare share with people. Or they may write of such feelings in school essays or poetry.

A suicide threat can represent a sincere, intense wish "to be" no longer, or it can be a distress signal, yelling for help when all other forms of communication have broken down. It is essential to intervene before this point is reached, and to start talking. Don't be afraid to come right out and say the word *suicide*. Ask, "Were you thinking about taking your life? Sometimes people do feel like that, but there is always another way. Let us help you find it." Talking about the possibility of suicide this way reduces the person's tenseness and aloneness. If he can talk about it and feels he's being listened to, a teenager can regain perspective, and with it the hope of solving the problems that have driven him to such despair.

It is a serious mistake to be reassuring by saying "There's nothing to worry about" or "Things can't be *that* bad." If things were not serious, why would the child be so despondent? Instead, ask specific questions about what the trouble is. Also speak to other people in your child's life. Teachers have an especially good opportunity to know what goes on in a student's social life, schoolwork, and behavior in school. They have access to written work, which often gives clues to the student's frame of mind. Friends and relatives may be able to provide new insights into the situation, too.

If there are any suspicions at all that a suicide crisis is imminent, get immediate professional help. Psychotherapy creates a special trust between the therapist and the patient, almost a special kind of love. Through this relationship a teenager learns to rely on the therapist and can start rebuilding self-esteem, which means feeling kindly toward one's self and sure of one's ability to live up to one's own goals and standards. Often the problem with suicides is that their aspirations are so high they can't possibly be reached. Through therapy, these goals can be reset at more realistic levels, and once again, life becomes manageable.

Not all therapists are familiar with suicide cases, however, so it might be wise to get advice from a suicide prevention agency or crisis center also. Most cities now have organizations that specialize in suicide intervention, such as the Samaritans. Or help can be found through local mental health centers and many city hospitals.

A teenager who has actually tried to commit suicide needs to be seen, evaluated, and treated, but some kids refuse. Urge and beg them to seek help. Going yourself may compel them to follow, and your support shows that you care. This is essential to the child's reestablishment of self-respect and love.

Sometimes people are bent on self-destruction. We naturally try to stop them but sometimes we fail. To an outside observer, the lives of poets Sylvia Plath and Anne Sexton seemed so filled with love, children and acclaim, yet these women could not, at the last, be prevented from ending their lives. Whether the death could have been prevented or not is of little comfort to the family of a suicide. It's an especially hard time, replete with shame and guilt and terrible grief. Parents inevitably wonder where they went wrong. During periods of sharp conflict in their young lives most children secretly wish a brother or sister were dead, and so they may feel unbearable guilt and responsibility if a sibling commits suicide. Therefore it is important for the whole family to examine the family conflicts that contributed to the suicide with a therapist. Generally the family can better pull through the shock and grief, once they have talked out the devastation the loss has caused the survivors.

Reading so much about depression and suicide may make it

seem as if most adolescents are deeply troubled and on the brink of collapse. This is not so. Often a teenager who seems withdrawn is simply daydreaming — fantasizing is a normal part of this age. An adolescent who becomes very introspective is usually not "sick" but working over an intense problem of some kind and will emerge with a new insight. This is also a normal part of growing up.

Everyone changes moods to some extent, but some people do so much that they seem like entirely different people at different times. Teenagers are famous for this changeability, but this is seldom a sign that professional help is needed. By and large the number of adolescents who need therapy is no greater than that of adults. In the end, most teenagers overcome these mood swings with serenity and success.

13. What's Wonderful About Teenagers

This has been a book about problems, problems, and more problems, but I don't want to leave readers thinking of adolescence only in terms of trouble. Sometimes we talk about teenagers as if they "had adolescence" as a kind of disease. You may look at your teenagers and see only people who never pick up their rooms, drive too fast, and probably use marijuana, too. Or you might see young people with energy and humor, inquisitiveness and bravery, idealism and generosity. This period represents the unfolding of a new adult — a rich and sometimes scary drama, but most often one with a happy ending.

Parents who can watch their kids' struggles with a little detachment can relax and enjoy them more. One mother explains why this isn't always easy to do, however. "My children are eleven and thirteen, and we are very close. As they enter teenage, though, I find it harder to accept their missteps than I did when they were smaller. I know intellectually that these are the mischiefs and errors of their age, but I seem to feel more personally responsible. Why is it that parents can laugh at the mistakes of toddlers, but see themselves personally affronted when teenagers fail? — Tensing Up." One reason parents tense up is that bigger kids make bigger mistakes. Another is that as kids approach adulthood you may see more and more of yourself in them, which can arouse mixed feelings. They remind you of your own teenage, and it's hard to feel dispassionate about that. Above all, they are bound to you by all the care you have invested in them already. You feel their behavior reflects on your abilities as a parent, indeed, as a person. You have to remind yourself that your teenagers are reaching the point where they are their own responsibility, not yours. So step back, like an artist viewing a picture, and get more perspective on your creation.

Take a break from your critical job of molding this person and marvel that it is the one and only individual, just like this, in the whole world. And no one was ever like this before, or ever will be again. Pretty awesome. When you accept the uniqueness of your offspring, you allow their individuality to flourish. Don't be afraid of it.

One of the significant qualities of adolescents is their energy. They sparkle and snap with it. Like young colts, they toss their heads and stamp, and then go tearing off, just for the sheer pleasure of running and kicking up their heels. Sometimes it makes you tired just watching their restlessness, but you can feed off it, too. Capitalize on the enthusiasm of youth. Their commitment to a person, an idea, an event, may be transient, but it is all-consuming. Channel it, use it, and admire it.

Another quality to enjoy in your kids is their sense of humor. The young have a wonderfully silly streak, and when you can drop the generation gap for a moment, you will probably find yourself laughing at some foolishness until you are rendered helpless. What could bring two people closer together? Kids love to poke fun at the solemnity of adults. They can puncture pomposity with killing wit, and are irreverent about adults, relations, government, their friends, you, and sometimes even themselves. Sometimes they are corny. Sometimes raunchy. Sometimes they draw devastating cartoons. Let down your hair and enjoy some of it.

Along with humor comes some incredible acting ability. This letter shows how a teenager can dramatize a situation, especially one in which she is trying to draw her parent's attention to the unfairness of it all. "Are all kids such clever actresses? I told my daughter she could not go someplace. She flung herself onto the sofa in an attitude of utter despair. With melodramatic voice and gesture, she predicted social failure, ostracism, and permanent isolation. It was worthy of a first night on Broadway, and it began to get to me. So I relented. That produced Act Two. My daughter instantly shifted to joy and rapture. Flinging her arms around my neck, she trilled, 'Oh, Mom. You're super!' and, as Miss Ecstasy, flew out of the room on wings of happiness." Such a show is really quite marvelous. The trouble is, it is hard for the parent not to get dragged into the act. If you can keep some part of yourself out there in the audience, you will want to applaud the performance.

Teenagers are questioning everything, and if you listen they may lead you to take interesting new looks at some of your own assumptions. This isn't always comfortable, but it is vital to your continued growth. People are never "finished"; they need to keep expanding, changing, reevaluating. Your teenagers' eagerness to try new experiences and ideas can drag you out of a rut, if you'll let it. For to a large extent it is youth, in this country at least, who set new styles in popular music, dancing, hair, clothes, and movies. Let your teenagers give you a new look at social customs, family way of life, health, food, politics, goals. Not that their ideas are necessarily right, but they can get you to reassess your own. Sometimes you will reaffirm your own, and that's good. Sometimes you will find a different way that works better, and that's good, too.

Teenagers are developing rapidly in intelligence, judgment, and analytical ability. Of course, they can be naive and simplistic about many things, but test their reflections on political and moral and ethical issues sometimes, and you may have some good discussions that stretch everyone's minds.

Young people's idealism doesn't just inspire parents; it can affect the whole country. The ideals and purposefulness of young people in the sixties and early seventies made profound changes in our national view of a war and of minority rights and social traditions. You may not like these changes, but you have to credit kids with the power to effect change and to make us be more honest with ourselves.

"Youth movements" seem to come in waves. Some generations are activists; some, like the adolescents of the eighties, are more passive and concerned with their own affairs. The economic situation doubtless has a lot to do with it, but idealism is always a big part of adolescence, and we must encourage it because our country's growth depends on it. If we don't take a fresh look at ourselves every few years, our society will stagnate. Sure, much of young people's idealism is unrealistic, but some of our adult goals, such as an arms race for peace, don't make much sense either.

Admiring your kids may be a pleasure mixed with nostalgia. A parent writes "I love to watch my sixteen-year-old daughter preening herself for a very special date, but I wonder why it always makes me feel a little sad, too. Is it because I miss the little baby she used to be? — Nostalgic." Parents do regret the childhood lost, and they also feel sad about the approaching independence, knowing their kids will soon be moving away from them. Enjoy the present: This wonderful moment when the mature character is first showing itself in your teenager's soft, childish face is so exciting. It does not spoil teenagers if you admire them openly and enthusiastically. "Oh, Mo-*ther*!" they may say, but your pride does double duty; it makes you both feel better.

Resiliency is strong in teenage, and you can rely on it. This is important to you in two ways. It helps kids bounce back when they make a mistake, and it gives you second and third chances when you do something that doesn't work well. No one is infallible. If one method of discipline or guidance isn't effective, you have to shift gears and try another. This doesn't ruin a resilient teenager. Like Silly Putty, they can take new shapes and adapt to new parental methods. They can adapt, too, when they use poor judgment or make bad choices — even serious errors seldom mar them for life. They usually recover and use the experience to good advantage.

As parents, you need to remind yourselves frequently that there are limits to how much you can control your children's thoughts and behavior, and these limits grow narrower and narrower with each year. Your job now is to be a helpful guide, not an invincible warden. The kids are almost on their own, and you can't and shouldn't hold them back. So don't penalize yourself for what you cannot do. Expect that your teenagers' resiliency will pull them through.

Let yourself glow about your children's growing maturity and self-confidence. Think of all the things they have resisted to get where they are. Most kids weave their way successfully through the tangled web of drugs and alcohol and copping out and sex. For some, adolescent problems may take a long time to resolve. With luck and hard work, most kids are getting it all together and are approaching college or a vocation in remarkably good shape.

Above all, teenagers can be loving, not every minute or even every day, but the quality is there. Watch a fifteen-year-old daughter flirting with her father or a sixteen-year-old son bending to pat his mother on the head. It makes it all worthwhile. It bothers parents that their teenagers do not often seem grateful for all they have done and all the worries they have suffered for their kids. Kids are not grateful. They take it as their due, which it is. They are single-minded in their work to split off from you, and actively ungrateful for anything you do that seems to interfere. However, as you acknowledge their readiness to take responsibility and share in the planning and management of their lives, they will start to appreciate you more and more openly, and be more loving.

You have been through a lot together. Neither of you will ever be the same. You have had a trial by fire, and you are emerging stronger and more sure of yourself, yet at the same time, more openminded and tolerant of others. Your values have been tested and retested, until they are honed down to a core of firm beliefs. Most likely you've become more patient and self-aware, and more grown-up.

So you have grown as your child has grown. You have struggled with each other, but if you have both struggled with love, you have tried not to inflict irreparable scars. You will win through to mutual affection and respect, which will give both of you comfort and joy, the rest of your lives.

What of the Future?

I have written a lot about how tough life is for teenagers today, so it may be a comfort to remember how very recent the whole concept of adolescence really is. In the 1900s, only 10 percent of American teenagers went to high school, and the rest worked like the adults they were considered to be. In the 1980s, the situation is just the reverse; 90 percent go to high school and only 10 percent work. We worry that our children grow up too soon, but in fact, an extended period of training and education is a new feature of childhood. World events once more impinge on young people earlier, so now perhaps our kids need to grow up faster again.

Our lives get more complicated in every way, technologically, socially, demographically, politically. It may not be possible for adolescents to cling to childhood as long as they have been doing and still get the requisite knowledge and experience to cope with such a life. I believe that the potential of teenagers is much underrated and that they are capable of participating in many more aspects of adult life, if they are given the training, respect, and responsibility to carry out adult tasks.

We are obviously in the midst of great change. The status of men and women is altering and their responsibilities shifting. This affects the roles of children as well. Our understanding of human psychology is improving, and though young adolescence is one of the least studied ages, we are gradually learning more about this age, too. This will change our ways of raising and educating teenagers.

As the population explodes, our world is suddenly shrinking and our resources dwindling, and this will dramatically change the way we live. Saving, conserving, and reusing resources will become the way of life for rich and poor alike. It is reminiscent of the small family farms in times past, when the whole family worked together and nothing was wasted. This is promising, for children thrive when they are important, needed, respected members of the family household.

Parents Are Still the Answer

Other aspects of future life are not so hopeful. The possibility of nuclear war heads the list of dreadful dangers, with pollution, dwindling natural resources, and a shrinking job market hard upon us. Adults have much to be anxious about, but we have to give hope to our kids. If we allow ourselves to be constantly grim and pessimistic, it only further threatens their future. Parents must provide a home atmosphere that is hopeful and positive. It may be the hardest thing you have to do, but it makes the difference.

Some people become so concerned about dire events that they

seem actually to relish the destructive and dangerous. See to it that your attitude isn't perpetually negative. With determination, you can express optimism and hope, much of the time. In fact, the kind of gossip that makes fun of other people's personal faults and failures, entertaining as it may be, ought to be kept to a bare minimum. Instead foster an attitude of kindness and faith that will help your kids believe that things can get better.

This may sound Pollyanna-ish, but haven't you come through some hard times and survived? Be proud! Aren't there some good things in your life now — your family, your house, your job, your hobbies? Take joy in them! Be playful sometimes. Sing or laugh or hum, or whatever you do when you are happy. One thing you want very much for your kids to know about life is that it's worth living!

People who are hopeful and trusting are much better off than those who are perpetually suspicious and dubious. Work on being trusting — even at the risk of being a bit gullible. High trusters are happier, better adjusted, more trustworthy, and more likeable. Pass this along to your kids. Parents who create an atmosphere of trust and acceptance, of hopefulness and flexibility are going to have children who mirror these attitudes. These will be the kids who bob up again when experiences try to push them down. These will be kids who will like and respect their parents.

As children reach the end of teenage, they usually leave home for college or for work or to explore adult life some other way. Even those who may live at home a few more years find that the center of their lives is elsewhere, with other friends, other interests. Now is the time you may see your long job paying off. If you respected your kids, it has built their self-respect, so they can enter adult life with confidence. If you shared responsibilities with them, it gave them the skill to tackle difficult jobs and carry them through. If you set limits for them in the past, these have become the patterns by which they organize and govern their own affairs. And if you enjoyed honest communication with them, it has enabled these children to look deep within themselves at all those positive developing human qualities — the wonderment, courage, and ideals, the appetites of spirit and body — and now they can bring them forth and offer them to the world, unafraid.

One thing I haven't talked much about is love. It goes without saying, love is *the* ingredient without which nothing else works. Every child needs constant, special, enduring, unqualified, crazy love from a parent or devoted guardian. This special love and admiration, even while it may seem to be actively rejected, is still being soaked up by your teenager. This is what helps all young people to grow up knowing they are worth something, that they are lovable, special, and important. It enables children of any age to shape and sharpen their unique talents. And they will give their love back to you in full measure when, as adults, they may become your best and most cherished friends.

Suggested Reading

Index

Suggested Reading

Puberty and Adolescent Development

Adelson, Joseph. *Handbook of Adolescent Psychology.* New York: Wiley, 1980. Addresses, lectures, and essays about adolescent development.

Blos, Peter. *The Young Adolescent: Clinical Studies.* New York: The Free Press, 1970. Discussions of teenage by a preeminent child psychiatrist.

Friedenberg, E. G. *Coming of Age in America: Growth and Acquiescence.* New York: Random House, 1965.

Johnson, Eric W. *How To Live Through Junior High School,* rev. ed. Philadelphia: J. B. Lippincott, 1975. A practical picture of student life by a wise and experienced teacher.

Kagan, Jerome, and Robert Coles, eds. *12 to 16: Early Adolescence.* New York: W. W. Norton, 1972. Topics such as physical maturation, social characteristics, and discovery of oneself, discussed by experts such as the editors and Joseph Adelson, Peter Blos, J. M. Tanner, and Thomas J. Cottle, all of whom write well for lay readers.

Schowalter, John E., M.D., and Walter R. Anyan, M.D. *The Family Book of Adolescence: A Comprehensive Medically Oriented Guide to the Years from Puberty to Adulthood.* New York: Knopf, 1979.

Face and Figure

"Acne: New Approaches to an Old Problem." *Consumer Reports,* August, 1981.

Bennett, William, and Joel Gurin. *The Dieter's Dilemma: Eating Less and Weighing More.* New York: Basic Books, 1982.

Bluestein, William J., and Enid Bluestein. *Mom, How Come I'm Not Thin?* Minneapolis, Minn.: CompCare Publications, 1981. Written for young people, this book give insights and advice about how parents can help by giving praise and hugs instead of food for rewards.

Bruch, Hilda, M.D. *The Golden Cage: The Enigma of Anorexia Nervosa.* Cambridge, Mass.: Harvard University Press, 1978. The classic on anorexia by a doctor who treats anorexic patients.

———. *Eating Disorders: Obesity, Anorexia, and the Person Within.* New York: Basic Books, 1979.

Edelstein, Barbara, M.D. *The Woman Doctor's Diet for Teen-age Girls.* New York: Ballantine, 1981. This takes into account physical differences as well as nutritional demands of teenage lifestyle.

Kuntzleman, Charles T. *The Exercise Handbook: How to Get More Out of the Exercise You Are Doing—Jogging, Weight-lifting, Swimming, Tennis, Bicycling, or Any Other Serious Exercise.* New York: David McKay, 1978.

Levenkron, Steven. *The Best Little Girl in the World.* Chicago, Ill.: Contemporary Books, 1978. The novelized story of an anorexia patient, her hospitalization and treatment.

———. *Treating and Overcoming Anorexia Nervosa.* New York: Scribner's, 1982.

Orbach, Susie. *Fat Is a Feminist Issue: The Anti-Diet Guide to Permanent Weight Loss.* Berkeley, Calif.: Berkeley Pub., 1979.

Palmer, R. L. *Anorexia Nervosa: A Guide for Sufferers and Their Families.* New York: Penguin Books, 1980. Symptoms and treatment discussed in a clear, basic, and compassionate manner.

Parrish, John A., M.D., et al. *Between You and Me: A Sensitive and Authoritative Guide to the Care and Treatment of Your Skin.* Boston: Little, Brown, 1978. Dermatologists' advice about everything from acne to freckles.

Wurtman, Judith J. *Eating Your Way Through Life: a No-Nonsense Guide to Good Nutrition for All Ages and All Eating Styles.* New York: Raven Press, 1979.

———. *The Carbohydrate Craver's Diet.* Boston: Houghton Mifflin, 1983. Said to be "the first diet that succeeds where others fail because it satisfies your daily need for sugar and starch."

Sexuality

General

Am I Parent Material? Washington, D.C.: National Alliance for Optional Parenthood, 1972. Pamphlet available from the publisher, 1439 Rhode Island Avenue, N.W., Washington, D.C. 20005. Questions to help teenagers face the consequences of a possible pregnancy.

Boston Women's Health Collective. *Our Bodies, Ourselves: A Book by and for Women,* rev. ed. New York: Simon and Schuster, 1976. The classic on women's sexuality, physical, psychological, and medical.

Brown, Howard. *Familiar Faces, Hidden Lives.* New York: Harcourt Brace Jovanovich, 1976. Life stories of growing up gay, by a doctor who was formerly a New York City official.

Brownmiller, Susan. *Against Our Will: Men, Women and Rape.* New York: Simon and Schuster, 1975.

Burgess, Ann W. *Rape, Victims of Crisis.* Bowie, Md.: R. J. Brady Co., 1974. The first book to address this problem from the victim's point of view.

Calderone, Mary S., and James W. Ramey. *Talking with Your Child About Sex: Questions and Answers for Children from Birth to Puberty.* New York: Random House, 1982.

Calderone, Mary S., and Eric W. Johnson. *The Family Book About Sexuality,* rev. ed. New York: Harper and Row, 1981. An encyclopedia of information about sexuality by the founder of SIECUS (Sex Information and Education Council of the U.S.) and a teacher of sex education who has authored many books on the subject.

Corsaro, Maria, and Carole Korzeniowsky. *STD: A Commonsense Guide.* New York: St. Martin's Press, 1980. The necessary information about sexually transmitted diseases.

Csida, Jane Bundy, and Joseph Csida. *Rape: How to Avoid It and What to Do About It If You Can't.* Chatsworth, Calif.: Books for Better Living, 1974.

Fairchild, Betty, and Nancy Hatward. *Now That You Know: What Every Parent Should Know About Homosexuality*. New York: Harcourt Brace Jovanovich, 1979.

Gittelsohn, Rabbi Roland B. *Love, Sex, and Marriage*. New York: Union of American Hebrew Congregations, new edition, 1980.

Gordon, Sol, et al. *Living Fully: A Guide for Young People with a Handicap, Their Parents, Their Teachers and Professionals*. Ed-U Press, 1975. Out of print, but worth searching for in libraries, as there is so little other information available.

Hanckel, Frances, and John Cunningham. *A Way of Love, a Way of Life: A Young Person's Introduction to What It Means to Be Gay*. New York: Lothrop, Lee and Shepard, 1979. How to know if you are gay, and if you are, to feel all right about yourself.

Johnson, Eric W. *V.D. and What You Should Do About It*, rev. ed. Philadelphia: J. B. Lippincott, 1979. Good, basic description of the symptoms, how they spread, and how they are treated.

Kappelman, Murray. *Sex and the American Teenager: A Guide for Parents*. New York: Reader's Digest Press, 1977. Advice from a pediatrician who counsels adolescents and their parents.

Kempton, Winifred, et al. *Love, Sex and Birth Control for the Mentally Retarded: A Guide for Parents*. Philadelphia: Planned Parenthood of Southeastern Pennsylvania, 1973. Available from the publisher, 1220 Sansom Street, Philadelphia, PA 19107 ($2.24).

LeShan, Eda. *Sex and Your Teenager*. New York: David McKay, 1969. Honest and forthright acceptance and discussion of teenage sexuality.

McKee, Lyn, and Virginia Blacklidge. *An Easy Guide for Caring Parents: Sexuality and Socialization — A Book for Parents of People with Mental Handicaps*. Walnut Creek, Calif.: Planned Parenthood of Contra Costa. Available from the publisher, 1291 Oakland Boulevard, Walnut Creek, CA 94596 ($5.95).

McNaught, Brian. *A Disturbed Peace: Selected Writings of an Irish Catholic Homosexual*. Washington, D.C.: Dignity, Inc., 1981.

Money, John, and Patricia Tucker. *Sexual Signatures: On Being a Man and a Woman*. Boston: Little, Brown, 1976. The development of gender identification, from conception to maturity.

Oettinger, K., and E. Mooney. *"Not* My *Daughter": Facing Up to Adolescent Pregnancy*. Englewood Cliffs, N.J.: Prentice-Hall, 1979.

Pogrebin, Letty Cottin. *Growing Up Free: Raising Your Child in the 80s.* New York: McGraw-Hill, 1980. Encouraging nonsexism in children, with emphasis on sex education.

Pomeroy, Wardell B. *Your Child and Sex: A Guide for Parents.* New York: Dell, 1976.

Rush, Florence. *The Best Kept Secret: Sexual Abuse of Children.* New York: McGraw-Hill, 1980.

Silber, Sherman D. *The Male: From Infancy to Old Age: Understanding Male Sexuality, Impotence, the Prostate, Circumcision, Bedwetting, Puberty, Homosexuality, and All Aspects of Being a Man.* New York: Scribner's, 1981.

Silverstein, Charles. *A Family Matter: A Parent's Guide to Homosexuality.* New York: McGraw-Hill, 1977. A doctor's advice to parents about how to accept their child's different sexual direction.

The following pamphlets are available from the Public Affairs Committee, Inc., 381 Park Avenue South, New York, NY 10016. They cost 50¢ each and can be ordered by number.

Bienvenu, Millard J. *Parent-Teenager Communication* (#438).

Dickman, Irving R. *Sex Education for Disabled Persons* (#531).

Gordon, Sol, and Irving R. Dickman. *Sex Education: The Parent's Role* (#459).

Hofskin, Sadie. *Talking to Pre-Teenagers about Sex* (#476).

Hynes, James L. *How to Tell Your Child About Sex* (#149).

These pamphlets are available from the Planned Parenthood Federation of America, Inc., 810 Seventh Avenue, New York, NY 10019. They cost 50¢ each.

How to Talk to Your Teenager About Something That's Not Easy to Talk About: Facts About the Facts of Life.

Pregnancy Resource Books 1–3: *Considering What to Do, Caring for Two,* and *Deciding on Abortion.*

Preteens

Johnson, Eric W., and Corinne B. Johnson. *Love and Sex and Growing Up,* rev. ed. Philadelphia: J. B. Lippincott, 1979. The major topics, covered in an unthreatening way.

Kaplan, Helen Singer. *Making Sense of Sex: The New Facts About Sex and Love for Young People.* New York: Simon and Schuster, 1979.

Lyman, Marilyn. *Growing Up — Specially for Pre-teens and Young Teens.* Syracuse: Planned Parenthood Center of Syracuse, 1973. This useful pamphlet can be ordered from the publisher at 1120 East Genesee Street, Syracuse, NY 13210.

Mayle, Peter. *What's Happening to Me?* Secaucus, N.J.: Lyle Stuart, 1975. A clear, matter-of-fact guide to puberty.

Early Teens

Gordon, Sol. *You Would If You Loved Me.* New York: Bantam Books, 1978. A paperback full of the lines kids use to egg each other on, and some suggested replies.

———. *The Teenage Survival Book,* rev. ed. New York: Times Books, 1981. A paperback with lively format and many illustrations, for kids who don't like to read.

Hamilton, Eleanor. *Sex with Love: A Guide for Young People.* Boston: Beacon Press, 1978. Suggestions about how to be loving without intercourse.

Johnson, Eric W. *Love and Sex in Plain Language,* rev. ed. Philadelphia: J. B. Lippincott, 1979. Basic information about intercourse, masturbation, homosexuality, etc., in terms of personal responsibility.

Hettlinger, Richard F. *Growing Up with Sex: A Guide for Early Teens,* rev. ed. New York: Continuum Publishing Company, 1980. Sex education in the context of Christian values.

Lyman, Marilyn. *Teen Questions About Sex — and Answers.* Syracuse: Planned Parenthood Center of Syracuse, 1973. This pamphlet can be ordered from the publisher at 1120 Genesee Street, Syracuse, NY 13210.

Pomeroy, Wardell B. *Boys and Sex,* rev. ed. New York: Dell, 1981. The facts and feelings of sexuality in understandable and reassuring language.

———. *Girls and Sex,* rev. ed. New York: Dell, 1981. The same thing for girls.

What Teens Want to Know But Don't Know How to Ask. New York: Planned Parenthood Federation of America, Inc. This pamphlet can be ordered from the publisher at 810 Seventh Avenue, New York, NY 10019.

Older Teens

Balis, Andrea. *What Are You Using? A Birth Control Guide for Teenagers.* New York: Dial, 1981. Up-to-date information about contraception.

Bell, Ruth. *Changing Bodies, Changing Lives.* New York: Random House, 1980. The most comprehensive book on sexuality for and by teenagers, with copious illustrations and discussion by kids themselves. Also good for more-experienced younger teens.

Lieberman, E. James, M.D., and Ellen Peck. *Sex and Birth Control: A Guide for the Young,* rev. ed. New York: Harper and Row, 1981. Issues of decision making, with emphasis on contraception.

McCoy, Kathy, and Charles Wibbelsman. *The Teenage Body Book.* New York: Pocket Books, 1979. Thoughtfully presented facts about the rapid maturing process of teenage bodies.

Mazur, Ronald. *Commonsense Sex.* Boston: Beacon Press, 1973. Sexuality discussed in a religious but liberal framework.

Winship, Elizabeth, and Frank Caparulo. *Masculinity and Femininity.* Boston: Houghton Mifflin, 1978. A high school text, fully illustrated and including letters from students.

Relationships

Avery, Curtis E., and Theodore B. Johannis, Jr. *Love and Marriage: A Guide for Young People.* New York: Harcourt Brace Jovanovich, 1971. Helps teenagers analyze issues of adjustment, such as money, recreation, family, friends, sex roles, and so on.

LeShan, Eda. *Mates and Roommates: New Styles in Young Marriages.* New York: Public Affairs Committee, Inc., 1979. Available from the publisher, 381 Park Avenue South, New York 10016 (Pamphlet #468; 50¢).

Rofes, Eric, ed. *Kid's Book of Divorce: By, For and About Kids.* Brattleboro, Vt.: Lewis Publishing Company, 1981. Although written by schoolchildren, this book can teach parents and teenagers about feelings and how to cope with them honestly.

Zimbardo, Philip G., and Shirley Redl. *A Parent's Guide to the Shy Child.* New York: McGraw-Hill, 1981. How to build children's confidence by making them feel loved.

Discipline, Rights, Legal Problems

Helm, Alice K., ed. *The Family Legal Advisor, 1982: A Clear, Reliable, and Up-to-Date Guide to Your Rights and Remedies Under the Law.* New York: Crown Publishers, 1981.

Last, Jack. *Everyday Law Made Simple,* rev. ed. New York: Doubleday, 1978.

Lipstiz, Joan Scheff. *Growing Up Forgotten.* Lexington, Mass.: D. C. Heath, 1977. A review of programs and research on twelve- to fifteen-year-olds; the schooling, services, and family treatment of adolescents.

Paine, Roger W. *We Never Had Any Trouble Before: A Handbook for Parents on Subjects Including Appearance, Drugs, Living Together, Communication, Divorce, Discipline, Hitchhiking, Runaways, Sex, Suicide, Responsibility and Ethics.* New York: Stein and Day, 1975. Sensible advice from a youth and family counselor.

Drugs, Smoking, Drinking

Cross, Wilbur. *Kids and Booze: What You Must Know to Help Them.* New York: E. P. Dutton, 1979. How parental drinking habits affect children, and how parents can teach responsible drinking.

Dusek, Dorothy. *Drugs, A Factual Account.* Reading, Mass.: Addison-Wesley, 1980.

Grinspoon, Lester. *Marihuana Reconsidered*, 2nd ed. Cambridge, Mass.: Harvard University Press, 1977. The definitive study to date on marijuana research, history, usage, and effects in America.

Grinspoon, Lester, and Peter Hedbloom. *The Speed Culture: Amphet-*

amine Use and Abuse in America. Cambridge, Mass.: Harvard University Press, 1975.

Jackson, Michael, and Bruce Jackson. *Doing Drugs: Teenagers Talk About the Most Serious Problem Afflicting Them Today.* New York: St. Martin's Press, 1983.

North, Robert, and Richard Orange, Jr. *Teenage Drinking: The Number One Drug Threat to Young People Today.* New York: Macmillan, 1980.

Ray, Oakley. *Drugs, Society and Human Behavior.* St. Louis, Mo.: C. V. Mosby Company, 1978. Technical description of what psychoactive drugs do, and who uses them and why.

Silverstein, Alvin, and Virginia Silverstein. *Alcoholism.* Philadelphia: J. B. Lippincott, 1975. An objective presentation of the facts about alcohol, for teenagers.

Weil, Andrew, and Winifred Rosen. *Chocolate to Morphine: Understanding Mind-Active Drugs.* Boston, Houghton Mifflin, 1983. This how-to-live-safely-with-drugs advice is recommended for both teenagers and parents.

Worick, W. Wayne. *Alcohol, Tobacco, and Drugs: Their Use and Abuse.* Englewood Cliffs, N.J.: Prentice-Hall, 1977.

Depression and Suicide

Jewett, Claudia L. *Helping Children Cope with Separation and Loss: Divorce, Death, Absence, Adoption, Foster Care.* Harvard, Mass.: The Harvard Common Press, 1982. Though it primarily concerns younger children, good advice for parents of children of all ages is presented here by a family therapist.

Klagsbrun, Francine. *Too Young to Die: Youth and Suicide.* Boston: Houghton Mifflin, 1976. Information that can help both parents and children recognize problems that could lead to suicide.

Mack, John E., and Holly Hickler. *Vivienne: The Life and Suicide of an Adolescent Girl.* Boston: Little, Brown, 1981. The poignant story of one girl's despair, written by a doctor and teacher.

Schneidman, E. S., and N. L. Farberow. *Some Facts about Suicide.*

Washington, D.C.: Public Health Service, 1961. Available from the Government Printing Office, Washington, DC 20402 (Bulletin #852; free).

Miscellaneous

Ginnott, Haim G. *Between Parent and Teenager.* New York: Macmillan, 1969. Useful ideas for communication with teenagers, even if "instant success" seems unrealistic.

Norman, Jane, and Myron Harris. *The American Teenager.* New York: Rawson Wade, 1981. Over 160,000 teenagers reveal what they think and really do about parents, sex, drugs, drinking, peer pressure, and all the other concerns they may never discuss with adults.

Postman, Neil. *The Disappearance of Childhood.* New York: Delacorte, 1982. How the electronic media deprive our children of their childhood.

TV and Teens: Experts Look at the Issues. Edited by Meg Schwartz. Reading, Mass.: Addison-Wesley, 1982. Action for Children's Television (ACT) takes a look at the influence 25 hours of weekly TV watching has on our children.

Weiss, Robert Stuart. *Going It Alone: The Family Life and Social Situation of the Single Parent.* New York: Basic Books, 1979.

Index